Trayer

Courage FOR LAMBS

A Psychologist's Memoir of Recovery from Abuse and Loss

DR. JOANN NISHIMOTO

WESTBOW®
PRESS
A DIVISION OF THOMAS NELSON
& ZONDERVAN

Copyright © 2014 Dr. JoAnn Nishimoto.

All rights reserved. No part of this book may be used or reproduced by any means, graphic, electronic, or mechanical, including photocopying, recording, taping or by any information storage retrieval system without the written permission of the publisher except in the case of brief quotations embodied in critical articles and reviews.

Cover lamb image by Steve Pennock

Illustrations by Jen Jao

Scriptures marked NASB are taken from the NEW AMERICAN STANDARD BIBLE®, Copyright © 1960,1962,1963,1968,1971,1972,1973,1975,1977,1995 by The Lockman Foundation. Used by permission.

Scriptures marked KJV are taken from The Holy Bible, King James Version.

Scriptures marked The Message are taken from *The Message*. Copyright © 1993, 1994, 1995, 1996, 2000, 2001, 2002. Used by permission of NavPress Publishing Group.

WestBow Press books may be ordered through booksellers or by contacting:

WestBow Press
A Division of Thomas Nelson & Zondervan
1663 Liberty Drive
Bloomington, IN 47403
www.westbowpress.com
1 (866) 928-1240

Because of the dynamic nature of the Internet, any web addresses or links contained in this book may have changed since publication and may no longer be valid. The views expressed in this work are solely those of the author and do not necessarily reflect the views of the publisher, and the publisher hereby disclaims any responsibility for them.

Any people depicted in stock imagery provided by Thinkstock are models, and such images are being used for illustrative purposes only.
Certain stock imagery © Thinkstock.

ISBN: 978-1-4908-2996-8 (sc)
ISBN: 978-1-4908-2995-1 (hc)
ISBN: 978-1-4908-2997-5 (e)

Library of Congress Control Number: 2014905416

Printed in the United States of America.

WestBow Press rev. date: 07/30/2014

To Hope, my beautiful daughter,
and to my nieces and nephews,
Andy, Elizabeth, Katie, John, Anna, Joe, and Tom…
As the next generation,
I want to leave you the record of
struggle and lessons learned,
so that you can navigate your own lives,
and so that you may never feel that you're alone
when trouble finds you

To the many courageous clients
with whom I have worked

To my husband, Stuart,
whose devotion, emotional maturity,
and vision for this book
gave me the support to write it

Special Thanks

... My initial readers: Helen Pennock, Kris Umfress, Mary Thornsen, and Dorothy Grant. You helped to launch me on the writing waters.

... My early enthusiasts: Sam Kendrick, Kathy Richards, Cheri Bennett, Nancy Brown, Barb Carroll, Roberta Kitchens, Rod Rogers, Ginger Ratcliff, Heidi Furr, Ralph Brandt, Julie Rokusek, Renee Kessell, Sue Guilianelli, and Betsy Meade. When I saw your excitement, it helped me sustain the journey to publish.

... My long-term prayer team: Pat Scales, Mary Kendrick, Cheryl Kilburg, Julie Schawel, Laura Dennis, and Marisa Rogers. You lasted for the marathon.

... My church lobby friends: Thank you for asking, "How's the book?" Your encouragement spurred me on.

... My illustrator, Jen Jao, for your patience in developing the five drawings I envisioned, and Jeff Sliwa, for photographing her artwork.

... Our couples' small group: Maureen and Neal Schmidgall, Etain and John Bruss, Ana Maria and Dave Raymond, Mindy and Jeff Brainerd, and Mina and Dave Roller. You put up with the endless "pray for JoAnn's book" requests.

... My therapist friends Maggie Caudell and Leah Schaut, for shaping the last draft with your input.

... My final editor Amy Croft. Your energy to cross the finish line was a Godsend. You brought it up to excellence.

... My dog and co-therapist, Sadie, who helped to mediate the tension in the house that comes with a 12-year book project.

Introduction

As human beings, we're all broken. This book is the account of my own brokenness. My human limitations. My journey in overcoming tragedy. My "coming out of fear." The healing process of fighting my way back. It's an account of how I got broken by this fallen world and what it took to get healed. I don't always look good in it, but it's an honest account. I agree with American journalist Bill Stout, who said, "Whether or not you write well, write bravely."

Several years ago I was sitting with one of my counseling clients. At the time I was in training to be a psychologist. This particular woman had been in a seriously abusive relationship which had ended several years before. She had kept most of the painful legacy of it bound up in her heart until our recent sessions.

"I'm trying to understand myself," she mourned. "I don't know why it took me so long. Why didn't I get out sooner? I stayed in that relationship for eleven years! It took me eleven years to get out." Her self-deprecating attitude showed me that she was despising herself.

"It took me twelve," I said quietly.

She lifted her head and stared in my face. There was disbelief and questioning in her eyes.

"I was in an emotionally and spiritually abusive relationship myself," I stated, "and it took me twelve years before my eyes were opened to what was happening and I had the courage to leave." I sometimes alluded to my own life when I knew I could leverage a client toward healing.

"But you're a *smart* woman," she said, as if trying to put me in a different class than herself, since she saw me as the "doctor."

"So are you," I countered. "Listen, being smart has nothing to do with it. Lots of smart women have been in abusive relationships."

In later sessions this woman told me that this had been a turning point for her. She began to stop despising herself as an inferior or stupid person. If someone she respected had been through a similar thing, maybe *she,* too, was worthy of respect.

If the grace and love of God are real, and I know them to be, then I don't have to hide my life. The Bible doesn't shrink from recounting the sins, fears, and failures of its very human characters. In their stories we find hope for ourselves.

We're all looking for hope. In letting myself be real, hope also becomes real.

I used to be more concerned about protecting my image. I didn't want to look particularly defective, inferior, or stupid. I wouldn't want people to *really* know what I'd been through, what my failures were, how really human I'd been.

This book is about being human and being broken. It's a disorderly story. But it does move on past that. It moves on because there really *is* more. There is hope and healing and love and respect and stability to gain. There is recovery from shame. There is grace and understanding. There is actually even a destination called joy.

My own trials have certainly given me compassion. The more I've journeyed toward wholeness, the more I can embrace the messiness of others. Their crises don't scare me. Their brokenness doesn't shock me. Loving them doesn't terrify me.

I hope you'll understand, by the end of this book, that while you may be broken, you are lovable. Disorderly and human, but of infinite worth to God.

*** *Names have been changed except where I was given permission to use them.*

Dear Reader...

Reading a recovery book can be a dramatic experience. It can awaken emotions that you didn't know you were going to feel. If at any point in reading this book you feel overwhelmed, I want you to remember to stop and breathe slowly and deeply. Call a friend. Take a break. Hug your pet. Journal about the similarities with your own life. You also might want to read the book with a supportive friend so you have someone to discuss it with. You might want to seek out a trained counselor.

The essays at the end of the book were written especially to those who are dealing with difficult recovery challenges. During the book I'll be pointing out which essays apply to themes that you are reading. It's my way of coaching you and encouraging you in your recovery.

If you are a survivor of sexual abuse, I want you to know that the book isn't explicit and doesn't contain violence. I've hoped that this would allow you to read the book without feeling traumatized. If I were there with you I'd want to hear your story. I'd want you to feel that you are not alone.

There can be no authentic consent
in a relationship involving
unequal power.

Marie Fortune
Is Nothing Sacred?
United Church Press, 1999

CHAPTER 1
Assumptions of Security

Driving home from school that day, I calculated the months until my high school graduation. It was January, 1976. My senior year. I was savoring the thought of getting to the exciting world of college. I was tired of high school. There must be a wider world waiting outside my small, northern Louisiana town.

I loved my town, but I didn't dream of staying here forever. It did have its special features though. The tree-lined Main Street led to the Courthouse on the town square, its Greek-revival columns a surprise if you weren't expecting such a grand building in an out-of-the-way place. It was a source of pride for the community, being built before the Civil War. It had already been there a hundred years when I was born at the local Memorial Hospital. I recall only four stoplights in our town of 4,000 people, one at each corner of the square. The stores that faced the square were predictable: the two competing drug stores, The National Bank, a couple of clothing stores, the library, a barbershop…you can guess the others.

My father had been born and reared in this town. After service in World War II and then college, he had returned to join the insurance business with his father. Marrying my mom (a city girl) and building their first small house were milestones which many of the returning veterans achieved. My father's extroverted, friendly style fit his job. Being in insurance sales meant that he met everyone new in town. I grew up with the skewed view that everybody really did know everybody.

My best friend, Cindy, and I used to monitor the Main Street traffic from her yard overlooking the street. The game of pretending "you get this car" and "I'll get the next one" easily kept us busy for an hour. It was a victory in my ten year old mind if she got a rickety farm truck and the next passing car was a Cadillac for me. Simple games.

When the summer heat set in and the cicadas were loud in the trees, there was a suffocating humidity. Nobody liked it, but it was our norm. Come January we'd be comparing the advantages of living where the winters weren't severe.

The magnolia tree in our yard, a symbol of the Deep South, was actually a nuisance. The large white blossoms were pretty, but leaves fell off of it year round. It seemed it was always my turn to pick them up.

When I rode my bicycle to town I passed the historic Victorian homes with their porch swings, the Methodist church, the dry cleaners, and our family insurance agency. The post office was that red-brick-with-granite-steps type. When I was born in 1958 a postage stamp was four cents, President Eisenhower enjoyed high popularity, and economic growth was assumed. It was the peak of the baby boom, with my family doing its share in the 1950's with the birth of my sister, brother, and me. In TV-terms this was Mayberry. In actuality I really did know the sheriff and the mayor.

Although my parents didn't say it explicitly, they conveyed through attitudes and comments that we had social standing in our community. My parents weren't superficial, but they wanted us to keep the family honor. My grandmother, just one block away, seemed to have an acute awareness of social approval, and she was notably happy when we made the local newspaper for a school honor or Scout award. My parents and grandparents were involved with civic service and clubs, faithfully served as Boy and Girl Scout leaders, and enriched our lives with summer camp and dance lessons. Our small town life existed in a network of relationships and my parents had personal and business reputations of substance. They treated others well. There was also an underlying reality that gossip could be brutal and being targeted with criticism was something to be feared. Therefore, one should be careful to keep things quiet if something embarrassing happened.

I attended a small, private school with only 42 students in my grade. We knew each other well, and everyone saw I had more conservative leanings than most students. Ever since I made a commitment to living out my Christian faith when I was fourteen years old, the gap had been widening between my classmates and me. I prided myself in avoiding the adolescent stage of rebellion. It annoyed me that many thought it was cool to drink, sleep around, or lie to your parents about where you were going. I was offended with the immaturity of high school life and eager to get out of there. Feeling ignored by other students, I had pulled out of most activities at school.

During my senior year I had been taking classes only in the morning, then working at my parents' insurance and tax preparation business in the afternoon. By leaving at the beginning of lunch hour, I had avoided the awkwardness of classmates who didn't seem to want to sit with me anymore. Things had felt lonelier during the last two years since my older brother, Sam, had left for the Air Force Academy in Colorado. We'd been close during his last years in high school, and we'd supported each other in our spiritual commitments. Once popular, I now felt like a loner at school. *Oh, well, stick it out,* I thought. *Mom keeps reminding me that I'll be at college soon enough.* I'd been accepted at a Christian university in Oklahoma, where I thought I'd be respected for my faith. Meanwhile, I had my church family as my friends.

Despite my uncomfortable circumstances in high school, I had one place where I fit in. Our small, independent church might have had only 75 people in attendance, but the love and fellowship were in abundance. The church had started only a few years before and my parents had been founding members. The location right on the courthouse square was a remodeled store front, rather undignified by local standards. This raised the eyebrows of the traditional Baptist, Methodist, and Presbyterian churchgoers who were used to stained glass windows and vaulted sanctuaries.

Tonight was the Wednesday Bible study, one of my favorite parts of the week. I never missed a Sunday morning or evening service, or the Wednesday Bible study, unless I was out of town. I had become an excited theology student, and I never attended without taking notes and following along in my Bible as the pastor spoke.

Entering the building, I was quickly enveloped in a hug from Betty. Effusive and smiling, she was always affectionate. Another member, Francis, gave me a wink. I knew I held a special place with her. Her son, Todd, was about my age, and she'd known me since I was born. Ray and Melba were like second parents to me; they'd been my parent's friends for 25 years. Some of these people had held me when I was a baby. There weren't many teenagers in the church, but it didn't matter. I felt more validated by adults. Here in my support system I was accepted, even admired, for my spiritual commitment. I felt mature here, but most importantly, loved, and this seemed to make up for the rejections at school.

The service started, and after a few rousing praise songs there were announcements. A local family had lost their son and prayer was requested. An upcoming baby shower was announced for a member. So-and-so was going on vacation and wouldn't be there next Sunday. We shared the most ordinary family news, usually punctuated with laughter. Feeling affectionate and safe, I sang, "I'm so glad I'm a part of the family of God." *I love it here. I wish everyone understood what this kind of Christian love is about. This is my spiritual home.*

When Brother Hansen got up to teach, I was ready with my pen and notebook. Tonight we were continuing in the book of Romans. Everyone agreed he was an excellent Bible teacher and pastor. Going verse by verse through a book of the New Testament, he was astute at explaining the meaning of the text, making everyday applications to life, and keeping one engaged in the process. *This is Bible teaching the way everyone should hear it.* When the service was over, several people remarked about how much they were learning. For many, their faith had never been as meaningful or vibrant as it had been since he'd become our pastor. My opinion of him as competent and godly was frequently confirmed by others. I still had notes from many of the 200 messages I'd heard him preach.

Brother Hansen had moved to our town about three years before. As a congregation we'd always called him "Brother" instead of "Reverend," a practice used in some southern churches as a term of friendly endearment. He'd been an independent evangelist and pastor for years. He was high-energy for a 69-year-old, and could pass for someone ten years younger. When I'd first seen him I thought he looked friendly, his appearance at 230 lbs. being somewhat of a mix between Colonel Sanders and Santa Claus. He was six feet tall, with a barrel chest. He had a personal charisma, but most importantly, he was seen as someone who would teach us the Bible.

Brother Hansen was highly valued by the congregation. We felt lucky to have him as a pastor. His dedication to Scriptural teaching aroused intense loyalty in many people for whom being true to the Scriptures was the litmus test of a solid pastor. His wife, Blanche, was also our church pianist. Together, I felt they were two of my best friends. After exchanging hugs with both of them, I left with my parents to go home.

Sometime during 11th grade I had started meeting Brother Hansen once a week for spiritual discussions. When I arrived at his home each week, I stopped by the kitchen to say hello to Blanche, pet the cats, grab a cookie, and head into his study for our engaging and spirited conversations. A number of people came to his home to meet with him, even though he had an office in the store-front church building. Often I met other church members on my way out the door as they arrived for their appointments.

Although my parents had always applauded my individuality and abilities, I took it for granted that they would say I was special. *They're supposed to love me... they're my parents.* But it also felt good to hear Brother Hansen say that he respected me. When he affirmed my gifts and maturity, even though I was only seventeen, it encouraged me deeply. He acknowledged my commitment to God and assured me that God had good things in store for my life. This recognition helped to shore up my self-esteem that felt so diminished at school.

Although my discouragement at school was sometimes the topic, more often our Thursday meetings were spent in lively banter over spiritual themes, Bible interpretation, and questions about life. He seemed to be such a trustworthy guide. I endowed our relationship with immeasurable value. He was helping me develop myself, and I trusted him unconditionally. I usually had several questions that I was eager to present to him at each meeting.

Sitting behind his large oak desk, Brother Hansen would sometimes remove his glasses and furrow his thick gray eyebrows before he spoke. I felt mature for discussing philosophical questions that I knew many my age would avoid. With all the clout of his pastoral role, he was affirming my relationship with God and encouraging me to further growth.

I felt fortunate to have a pastor who was such a resource for my spiritual quest. He had what I valued and wanted, a personal closeness to God and a commitment to the Bible as the Word of God. A year earlier I had spent a great deal of time thinking about deepening my walk with God. We had spent several sessions talking about it and concluded the sessions with a brief prayer together. On one occasion when we prayed, I felt God's presence in a special way. Afterwards, my connection with God seemed clearer, and my appreciation for Brother Hansen only deepened.

At home after church that night, I continued reading one of the missionary biographies that Brother Hansen had loaned me. Eager to please him, I usually completed any reading suggestions he made. He'd introduced me to inspiring stories of Christian believers who had made a difference with their lives. Idealistic and motivated, I wondered what God was going to have me do with my life. One of my frequent prayers had been, "Lord, use me to do something special that no one else would do." I felt gutsy, yet a bit guilty. I also wanted to be famous.

Maybe a Christian singer? Would God let me have public visibility, or would I be a missionary somewhere in a remote place? More eager for the former, I also remembered that God's will should be put before mine, so I tried to submit my ambition to God.

My sister, Helen, and her husband, Steve, were on the staff of Campus Crusade for Christ, a respected Christian organization. They lived in Virginia and worked with college students. If I chose a similar vocation, I would certainly have the support of my family. Still undecided, I was open to pursuing anything from business to art. My parents had always said that we could major in anything we wanted, but we had to go to college. That wasn't a problem for me; I had always wanted to go to college. I wanted to be a leader. My experiences at summer camp confirmed my belief that I could lead others and that others looked up to me. I could clearly see that this was to be used for Christ.

Me as an idealistic teenager heading off to college

I had grown up in a small, safe world. My family was stable and loving. Both sets of my grandparents lived nearby and had 50-year marriages. My world was predictable and full of loving individuals I trusted. There was little skepticism about trusting others or trusting life to be good. My parents' love, coupled with my inborn sunny temperament, had given me a deeply internalized optimism about life. I believed that I could be successful. *If I can just get out of this silly high school, I'll get on with my life.*

Buoyed with encouragement, especially after my sessions with Brother Hansen, I kept counting the weeks until graduation. He was also excited about my college choice. He had previously lived in Oklahoma, where the university was, and validated my plans to go there.

Although I didn't speak of it often, I looked forward to having the opportunity to date in college. I'd had only minimal dating experience in high school, and I pictured an available group of guys at college. Surely there would be some boys at a Christian college who would be attracted to a girl like me. There was no question I wanted to be married eventually. I reflected briefly on Phil, a boy I'd liked in North Carolina who worked at the summer camp I'd attended. The summertime relationship had fizzled out, and I thought he liked another girl now.

Laying my reading by the bedside, I was already rehearsing a question I wanted to pose to Brother Hansen at our next meeting. It was something to look forward to.

> **Relationships of trust are the most important assets in life. When we trust someone we hand them our heart. We believe they are going to value it.**

Let us look for a moment at the delicate balance between power and trust. Because of the power imbalance in our society, a man often has the key to a woman's career, health, and future. If there is any legitimacy to this power, it must be wielded in trust as part of an ancient moral bargain that endows men —fathers, teachers, physicians, religious, economic, and political leaders —with such authority.

A man in a position of power over a woman holds a sacred trust to guard her welfare, guide her safely into life in the wider world, and eventually share the power with her so that she can, if she wishes, leave him and go her own way.

Peter Rutter, M.D.
*Sex in the Forbidden Zone:
When Men in Power – Therapists, Doctors, Clergy,
Teachers, and Others – Betray Women's Trust*
Tarcher, 1989

CHAPTER 2
The Betrayal

Arriving for a church service, I headed toward the restroom downstairs. I was an early arriver tonight and few others were here. As I approached the stairs, Brother Hansen came around the corner. Glad to see him, I extended my arms for the usual hug. Rather than merely hugging me, he raised my chin with his finger and placed a solid kiss on my mouth. I was startled. Without missing a beat, he said, "Glad to see you," and was off down the hall. His facial gestures didn't indicate anything unusual, but I inwardly felt a sense of embarrassment.

Taken aback by the surprise kiss, I thought: *What was that?* I didn't like kissing others on the mouth, and it violated my sense of internal boundaries. I knew some families kissed mouth-to-mouth, but we'd never done it in my family. An affectionate kiss on the cheek was the norm in my other relationships. This felt inappropriate...*a married man kissing me on the mouth?*

He had planted the kiss with assertiveness, and he had acted as though it was perfectly normal. Trying not to believe it was inappropriate, I dismissed it from my mind. I thought I must be exaggerating my own uncomfortable feelings and felt somewhat ashamed to even question whether my pastor had done anything improper.

Although I had reflected briefly on the kissing incident a few times, it wasn't on my mind when I arrived for my usual Thursday session later that week. As Brother Hansen and I talked, we were both sitting on the couch in his study. Suddenly, in the middle of our topic, he scooted over to me, put his arms around me, and started to kiss me.

Danger. Red light. Danger. Warning bells were going off inside me. My surprise turned immediately to fear. I felt physically frozen and emotionally intimidated.

In a seductive tone of voice, which I had never heard him use before, he said, "Let's put our tummies together." With one motion he pulled up my shirt and pulled me tight against him.

Repulsed, but mute and frozen, I couldn't get my bearings. *I don't like this, something's wrong!* After several seconds I began trying to push away. He released me, and I stood up and started trying to pull down my shirt and straighten my clothes.

Trying to break the spell of my own confusion, I said, "That...that was a good sermon on Sunday. I had never understood that passage in Revelation before. I have to be going." Groping to normalize the awkwardness, my deeply internalized values took over. My voice was polite. I was respectful to my pastor.

Looking to him for signals about what had just happened, I couldn't get a "read" on the situation from his facial expressions. He appeared calm and in control. "Sure," he said, "see you Sunday."

Returning home, I wanted to avoid thinking about what had happened, but I felt sick about it. *Why did he do that?* Normally, I talked to my mother about nearly everything that happened to me, but, ashamed about the pastor's behavior, I kept the incident to myself. Yet not talking to my mom when I was anxious was foreign to me, and my anxiety rose during the evening. *I'm not even sure exactly what happened.*

In bed that night, I replayed the scene. I tried to quell my anxiety through prayer. *Lord, show him that he shouldn't have done that. I didn't like it.*

During the next few days, I tried to put the encounter out of my head. When I couldn't, I tried to make meaning out of it. As I thought about it, an interpretation formed: *This is a one-time incident. He didn't mean to do that. It won't be repeated. I know him; he is a godly man. He'll probably be calling me soon to apologize. He'll take responsibility for it and then I'll say, "I forgive you," and then everything will be all right again.* Given the values I had heard him preach and what I had always seen of his behavior, expecting him to do the right thing seemed reasonable.

Unaware of my psychological need to deny the incident, I minimized it. *It must not mean anything. Just forget it.* It was too threatening to believe that there was inherently something wrong in him. I didn't want to see him as anyone other than my wonderful pastor who had taught me so much. Understanding the event as a brief slip on his part was the only explanation I could think of or mentally tolerate.

In light of this interpretation, there was nothing for me to do but wait for his apology. I never considered approaching him first about it; on no occasion had I confronted an adult in my life. He would do the right thing, I was sure. I just had to wait. With my generally trusting nature shored up, I tried to see our relationship as before.

At the next church service, Brother Hansen acted completely natural, greeting me in the ordinary way. I relaxed. *Things must be okay.* I reflected on what a good man he was and the church service at hand. Confirming my hope that everything was normal, everyone complimented the sermon message as usual. He had fulfilled our expectations once again. It was a challenging and meaty message. The joy and fellowship of the service uplifted me, and I felt optimistic. *He'll be apologizing to me soon, probably this week.* I was eager for him to apologize so we could clear the air and resume our predictable friendship.

Meanwhile, two weeks passed since the initial incident. Hansen had called me briefly on the phone about a church matter, but still did not mention the incident. There were Biblical topics and ideas I was waiting to discuss with him, so I headed back to his house for our usual Thursday meeting.

Confident he'd clear the air when I saw him privately, I arrived at his study. Things seemed normal enough. He sat down behind his desk and I took my seat in a chair. *Great, we're talking normally like we always do.*

It seemed an ordinary enough meeting. His friendliness disarmed any anxiety and made me feel like a peer. We discussed a missionary biography I'd just finished. A missionary to China, Hudson Taylor, was a model of spiritual devotion to his ideals and love for Christ. Brother Hansen related what reading about Taylor had meant for him. I said that I was also impressed by Taylor's faith when others around him wanted to quit. *I can tell everything's okay. This is how we usually relate.* I relaxed more.

We discussed how school was going and several special events which were upcoming at church. The hour passed quickly, as it usually did, and I stood up to leave. I had to get home; I was cooking supper for Mom, Dad, and myself this evening.

Approaching me, it looked as if there was something he was going to say. *Good, he's going to apologize.* He reached out both arms and touched my shoulders lightly.

"JoAnn, I'm in love with you." His voice took on a firm tone. Instantly, I felt the fear return. "I've been in love with you for quite a while, and you should know it." Then he pulled me hard against him and kissed me overbearingly. With one hand he reached below my skirt, behind my knee, and slid his hand up to my bottom.

Warning. Danger. Red light. Danger. I couldn't quell the sick, threatening feelings that were washing over me. Again frozen, I couldn't put my panicky confusion into words.

"You're a beautiful woman. I love you so much."

Frightened and intimidated, I tried to respond with an objection. "I love you, too, but..." I wanted to convey that I loved him in the brotherly way.

He interrupted me, "I'll see you next week." Releasing his grip on me, he pivoted to open the door. I lowered my eyes as I left, hoping not to encounter Mrs. Hansen on the way out of the house.

That night, it all seemed surreal. *This couldn't have happened.* I could hardly think about the passion he put behind the kisses. *He may have kissed me, but I didn't kiss him!*

My anxiety sky-high, I began praying. *Lord, you've got to convict him. I love him as my pastor, but please make him love his own wife. I don't want anything to happen to him or to our church.*

I felt sick every time I thought of him touching or kissing me. I just couldn't integrate this image of him with the image I had of him being my pastor and spiritual guide. He had done so much for me, and I felt indebted to him.

My thoughts were racing; I could hardly finish one thought before another crowded my mind. *I can't tell anyone about this. I just have to pray about it. If it gets out it might hurt our church, and there might be rumors.*

Admittedly, in our quiet community, there was some uneasiness about people leaving the mainline Baptist, Methodist, and Presbyterian churches to attend our church. Most churches had no more than a few hundred members, so it was noticeable when members left. This created some resentment about our church in the community; some perceived our church as "sheep-stealing." As members we worked hard at defending our church to those who were critical. We were invested in supporting our pastor and promoting him as a man of integrity. I often thought: *If anybody would just see the loving relationships and hear this wonderful Bible teaching, they'd know why we love it here so much.*

I didn't want anything to hurt these people I loved so deeply. I also firmly believed in the effectiveness of Brother Hansen's ministry. So many people seemed to be helped by him. I wouldn't want his ministry to be hurt. I didn't want to embarrass him. My longstanding loyalty to him was strong.

I prayed again, pleading to God to speak to Hansen, and tears came. *I believe in prayer; this is the right way to handle this.* Minimizing the violation to myself, I focused more on his and the church's welfare. The anxiety had hardly abated as I fell asleep, unaware of the strength of my two companions: fear and ignorance.

We can mistakenly believe that protecting our church, teacher, or family friend should always be our guiding principle. What we are really doing is avoiding our own pain, embarrassment, and confrontation of the abuser. Truth telling is almost always the most prudent choice, although we must be willing to face the pain it may bring.

For more understanding of the dynamics of sexual abuse and unequal power in relationships, see Essay #14, Bathsheba the Lamb.*

* I have written fourteen short essays at the end of this book to address important topics. The essays may be read at the conclusion of the book or periodically as I reference them in the text. May this information bring you additional insight and hope.

The clergy role carries a great deal of power in and of itself, and one of the most insidious aspects of that power is the role of "man of God." In some sense the minister carries ultimate spiritual authority, particularly in the eyes of a trusting parishioner who looks to him for spiritual guidance and support.

But the male minister also possesses other forms of power: as a man, he carries the power society confers upon men and socializes them to hold over women, often in the guise of being their protectors. He is often physically stronger and more imposing. He may be an employer. He may also assume a teaching or mentoring role which encourages women to listen to his advice and correction. Often he also functions as a counselor, with all the transference inherent in such a relationship.

Pamela Cooper-White
Soul Stealing: Power Relations in Pastoral Sexual Abuse
The Christian Century, February 20, 1991

CHAPTER 3
Descent into Confusion

It had now been three weeks since Brother Hansen had kissed me at his house. No new thoughts had come to me about solving this situation. Waiting for him to repent and apologize to me seemed to be the only viable solution. I was fixated on praying for Brother Hansen and asking God to show him that he was wrong. It was absolutely out of the question for me to tell anyone. *I wouldn't know what to say. Someone might say I caused it. I don't want to hurt him. I'm embarrassed.* Those were enough reasons to be silent.

Inwardly I was still struggling, not wanting to believe that Hansen could do anything bad. I admired him spiritually. It might take time for him to see that what he had done was wrong, but I felt that given time, he would. *After all, he is a godly man, and he will do the right thing.* I rehearsed my basic beliefs about him, trying to soothe my fear. *He'll repent, and then no one will have to know what he did… it will save his ministry, and he can go on helping people.* I felt responsible to protect him from failure. Besides, Christians were supposed to be patient with each other. He deserved my confidence.

Hansen phoned and said that he'd like to talk. In an upbeat voice, he said that God had been speaking to him. Relief flooded me, and I said that I'd be right over. His voice on the phone was reassuring and inviting, and his pastoral authority and charm easily overcame any sensible hesitations I had about going back to his house.

When I arrived he suggested that I just sit and listen. He said that there were important things that he'd been praying about and wanted to tell me.

"My love for you is from God," he began. "I want you to know that it's not lust, but love. You are a dedicated Christian woman, and we're right for each other." His tone was earnest and calm. "Yet no one would understand our love for each other and what we are doing, so of course, we have to keep it a secret."

He continued methodically in a controlled voice. "God had showed me that He was about to open up something special for me, and now I know that it's this love that I have for you. You've been sensing that God was preparing you for something special, too, and now I can see how it's coming together. I know that I can't live without you."

I was flabbergasted. I couldn't think of anything to say.

"Of course, you don't have to love me, but I know that if you don't, I'll just have to resign and move away from here. I wouldn't be able to stand seeing you every week if you don't love me."

Immediately my mind was a scrambled mess. *Was he saying that we were supposed to do ministry together? What does he mean, "What WE are doing?" What did he say that God was showing him?* The questions wouldn't form in my mouth, so I sat silent.

13

His facial expression was calm. He looked completely normal. *Was he talking about ME?*

"I hope God does use me." I stumbled to make some sort of comment.

"God is putting us together to be a team for Him. You know, I've never really been a team with my wife; she's never understood me. You're the kind of woman who understands my mind."

I recoiled at the implication that he was criticizing his wife to me. I felt embarrassed. I didn't like his references to me as a *woman*; I felt childlike in his presence.

"I want you to love your wife," I mustered the courage to blurt it out.

"Nobody wanted our marriage to work more than I did," he continued, "but she has broken off all affection for me. God has told me that He has released me from my marriage to Blanche."

I couldn't put my finger on what was happening. A feeling of confusion was my only reality.

"The Lord has been using you to give me courage to go on in my ministry. I wouldn't want to go on without you." His voice was sincere and caring as he continued, "I know that I don't have to feel guilty about this. I've prayed about it, and it's okay."

I honestly can't remember anything I said in response to his statements. I felt mute again.

"We'll talk again in a few days," he stated flatly. He motioned for me to stand, and I did. He kissed me lightly on the forehead and said, "I love you, and I'm so glad you understand."

Later that evening, I tried to make sense out of his statements. He hadn't apologized, but he had said that God had been speaking to him. I tried to focus on that, believing that he must somehow have meant he was sorry for kissing and touching me. I tried to recall his comments. *Did he say something about needing me to love him, or he'd leave town?* I felt sick. *He couldn't leave! Everybody needs and loves him.* I wished that I'd said more. I felt responsible to show him how loved he was in the church, and I wanted to persuade him to love his own wife.

I reflected on the derogatory statements he'd made about Blanche. I sensed they were inappropriate. I was embarrassed to hear that their marriage wasn't close. They looked fine outwardly. *Why was he telling me these things?*

My emotions alternated between anxiety and numbness. I prayed for him again.

When I saw him at church Sunday, he was cheery and buoyant. I monitored his sermon closely. Several times he related how rich his relationship with the Lord had been lately, and his optimism spilled over to include the church....he thought we were on the verge of really growing. He knew that God was going to bring many needy people to our door. I watched him interact with one of the elders after church. He looked so normal. *I know everything's going to be all right.* I blocked out the fear that was becoming my constant companion. *I'm going to have faith. No one else seems to notice anything wrong. No one else looks alarmed.*

Several days later I answered the phone at my parents' office. It was Brother Hansen, and he sounded depressed. "I've got to tell you some things soon," he said mysteriously, "because Satan is going to try to get to you."

I believed in the reality of Satan, and I certainly wouldn't want to be playing into his hands. "OK, I'll drop by after work," I offered.

Arriving in his study, he quickly shut the door. "I was awake nearly all last night. God showed me that Satan is going to try to make a play for you. God has put us together and Satan is going to try and break us up."

His face had a strange sadness. I had never seen him depressed like this. "I've just got to hear you say that you won't leave me, so I'll have ammunition to fight off Satan's attacks." He sounded almost pitiful, and I felt drawn to comfort him.

"You're a wonderful pastor. Please don't be discouraged. You know that I appreciate and love you." I felt distressed to see him like this. This was no time to try and tell him the doubts that I was having about what he had said a few days before.

Almost crying, he continued. "You're just a young girl, I know. And you could have any man you want. I just don't know if you're going to be able to cling to your calling of being with me. I might as well quit now and leave town."

"No, really, I think everything is going so well in the church right now... please just keep trusting the Lord. Really, Satan is not going to do anything." I was shaken to see him so melancholy. I found myself groping to encourage him and to lift him from this mysterious sadness.

"Of course, I'm not going to leave you," I assured him, meaning that I believed in our friendship and loyalty to one's friends. He'd been my good friend, and I didn't betray my friends.

During March and April, my anxiety grew. I was finding it hard to keep up a normal face at home. He began to phone me at home and summon me to his house; he had to tell me the newest thing that the Lord was showing him.

When I was by myself, I could articulate an objection and practice saying it to him in my head. "You shouldn't be loving someone who isn't your wife. It's against Scripture." I knew he'd understand that. Hadn't he been emphasizing obedience to the Scripture? But when I arrived in his office, he could talk faster than I could think.

"You're probably thinking that I am still married and shouldn't love someone other than my wife," he was rebutting my objections before I even voiced them. "But Blanche and I have a spiritual divorce which the Lord has given me, so it's not wrong for you and me to love each other this way. Of course, others wouldn't understand why we love each other like this." He was implying that we were both consenting partners and equals.

At times he kissed me, and progressed to touching my breasts.

But mostly he lectured me.

Like water rushing down a river, I was swept along with his diatribes. There seemed nowhere to get a word in, and I felt more and more overwhelmed by his speeches. Everything he said was coated in a kind of "God-talk." "God showed me this." "The Lord would want you to..." With my deep respect for God and His Word, the effect of this type of manipulative language was to prevent me from doing any real critical thinking.

The speeches came several times a week now, and he continually reminded me of how much he needed me and loved me. I was the key to his staying here, to God using him, to his overcoming Satan. I was to be his partner. I was left mentally exhausted by the intensity of listening to him.

Whenever I managed to try and confront him, he became dejected again, saying that he was afraid I wouldn't have the courage to live up to God's best... loving him. In his depressions he would sometimes cry on the phone, baiting me to reassure him that I loved him. I complied, feeling sorry for him and also feeling obligated to support him.

He particularly surprised me one day by saying that now he had "peace... ever since I had declared that I loved him like he loved me." Unable to object to the obvious twisting of my statements, I couldn't remember when or how I had said that. In his presence I felt speechless. Meanwhile, he was becoming more over-bearing.

My anxiety was growing to unmanageable levels, yet it was hard for me to believe that he was mistreating me. I began to cry alone regularly now, begging God to change Brother Hansen and stop him. The confusion in my mind made rational thought impossible. Since I felt fearful of talking to anyone else about him, I had no one but him with whom to sort through my feelings and questions. I tried to override the increasing feelings of fear which I had while around him. He hadn't repented. *I will try and talk to him again. I have to pray more.*

It was a welcome distraction when a family from our church asked me to make a weekend trip with them to Houston. Bob and Doris had two girls younger than myself, and I knew the family well. They had been in the church for two years and we had spent time together; I was comfortable with them. Bob was an elder in the church, and he and Doris were part of my circle of church family whom I highly respected.

I was surprised when Bob raised an issue about Brother Hansen while on the trip. Bob thought that Hansen had been irritable and unfair regarding a church matter. What did I think about it?

Flattered to be asked for an opinion, I discussed Bob's concern. Parts of me cringed that Hansen was seen by others as being contentious. This validated the feelings I had that something was terribly wrong with him. This thought was terrifying to me, and I tried to shove it down inside whenever it surfaced. If I followed this line of thinking to its logical conclusion, then my mentor was spiritually sick. This whole thing could blow sky-high. If he were deeply flawed, he would have to be asked to leave the pastorate, and people would be wounded and disillusioned. But my seventeen year old idealism rejected this. It was going to be okay. I could save anything bad from happening by intervening with Hansen. Assuming an adult role, I told Bob that I'd be glad to talk to Hansen when we got back. I did not realize that Bob should not have been discussing this with me at my age. In addition, I should never have tried to intervene in any problems Hansen caused among the church members. Blurred boundaries were everywhere.

The next week, when I managed to bring up the topic with Hansen, he exploded with sarcasm. "Oh, so now you're one of the elders, are you?" He was willing to play hardball with sarcasm.

I felt immediately deflated and pierced with guilt for confronting him. He continued with heated criticism about Bob, casting doubt on Bob's spiritual integrity. I was shocked. I'd never heard him use this tone before. I felt bewildered and afraid to continue the conversation. I couldn't believe that he'd say such harsh things about Bob. His voice was ugly, his tone authoritarian. I'd never seen him like this.

"Maybe you'd better pray about things before you just go assuming that you know what I've done wrong!" His voice was shaming.

I felt powerless and scolded like a small child. The manipulation had worked; now I was willing to assume *I* was wrong. "I'm really sorry. I didn't know the whole story. Please, please, forgive me for asking. It wasn't any of my business." I was in tears. I'd always been particularly sensitive to anger. I was the most compliant of the three children in my family, and the one who apologized first.

Returning home, I couldn't find my sense of equilibrium. Too frightened and shaky to be angry with him, a cloud of dread and fear gripped me like a vise. His wrath had hurt so badly. I cried from the pain of it.

Sinking into my fear, I tried not to think. I didn't have names or categories for what was happening. I didn't have answers. *I don't know what to do.*

The emotional manipulation I suffered took many forms: playing on my desire to please God, obligating me to support the abuser in his low moods, declaring that my objections are the "work of Satan," shaming me for attempting a confrontation, and intimidating me with anger and sarcasm.

The reason that sarcasm is very harmful is that it adds an emotionally-laden twist to the words that evoke shame in the hearer. Heavy-handed sarcasm is similar to a tricky wrestling move: it disables and destabilizes the hearer so that it is hard to make a comeback. You're emotionally pinned.

Dr. Peter Rutter, a psychiatrist who has studied sexual manipulation, offers a look into the mental progression of a manipulator's mind. The manipulator thinks:

1) I'm looking her over.
2) I wonder if she's interested in me.
3) I wonder what she'd be like to touch.
4) I can't stop fantasizing about her when I'm away from her.
5) I'll ask her about her sex life. (Dr. Rutter says this step begins the exploitation and boundary violation.)
6) I'll ask her whether she has fantasies about me. (Dr. Rutter says this is a proposition in disguise.)
7) I'll begin to close the physical space between us and see how she reacts.
8) I'll become more overtly suggestive, hoping she will respond.
9) I think she's being seductive toward me. (Dr. Rutter says the abuser is projecting the fantasy onto her.)
10) I'm fantasizing about how exactly I will seduce her.
11) Can I get away with it? (Practical considerations...will I be caught?)
12) The abuser's emotional justification: Can something that feels so right be wrong?
13) The last barrier: Can my values, or my inner self still be heard?
14) All restraint gone: I'll move ahead and sexualize the relationship.

After exploiting the victim, most perpetrators admitted that they knew the victim wasn't really a willing partner to the sexual fantasy, but was being compliant because of psychological coercion...quickly sapping the relationship of the euphoria.

Peter Rutter, M.D.
Sex in the Forbidden Zone:
When Men in Power – Therapists, Doctors, Clergy,
Teachers, and Others – Betray Women's Trust
Tarcher, 1989

CHAPTER 4

Breaking the Secret

Although drowning in anguish, I felt unable to disappoint him or leave the relationship. The association with Brother Hansen had represented so much hope to me during the past three years. Naively believing our pastor-parishioner friendship could be restored to its sanity, I resolved to pray harder. I couldn't just abandon him or refuse to accept his calls. I felt I owed him more than that. I didn't want to hurt him. I defaulted to believing the best about him, my tendency in all my relationships.

Due to my deep dependence on him, my fantasy that he would repent, and the inequality of power between us, I couldn't see that I was at risk of accepting the relationship on virtually any terms he set. Despite rehearsing positive thoughts, anxiety would overwhelm me at times. One afternoon in April I was at home alone after school. I was having trouble focusing on my homework. I couldn't control the fear. Crying, I began a vehement prayer time.

"Please, please, Lord, help me know what to do!" I felt frantic, and the tears streamed down my face profusely. I cried for half an hour. My face was bright red and my eyes swollen. Prior to this, I had done most of my crying at bedtime when my parents wouldn't notice, but today I couldn't hold it back.

Suddenly, I realized that my mother had driven up the driveway, home early from work. She came straight in the house looking for me. When she saw me, fear came over her face.

"What's wrong?" She was frightened, and her voice showed it.

I put my head in my hands and continued to cry. *Now what was I going to say?*

She put her arms around me and said that she'd been at work, but suddenly felt a compelling need to come home and check on me.

"Please, talk to me," she said, urging me to look at her. My mother and I had been close, and I'd always come clean when she demanded it. I broke.

"Brother Hansen has been doing some stuff to me. He's kissed me and stuff." I was shaking and hated to hear myself even utter the words. It sounded as awful to me as I knew it was sounding to her.

"What? What do you mean? When? Where?" she had four questions at once. I spoke of one of the occasions early on when he'd first begun approaching me. I didn't want to give many details.

Shame washed over me. This felt terrible. I hoped she wouldn't press me for more information. I had feared anyone finding out about Hansen's actions, and talking about it was proving as shaming as I'd subconsciously feared it would be.

Mom looked shocked and stunned. "Was there anything else?" she pressed for more information.

"Well, he…uhhh…he…he did touch my breasts." It felt dirty to say, and shaming. I felt like a worm.

"Is that *all?*"

"Yes, that's all." I just couldn't go on. It was too terrible. I couldn't tell her about his believing God had told him to love me. That it wasn't lust, but love. That he and Blanche had a "spiritual divorce" and he didn't think loving me contradicted Scripture. That he had begun to be sarcastic and angry with me, and that in between times he was melancholy, and I'd been trying to encourage him.

I had only told Mom the tip of the iceberg. I had mentioned the sexual violation in a minimal way. I couldn't even give words to the ways he had violated my emotional and spiritual boundaries. I didn't have the language for it. I could hardly make sense of that myself, much less communicate it to someone else.

We sat for a few moments in silence. Her face showed her own mental chaos. I felt sorry for my mom. I didn't want her to have to hear what I'd said.

Attempting to buy time for thinking and to quell her anxiety, Mom suggested that we get in the car and go for a ride. There was only one thought in the forefront of my mind.

"Please, please, Mom, don't tell anybody. Please don't tell Dad." I couldn't face being shamed in anyone else's eyes. Telling my mother had proved to be as painful as I had dreaded such an occasion would be.

We rode around for an hour, both of us in a mental fog. Mom made vague references to men and sexuality. "Men don't behave themselves sometimes. What Hansen was doing with you could have led to something else." I knew that she meant sexual intercourse and the implication of that sent me in another spin of shame. I felt nauseated. These were thoughts that I didn't want made explicit.

Although she didn't indicate that she thought I was responsible, she didn't absolve me either. She was also confused, and there was no clear statement from her that "this is all Hansen's responsibility, and you are innocent."

After an hour of awkwardness and semi-communication, we returned home. I had extracted from her a promise that she wouldn't tell anyone else, even Dad. I pushed my interpretation that Hansen had only made a "slip" and that everything would be okay. We wouldn't want to hurt the church. I also promised her that I'd call Hansen and tell him not to contact me anymore, and that I had told my mother about what he'd done.

Hansen called before I could call him, and he knew immediately by my voice that something had happened. "I told my mother." I was cautious in forming my words.

"Told her WHAT?" He was instantly defensive.

I related briefly that she had caught me crying and demanded to know what was going on. "I told her that you'd kissed me and touched my breasts."

"Well, you've ruined me. I might as well resign now." His voice had that angry and shaming quality again. He hung up quickly.

The next twelve hours passed fitfully, and I dreaded all the scenarios I had played out in my head. The double bind I had been in had finally exploded. I was destined to lose no matter what course of action I had taken. I saw it as losing my pastor and possibly our church if I told, or losing my integrity and sanity if I kept quiet. It was all too confusing. I didn't feel mature anymore. A sense of stupidity and failure surrounded me.

A surprise phone call came later that evening. A church member told us Brother Hansen had developed chest pains and had been hospitalized. There was no mention of him resigning or any other problem. *Is he having a heart attack, or is he reacting to the shock of me telling my mother?*

Immediately there was a swell of concern for him from the congregation. The consensus was that maybe he'd been working too hard. He might need a vacation, a sabbatical, or some extended time off. I defaulted to the belief that he was probably really sick. Projecting goodwill on him, I thought perhaps he was in such sorrow over his behavior toward me that it made him sick. I was sure he had been inwardly repenting of his actions toward me. Still, I didn't know what would happen.

Although my mother had told me not to contact him in the hospital, I felt that I should write a letter to him and tell him that I was sorry and that I had not meant to hurt him. I wanted to express that I forgave him of what he had done, and I was sure that he would continue to be a useful servant of the Lord. I wrote the letter and walked to the hospital. I saw another church member going in to visit him and that solved the problem of how to get the letter to him.

When he got out of the hospital three days later, he called me on the phone.

"You'll never believe what happened," he said. "An angel appeared to me in the hospital and let me know that everything was going to be okay." I was unsure of his meaning, and didn't ask.

He finished by telling me that he and his wife would be leaving on a one month sabbatical to Oregon, their home state. He wanted me to write to him while he was gone at a post office box in Enterprise, Oregon, where they would be staying. He gave me the post office box number. I agreed, glad to hear his voice was upbeat and that he didn't seem angry at me anymore for talking to my mom. I decided that if writing him would normalize our relationship again, it would be good.

I believed his story about the angel. Maybe this was God's way of saying that he would continue in his ministry and all this could be put behind us. I wanted to interpret it as a sign that Hansen was his old, spiritually-healthy self again. I was sure that he'd been sorry for his behavior toward me, even though he never indicated that he thought it was wrong. I was eager to endow him with a wholesomeness and innocence again. I projected that he must be repentant even though he never acknowledged being sorry. I was relieved by his contact, and happy to hear that he hadn't immediately resigned. I didn't tell my mom that he had called or that I had agreed to write him.

A week after I'd told my mother, she brought up the matter in front of my dad at the dinner table. I was mortified. She had told him, and a sense of disgrace enveloped me to learn that Dad knew. The conversation was awkward. I learned that they didn't plan to talk to Hansen or the elders. They had decided that I should just stay away from him until I left for college in August. In addition, I would be returning to North Carolina for the summer as a junior counselor at a girl's camp. There were only a few weeks overlapping when Hansen would be back from Oregon and I would not yet be at camp. Soon after camp I'd be leaving for college. I agreed to keep my distance. That was all that was said.

I was relieved that my parents weren't planning to confront Hansen or talk to the elders. I intuitively knew that would cause some sort of blow-up in the church or else Hansen would resign. I would have felt responsible for ruining Hansen's ministry or embarrassing the church. I believed that everything was all right now.

Although I could see their anger at Hansen, my parents chose not to react. The same forces of denial and fear, as well as their inexperience in situations like this, had shaped all of us. They probably feared embarrassing me, the church, and themselves. Knowing that I'd be leaving for college in Oklahoma, seven hours away, seemed sufficient. Meanwhile, I would stay away from Hansen.

Hansen had more cards to play than my parents did. During this era of the 1970's, clergymen who engaged in sexual misconduct were rarely taken to task. There was an absence of cultural and religious power to confront a minister. In a small, independent church such as our own, there was no organizational board above the local elders to turn to. Our church had no ties to any other body of churches, leaving it no recourse to a broader denominational policy for dealing with these matters of impropriety.

On a personal level, the traditional respect for the office of minister and both my parents' and my own unwillingness to believe we could have misjudged our pastor were a powerful social protection for him. Dealing with a minister's indiscretions isn't usually in one's comfort zone. In our minds, this person was placed in leadership because he was esteemed as being higher, smarter, more gifted, more experienced, and more spiritual than the rest of us. A pastor was a respected community leader. How would we go about confronting *him*?

As the Hansens left on their trip, I was entering my final month in high school. I was notified that I was the 3rd honor graduate, and I'd be giving a speech at graduation. It felt good. Helen had been second in her class, and Sam had been valedictorian. Mom and Dad were proud.

It was a relief to have other things to think about. There were graduation presents and parties and it was a happy time. On the night of my graduation, I began my speech by recognizing my paternal grandparents. That evening was their 53rd wedding anniversary. Everyone clapped. A sense of normalcy and family togetherness seemed restored, especially between my mother and me. It was a relief. At church, everyone was functioning normally in Hansen's absence. I was relieved that the crisis seemed to have passed without his resigning and now things could get back to normal.

I wrote Hansen three times during his month in Oregon. The letters were generic, and probably all sounded alike. I related graduation events, upcoming plans for camp and college, and trivial news from the congregation. I didn't mention any of his misconduct with me. I was eager to forget it myself. It now seemed easier to pretend it had never happened than to dissect it anymore. I didn't want to reflect on the bizarre ideas he had been having about me the past few months. I had no doubt he'd quickly dropped those ideas when he'd been recently shaken back to reality.

I knew my parents wouldn't approve of my writing him, but I felt obligated. I didn't want him to think that I'd just rejected him as a person or a friend. I believed in forgiving people and moving on. I didn't want the relationship to end on broken terms. Everyone deserves a second chance.

I thought of the principles of my faith as I understood them. *Wasn't that the way Jesus would want it?*

The disclosure of sexual abuse impacts everyone with fear, denial, and confusion about what to do. It is common for families to deal with it ineffectively. Most often they respond with silence or secrecy, not seeking outside counsel, and minimizing the abuse. This is especially true when the abuser is within one's circle of loyalty (church, family, or friends).

In these situations, it is absolutely necessary to seek professional help from a trained counselor. A counselor or therapist could have brought objectivity to my parents, helped them to understand the dynamics in the situation, and supported them in making the uncomfortable disclosures necessary to protect me. My parents needed an outsider to challenge them about their fears of community embarrassment and of the church's potential collapse, but they chose not to talk to anyone about it. Even if my parents had gone to the elders, the elders might have minimized the abuse and given in to rationalizations, influencing my parents to stay quiet.

A therapist would have created a safe zone where I could have disclosed all the ways Hansen was manipulating, grooming, and abusing me. Although I had begged my parents not to tell anyone, this was my immature, fearful perspective. I needed them to have confronted Hansen and sought support for both me and themselves. They were my parents and I needed them to do this. The abuse should have ended there.

In later years my parents felt a strong sense of guilt when they realized the serious error in judgment for not reporting Hansen to the church leadership and confronting him directly.

Because I was older than sixteen, I did not have legal protection under Louisiana law, otherwise reporting Hansen to child protective authorities would have been an essential step.

A pastor possesses a unique amount of power.
Like a doctor or a therapist, he sees people at their most vulnerable.
But unlike the other two, his interest is freighted (burdened)
with a divine imprimatur (sanction).
A sexual encounter between pastor and counselee is a profound
violation not only of the body,
but the spirit as well.

Ann-Janine Morey
Blaming Women for the Sexually Abusive Male Pastor
The Christian Century, October 5, 1988

CHAPTER 5

The Recapture

I had no real understanding of the dynamics of what had happened during the past four months. I could not articulate that Hansen had misused his power and that I had felt bound to silence by his authority. I was too embarrassed to process my confusion about Hansen with my mother, and she didn't try to talk about it either. All the fear and confusing thoughts still lay in my mind in a muddled mess. I tried to detach from the bewildering pressure of it.

I had absolutely no sense of the depth of his narcissism, that is, his excessive self-absorption and lack of empathy for others. It was exceeded only by the vastness of my own denial. Against every evidence I kept trying to believe that he was good. Overcompensating for his guilt, I had been willing to absolve his responsibility. I was trying to absolve someone who had not repented.

With no understanding of the nature of abuse, or even that this *was* abuse, I was unaware that the door was still open to danger. I had no insight about how to defend myself from future manipulation.

We heard that the Hansens had returned from Oregon. A welcome-home gathering was planned at their house for the church members. I tried to convince my parents that I should greet them.

"I don't think you should go there. Remember, we said that you'd keep your distance," Dad spoke his opinion. His mouth showed tension even though he continued to pass the food at the dinner table. I felt awkward and we broke eye contact.

"Really, it will be all right. I just plan to say hello for a minute," I managed. I felt that it was better to act like everything was normal and visit them.

I arrived at the Hansen's house and there were a few other church members there. *Good, others are here. I'll just make it a short visit to sort of break the ice.* After all, I hadn't seen him since before he went in the hospital.

After a brief visit he followed me out to the car as I was leaving. "I got your letters. I knew you'd write me," he said.

"Yeah, sure, I didn't mind." I tried to smile normally.

He lowered his voice. "At first I was thinking that you had rejected me, then I saw that you felt the same way I do…I could see that you loved me. You know, you almost shook me up last month."

The ambiguous nature of the words sounded strange. Deja vu was happening inside me. I had the same fear that I'd had previously, but I was not emotionally mature enough to have a name for what was happening. I could not form responses to his manipulative techniques. I was unable to object, to say, "You're projecting your own feelings onto me." I was afraid to say anything, and I didn't know what he meant by "rejected me" and "shook me up." He was masterfully using his psychological advantages of age and control.

"We'll have to meet to talk it over," he said.

I felt incapable of doing anything that might disappoint him. I agreed to meet him tomorrow at the church. I supposed that he must have some legitimate questions.

As I thought about it later, I told myself that we did have some straightening out to do between us. I knew my parents wouldn't approve, but I felt maybe he wanted to tell me how he'd resolved things in his own mind, and how he'd been mixed up about me. I still believed that he would want to apologize to me. It would be good to tell him in person that I forgave him.

When I arrived at his office in the church, he was quick to speak first. "You should know that the Lord showed me some things while I was in Oregon. First, when your mother came home unexpectedly that day, Satan was sending her home to try and break us up. It nearly worked."

This was surreal. I felt my whole body tense up. I felt that I had been transported back to six weeks ago, the last time I was in his office.

"No one would understand the love we have because this is a special situation from God. By your letters I could tell that you loved me like I love you."

His voice had that strange tone to it again. "Your parents think that they're so spiritual, but I could tell you a lot of things that people say about them." His voice twisted with sarcasm. He seemed intent on severing my loyalty to them.

I began to cry. I felt no strength to try and reason with him. I had sent him the generic letters about school and summer activities. I didn't know what he was talking about. I was shocked that he seemed to have picked up where he left off in April.

The next ten minutes were a mixture of his sarcastic remarks about my parents and what "the Lord had shown" him about us. He said that the Lord had put us together for a special purpose to do His work. He hoped that I was dedicated enough to pursue it.

Before I left, he cautioned me about not letting my parents know a thing.

Back at home, the sickening feelings, so familiar from the spring, were all over me. I was having a hard time keeping my head straight. *Maybe I'm supposed to work with him, or maybe help him in the ministry. Lord, are You trying to tell me that?* I was more hurt than angry that he had made unkind references to my parents.

During the next three weeks before camp I met him at his church office at times when my parents wouldn't have missed me.

He spent hours convincing me of his ideas. He had always been thwarted in the past by difficult people in his churches. He knew that there were greater things that God wanted him to do. He saw things in me that were meant to compliment his gifts. He was certain God had put us together.

He also began to grill me for every detail in my life. He especially wanted to know the history of every boy I'd liked and whether I'd kissed them or had sexual thoughts about them. He said I needed to be educated about sexual matters and he began to explain sexual terminology. I was embarrassed but felt helpless to object.

Too powerful for me to get past, his intimidating presence seemed larger than life.

The most shocking thing he said occurred just before I left for camp. "I know this sounds strange for me to say," he was speaking cautiously, "but the Lord has shown me that Blanche is going to die and you are going to marry me."

I felt more numb than startled. His bombardments on my mind had taken their toll.

"A lot of Christians in the past, like those in the books you've been reading, had to give up their own dreams to do what God called them to do. We have to be willing to do whatever God asks of us. When God puts us together we won't be able to stay around here because no one would accept our marriage. We might have to run off to Mexico."

He ended our meeting by kissing and caressing me. In my fear I felt detached from my body, and the marked feelings of disgust which I'd had earlier were distant. I could neither feel nor object.

Panic would set in between the times I saw him, but I felt inexplicably drawn to obey him and return for the next meeting. Right before I left for camp he fell into another one of his morose spells. He was pitiful and near crying. "You're going to go back to your old boyfriend in North Carolina. I know you won't be strong enough to follow God's call to love me," his voice was whiny and self-pitying.

"That boy and I don't like each other anymore," I said with mild defensiveness. "Besides, I haven't even talked to Phil in a year."

"Satan is going to set you up to see him, I'm sure of it," he said confidently.

He said so many absurd things to me that I had begun to stop reacting. He spent hours convincing me with his endless, well-thought-through rationalizations. He wanted me to agree with him, and he hounded me until I did.

Although he regularly insulted my parents and sometimes me, I felt incapable of saying, "I feel disrespected." It would only have triggered a lecture. In those instances I buried all my own feelings. He was intent on severing my loyalty to my parents and casting doubt on their character.

Subconsciously, I was adopting the role of taking care of him. When he was morose, I sought to buoy him up. I was worried that his moodiness would show in the church, and others would get suspicious. Meanwhile, he appeared to be normal in all the worship services.

I was no longer arguing with him. I recoiled at the thought of marrying him when Blanche died. I cried about it some nights. *I don't want to marry him!* It was easy to say when I was alone, but in his presence I was voiceless. *I don't want to leave the people I love or run off to Mexico!* The idea of running off to Mexico made me sick. *These weren't the plans I had for my life!* I felt repulsed by his age and did not find him attractive, but I never told him this because I was too polite to insult him. I knew he saw himself as youthful and appealing.

I began to consider that maybe God really had told him these things. His speeches had begun pickling my mind. Although it seemed crazy at first, my objections were receding, and I was becoming blind to the insanity of his ideas. His rationalizations were finding a foothold. My "eye for truth" was fading.

He returned from a men's Bible conference in a bright mood. "The last 20 years I've had a recurring dream," he said. "In the dream I would be tired and lonely, and wishing someone loved me. A woman would come to me in the dream and comfort me. While I was at the conference I had a vision that the woman was standing next to me, and if I turned I would be able to see her face and know who she was. When I looked, I saw you." His face was practically glowing and his voice was kind. It was a relief after the heavy-handed way he usually presented his ideas.

According to his vision, I was the one he had waited for and needed. God had given me to him. He told me this with eagerness and convincing intensity. He believed it. His interpretations had made a beachhead in my mind and I started to agree.

I knew that I was living deceitfully by continuing to see him. I had to work harder than previously at keeping up a normal face around my parents. I tried to fill the conversation at home with talk of camp and college. Meanwhile my 18th birthday came and went. With practice, I had gained some skill in blanking out my feelings when I wanted to. I was guilty over my behavior, but still tolerant of his.

One day I couldn't hide my depression and confusion when I saw Hansen. "I can see that you're having a demonic oppression," he stated. He prayed for me that it would leave.

Before I left that day he pushed the sexual contact further. "Don't worry. I'm not going to have sex with you. This isn't lust, remember?" His confident presentation masked the treason in his logic.

I arrived in North Carolina to spend a few days with an older friend, Carolyn, before camp started. While looking through her magazines, I saw an article by Bill Gothard, a Christian educator I respected. He described a situation where a married pastor thought he was in love with another woman in his church. The article pointed out the deception of the pastor who believed that "God had given him the love he had for the woman." It was practically a blow-by-blow account of Hansen's modus operandi. I felt unable to shove down the fear and dread. This made it clear: Hansen was sinning.

However, the article presented the woman as a co-initiator of the affair so I falsely assumed that I was equally guilty. I felt shamed. Also, if the article were right, Hansen was terribly sick in the head. I tried not to think too deeply. I had no more answers to this dilemma now than I'd had five months ago. I again felt as burdened as the day my mother had found me crying. *Lord, are You trying to speak to me? Again, I don't know what to do!*

When Hansen called that night, I was dreading his questions. My anxiety was so high, I felt I would explode. As usual, I could not hide my fear and he capitalized on my vulnerability. He demanded early on to know what was wrong.

I cautiously explained about what I had read in the magazine and the doubts I was having. I had already learned to edit everything I said.

He chided me for my lack of faith. I dissolved into tears. As his anger rose, I melted into an emotional pretzel. I was twisted every way his rationalizations pulled.

"You'll see I'm right." His voice was arrogant. Then he delivered the first of his many prophecies: "God told me that you are going to betray me by trying to see Phil while you are there."

He had recently begun to predict that "I was going to leave him because I didn't have enough faith to do what God had called me to do." His judgment about me felt so insulting. I had always wanted to do what God called me to do, and I fell into defending myself. I focused more on this than considering whether Hansen could have known what God's will was for me. The issues were confused in my head.

The next day, my friend Carolyn and I decided to go for a walk in a beautiful mountain area. We were walking and talking when I saw two men approaching us around a bend up ahead. As they walked toward us, I was astonished. One of the men was my old summer boyfriend, Phil. I was stunned and fear welled up inside me.

We made a bit of conversation, but I was so shook up that I brought the encounter to a quick close. I knew that we were at least 30 miles from where Phil lived and that the odds of having that chance meeting were one in a million. *How had that happened?*

On the telephone that night I felt incapable of hiding the day's events. *I'm going to get it. I hope he won't bawl me out.* As I'd foreseen, Hansen was angry and then self-righteous. "Now maybe you won't doubt me." He instantly made the interpretation in his favor. I worked to convince him that I hadn't planned the meeting with Phil behind his back.

Exhausted after our conversation and emotionally frozen, I packed my suitcase and moved into my camp cabin the next day.

This was my seventh summer to attend camp. My sister, Helen, had also been a camper and later a counselor here. This year I was a junior counselor. I had always felt wonderful when I was at camp. The mountains around Asheville were beautiful, and it was great to get out of the Louisiana heat. The previous summer I had been elected Princess by the other campers. It was an honor I valued deeply. I was liked here, and I had a history with this place. Every year for the past six years I had come for a four-week session. It was usually the highlight of my year.

During the month at camp I continued to function in the same split-like state of mind. Outwardly I went through the motions of camp life and activities, as predictably fun as always. Inside me, however, raged a war of confusion, fear, and denial. Hansen called the camp every two to three days and continued the same indoctrinating speeches. I was embarrassed at being paged to the phone from activities and meals. When the camp director overheard me crying on the phone,

I lied and said that I had a very sick friend at home. I said that I was worried about my friend dying, and I was getting regular updates on the phone. The director believed me and started accommodating the calls.

When I flew home from camp, there was only a week before I was due at college. Hansen had picked out a place in the woods for us to rendezvous that was less risky than his office. He had begun lectures about how blue he'd be without me here, but that I had to leave because my parents might get suspicious. He made his predictable speech that I might not choose to follow God's calling for me and stay true to him around the college boys. I repeated my robot-like response that I really did love God and wanted to obey Him.

As I said goodbye, he presented me with an opal ring surrounded by small diamonds. "It's your engagement ring. I'm hoping we'll be together by Christmas."

I was too afraid to ask the details of what he meant by this. In his presence I was functioning in a numb state. I acted ever more helpless and vulnerable. His intense program of reforming my thoughts was working. I was looking and acting brain-washed.

I took the ring and left.

An abuser may exploit a woman's innate capacity for compassion and nurture, working to get her to set aside her own best interests to nurture *him*.

For additional insight, see Essay #13: Who is a Pathological Man?

The power of the pastor over the congregant
is tremendously enhanced by his authority,
if he wishes to exercise it,
to describe to a woman her status with God.
A sexually abusive clergyman can easily exploit this authority
by telling a woman that her sexual involvement is part of
a divinely ordained plan.
Even sophisticated women can have difficulty
resisting this argument if they are
devoted to the religious vision that the
clergyman represents.

Peter Rutter, M.D.
Sex in the Forbidden Zone:
When Men in Power – Therapists, Doctors, Clergy,
Teachers, and Others – Betray Women's Trust
Tarcher, 1989

CHAPTER 6
Assault on My Identity

My room on the sixth floor of the college dorm looked out over the prayer gardens, a large area in the center of campus. The Prayer Tower, an eight-story slender tower finished in mirrored glass, was at the center of the garden. Beautifully lit at night, it was an impressive sight.

When I arrived in Oklahoma I was in such a state of fear toward Hansen that I was unable to think rationally about our relationship. I had not dared to ask how often he might try to contact me. I soon found out that he intended to talk to me at least twice a day, and more often if he felt necessary. In order to keep Becky, my roommate, from overhearing any of my phone conversations with Hansen, I located several pay phones in the student lounge areas around campus where he would call me at prearranged times.

Becky and I attended a local church one Sunday and introduced ourselves as new university students. The congregation was supportive of students who might be many miles from home, and one couple asked us to lunch after the service. I was alarmed to hear, on the way to their house, that they had also invited two freshman boys to eat lunch with us.

As we talked around the table at lunch, it was not hard to predict what the next conversation with Hansen would be like. I felt a compulsion to tell him that I had been eating with two boys. Intuitively, I knew there would be trouble. I limited my conversation with the boys and was uncharacteristically quiet. As we discussed a mutual class, they suggested that we exchange phone numbers as a way to help each other if we needed to discuss assignments. I hesitated, but Becky traded our phone number with them right away.

Later, on the phone with Hansen, he was immediately sullen about my lunch with the boys. Although I explained that it had happened innocently, I immediately fell into my pattern of avoiding his anger. Susceptible to his unspoken invitation to feel guilt, I began apologizing. "I'm really sorry I hurt you. I didn't know the boys would be there."

"How do you think that makes *me* feel? It seems like you'd know that people will always be trying to fix you up with a date," he said. "Of course, one of those boys is going to call you and ask you for a date."

He was quick to interpret every interaction I had with a male as a threat to our relationship. I was beginning to realize that he was going to make an issue of every contact I had with men. I could feel his moodiness on the phone, and I groped to hear from him that he knew I hadn't purposely set up the lunch with the boys. I was trying again to prove that I was sincere, especially since the incident with Phil in North Carolina was still a sore point between us.

"I guess you might as well accept that if you are going to be mine, you are going to have to live a different life than other college co-eds. After all, you're engaged to me. You won't be dating anybody. Everyone is going to think you are strange." There was that indoctrinating tone in his voice.

"I'm willing to be different. I've been telling you that." I automatically said what he wanted to hear as a form of protection against his anger. I looked down at the ring I was wearing.

"Maybe you'd better think it over again. Maybe this thing between us is not going to work after all," he replied. He hung up, and I felt that terrible sense of confusion that often came over me after we talked.

I had learned what "think it over again" meant. It had nothing to do with objectively trying to review our relationship to see if it was what I wanted. Rather than feeling freedom to make any real personal choice, I saw these challenges from him as unspoken directives to suppress my anxiety so that it didn't surface or threaten to make me run. "Thinking it over" merely meant that I redoubled my efforts at denying my feelings. If I showed any anxiety in my voice, he assumed that I was having thoughts of ending our relationship, and it would bring on another lecture or spell of depression in him. In response to those I was already trained to concede my doubts and support him.

During the evening, I rehearsed again the same circular reasoning that had been gripping my mind. *Since God has called me to be his, I won't be able to participate in the co-ed activities. I'm engaged to him. I have to be different, and I should be content in this.*

Self-examination was becoming a more frequent topic between us. I was expected to be able to say that I had been gut-level honest and to have spent time re-thinking and praying about any issues at stake. My deep sense of fear made it impossible for me to conclude anything except what he wanted me to conclude. I continued groping to feel safer by not threatening him.

The next morning I was at the pay phone in the student lounge for his six o'clock phone call. "You're late," he grumped. "I called three minutes ago. I figured you weren't coming."

"I'm really sorry. I'll do better next time. Sorry to make you wait." I placated his sulky attitude. Even minor offenses required a self-debasing apology.

"Well, have you prayed about what happened with the boys?" he asked in a badgering voice. He was waiting to see if I had searched out all my underlying motives.

"Yes, I'm more sure than ever that I love you. I'm happy that God has given me this call, and I'm obviously not going to accept a date from one of those boys if he calls me." I still wasn't sure what I was guilty of, but I knew exactly what he expected me to do, and I did it automatically.

"Well, when you know that God speaks to you, you just hold onto that. Sounds like you really know what God has shown you," he lent power to his words by coating them in spiritual language.

"I'm sure." By stating that I was sure, my own sense of integrity was at stake. Now I'd require myself to live up to what I'd said. After all, shouldn't I keep my word?

As the early weeks of college unfolded, I began asking permission from Hansen for everything. Could I eat in the cafeteria with boys? Could I attend a small devotional meeting where the girls from my dorm wing met with the boys from the brother wing that was paired with ours? Every event was a threat, and I never knew how he'd perceive it. The phone conversations grew lengthy, usually an hour in the morning and half an hour at night.

I had no conscious thoughts of turning back or trying to get out of the relationship. I was afraid to let these thoughts come to a conscious level. Somehow he would sense that I'd been thinking independently, and then there would be another emotional struggle where he'd demand that I examine myself again for my doubts. Each of these introspections resulted in my redoubling my efforts to be more faithful to him.

I began to totally lose my bearings about who and what I was and where I stood in relationship to Hansen. *I belong to him, and he says that we may be together by Christmas. I don't really know what that means, but I have to trust him.* Sometimes he mentioned again that he thought Blanche would die and then we would be legally married. I was becoming accustomed to hearing this and more receptive to the idea. I was falling more and more under the control of his brainwashing, willing to say and be whatever he demanded.

He surprised me occasionally by being sincere and kind at unexpected moments. I felt relieved when I made him happy. He said that he'd never felt whole until I became his. When he laughed, I felt suddenly reassured, and welcomed any reprieve from his interrogations and the tension that was a part of many of our phone conversations. Absorbing his moods, I was becoming enmeshed in his feelings, unable to feel happy unless he was feeling happy.

Several girls on my dorm wing were puzzled when they saw I had been crying one evening. Crying had become a daily occurrence, either during or after the phone calls. They inquired if I was all right.

"I'm fine, I'm just worried about a sick friend from Louisiana." I mentioned an older man (not Hansen) who was sick. "He may have to have his leg amputated." On the spur of the moment, it was the only excuse I could think of. I resolved to be more careful about others who might see me crying. Later, when I reflected on lying to my dorm mates, I rationalized that I had to keep the relationship a secret for now until it was the "Lord's timing" and Hansen and I were together.

Later that week, Cheryl, a resident advisor on my wing, inquired if I was doing all right. Apparently she was seeing some outward signs of my psychological distress. She said she was worried that I had been struggling since I got to school. I was alarmed that my emotions were more obvious to others than I'd thought.

"We have a counseling department here on campus. There's no charge for students to go there. I just wanted you to know that it's available if you wanted to talk to one of the counselors." Cheryl's voice was concerned.

"No, I'm fine. Really." My fear level shot up at the thought of telling anyone about my relationship with Hansen. That would be impossible. Besides, no one would understand, since it was a special situation from the Lord. In my mind I was dutifully repeating the rationalizations that Hansen had drilled into me. I made a mental note to try and be more "normal" around Cheryl in the future.

After nearly six weeks at college, Hansen surprised me on the phone by saying that he was planning to visit me in Tulsa in October. He would tell Blanche that he was checking out some evangelism/preaching opportunities in Texas and Arkansas, and that he'd be gone overnight. He would meet me in Tulsa and we'd stay at a hotel together.

I felt myself paralyzed with fear. I could hardly speak.

"The Lord has shown me that we should go ahead and make vows to each other to be spiritually married." He sounded kind.

I couldn't speak. It wasn't the first time I'd been mute when he said shocking and unexpected things to me.

"Are you there? Did you hear me?" He raised his voice.

"Yes, I'm here." I tried not to react with alarm. That would bring on a lecture. I was groping to find my bearings about what to do or say.

"Well, since we're going to be married anyway someday, we can just go ahead and seal our vows now. I think that this will give us some ammunition against Satan bothering me so much. I can just tell him that you've made your vows and it's sealed," he said.

I parroted the words that it would be okay. When we hung up I was numb. *What was this? Why did he want us to be married now?*

As the next day or two wore on, my anxiety grew. I had acted agreeable, but I was petrified. I felt sure that he wanted us to make vows because he wanted us to have sex. I felt such anxiety that I could hardly focus on school. I mustered the courage that I'd tell him that I couldn't have sex with him. Afraid to admit to him that I was deeply repulsed by the idea of sex with him, my mind rephrased it: *I don't want to have sex until we are legally married.* I had held a strong commitment to abstain from premarital sex. The pressure of him pushing for sex with me was deeply distressing.

When he called the next morning, I had marshaled my resolve. "I need to tell you that when you come to Tulsa, I can't have sex with you." My voice was shaky. It was better to speak in a timid voice that wouldn't come across as too threatening to him.

"What? What are you talking about?" He sounded accusatory.

"I just needed to say that I don't think it's right for us to have sex...we're not legally married yet." I tried to be cautious in my tone, fearing that an emotional assault was imminent.

"Well, you certainly have a twisted mind. What kind of a person do you think I am?" He sounded shocked that I would think this of him and sarcastically launched into a lecture. "I wasn't pushing for sex now. You're making it sound like I'm some sort of a bad guy."

"No, you're not a bad guy." I tried to head off the lecture by apologizing.

"You certainly have me pegged all wrong. After all the things I've done for you, I thought you would trust me. Do you think that I was just doing all this for sex with you? I'm just trying to do what the Lord has shown us to do." He was angry now and caustic. "You don't really know me, do you? How do you know about what I'm really thinking?"

I was crying now, apologizing for having challenged him and assuming that I knew his motives. I conceded that I had misunderstood him and that I felt fine about taking the vows. I felt humiliated. I had mustered the courage to confront him, and he had degraded me. I apologized again and we ended the conversation. The emotional pain from his cruel attitudes toward me seemed to short-circuit my ability to back track rationally or think critically.

Each act of humiliation had served to further erode my sense of dignity and injure my self-respect, making it less likely that I would rise up to challenge him the next time. I couldn't see that this was his game to keep me unstable and to think that my own discernment was unreliable. In the days before he arrived in Tulsa I felt more than ever like I was in a fog. I chided myself for having hurt him by bringing up the sex issue. It was much easier to be angry with myself than with him.

The barrage of the last few months had taken a toll on my identity. It had crumbled with the successive emotional attacks by him. I had shifted decidedly in the direction of giving in to nearly everything. It was increasingly easier to doubt myself. I was often afraid to question *him*, even in the privacy of my own mind. My mind felt like it was open and laid bare to him, and I worried that I'd accidentally have a thought that might be antagonistic to our relationship. He seemed to know everything I was thinking.

He had begun to probe my mind regularly. He often asked if I were "having any doubts today?" If I answered "yes," he'd lecture me, act depressed, or get angry. I was very afraid of lying to him and saying "no." The only other alternative was to not think about my doubts, suppress them, or deny them. Ironically, the more I suppressed and denied my doubts, the more "honest" I felt when I said to him, "I don't have any doubts about our love."

When I was alone, I rehearsed the *permitted* thoughts: *I love him. God has called me to him. I am happy doing God's will. Hansen is good to me. I am freely choosing to go through with the "spiritual" marriage ceremony.*

I prayed frequently, telling God that I didn't understand this, but I was willing to do what He wanted me to do. I asked Him to make it easier so that Hansen and I wouldn't have so many misunderstandings and to protect us from Satan's attempts to break us up. I was already too far sunk to even think of praying to be delivered from Hansen. It was clear. Hansen had decided. I was already entrapped so deep in fear that I didn't dare think my own real thoughts. I even denied to myself that I wanted anything different.

As I passed the mirrored glass of the Prayer Tower, I checked to see that my eyes didn't look swollen from crying. I slapped my face a little to bring color back more evenly to my cheeks. I had to get to my biology test.

I was dangerously close to betraying myself.

The central tactics of brainwashing, or thought reform, are to:

1) cause the victim to doubt her own reality, opinions, and discernment
2) create physical distress (exhaustion, pain, etc.)
3) evoke fear through intimidation
4) employ mental badgering and indoctrination until the victim accepts the abuser's definition of "truth"

No Defenses

He pushed open the door of my mind,
then wedged it with false guilt.

With access to my youthful vulnerability
he exploited my compassion for his weaknesses.

Blackmailed to silence by the power of his pastoral role,
I could not see that our relationship was a sham.

He got inside my defenses
and then I didn't have a way to make him leave.

Unable to see that the person who was my spiritual leader
had now become my abuser…

I embraced the lie.

JoAnn Nishimoto

CHAPTER 7
The Breaking Point

In the days before Hansen arrived in Tulsa, I was planning how I'd spend time away with him without my roommate and others suspecting anything. I decided to fabricate a story about spending the weekend with an older single woman I'd met at church. I'd conveniently omit her telephone number on my sign-out sheet I'd submit to the dorm mother. I didn't really feel comfortable with lying, but I overrode my guilt by telling myself that it was necessary to hide our relationship until "it was God's time."

When Hansen arrived to pick me up, I was a tense mixture of anxiety and excitement. I was glad to see him, and he seemed so happy to see me. I couldn't remember when I'd seen him so light-hearted. He suggested that we have dinner before we checked into the motel.

Once at the motel he presented "vows" which he'd handwritten on a piece of paper. In addition to language used in most vows ("for better, for worse," etc.), he had included statements about being true and faithful to him until we were legally married. He read them aloud to me and asked if I had any reservations about them.

"No, I'm ready." I was calm in my response. Given the manipulations he had wielded in the previous months, I was thoroughly re-educated and agreeable. To any observer I would have appeared a willing participant. In that moment there was no inward or outward duress.

I was detached from a conscious recognition of my true self. All my own wishes were buried under his carefully laid layers of rationalization, my fear of opposing him, and the obligation I felt to not let him down. It actually seemed like I wanted to do this…a sense of surrendering myself to the inevitable…to something I could not control. There seemed to be a relief in no longer fighting the emotional battle. It was the breaking point. I was ready to give in.

We knelt beside the bed together and repeated the vows before God, asking Him to be our witness. As I spoke them, there were no conscious reservations in my mind. There was no thought of outward compliance but inward rebellion. Hansen couldn't have picked a more honest partner. I sincerely believed I was pledging something sacred.

After the vows we had increased sexual contact, but he didn't push for intercourse. I was relieved. He was being kind and affectionate. I felt that I really loved him, and a strange kind of resolution was happening in me.

Now it all makes sense, I thought, *I don't have to feel guilty anymore. We're married now, and it makes it all right that we're touching and having sexual contact.*

Over the weekend we laughed a lot. We had conversation about thought-provoking topics, the way we previously had. I remembered how I'd learned so much from him in the past about the Bible, how he'd been such a support to me, and the admiration I'd always had for him. The weekend seemed void of conflict, and we created an atmosphere of mutual love. We prayed together and spoke of the time when we'd be together permanently.

Taking the vows seemed to quiet the anxieties which had seemed to overwhelm him in previous months. He said that now he'd no longer be depressed or doubt my love. I felt relieved to have a period of time when he wasn't interrogating me or being suspicious and angry. I felt peaceful.

As the weekend ended, he dropped me off at the campus entrance so no one would see me with him. We had an emotional goodbye. He expressed how deeply he felt about me, how reassured he was now that he knew I had committed myself to him, and how hard it would be to wait patiently until the Lord put us together.

Since taking the vows, there were no more psychological walls between us. As he drove off, I cried quite a bit. I had come to believe that it would be hard to make it without him near me.

Victims of intense mental programming may reach a point of "cracking." They give up critical thinking and fully embrace the new system of beliefs and ideas. They are no longer conscious of doubts. Doubts have been repressed to a level below consciousness. The abuser's thought reform or brainwashing techniques have been successful.

Teller, an illusionist, describes how he manipulates an audience to make false assumptions:

> Choice is not freedom.
>
> If you are given a choice, you believe that you have acted freely.
>
> This is one of the darkest of all psychological secrets.
>
> Nothing fools you better than the lie you tell yourself.

Teller
Trick of the Eye
Smithsonian, March, 2012

CHAPTER 8
Pickled

In the weeks that followed, I achieved a sense of harmony in my new role as a "married" woman. As I fell into step with believing that I was now married to Hansen before God, I understood what was expected of me and what I expected of myself. Having high ideals of marriage, I believed that a wife should be supportive, loving, respectful, and submissive.

I felt relatively calm for the first time since getting to college, no longer having the sensation of raw fear which had terrified me at times in the last few months. I took this as a sign that I was doing the right thing and that this was God's will. *After all, if I'm doing the Lord's will, I'll have peace.* I interpreted my lowered anxiety as an indication of having made the right decision. There was absolutely no awareness that I had taken the vows out of manipulation and the breaking down of my mind.

Being a wife to Hansen began to take on a feeling of reality. My re-fashioned identity was feeling like the real me. He had been successful in teaching me the "correct" view of our relationship. He had drilled and lectured me until I had finally taken on the full character of what he wanted me to be: his puppet.

His demands were now my self-demands: to be a good wife, to work hard at it, to be faithful to him, and to pray that God would put us together. I felt conviction about it. The vows were a turning point. Now it was "we." What *we* felt, *we* felt together. *We* were a team now.

In our daily phone conversations, we re-interpreted my behavior from the spring. We agreed that I had been "slow" to understand that God had called us together. We recalled my initial resistance to his overtures as my reluctance to understand God's will. I also had re-coded my sense of values. *It's okay to lie about this, because we're protecting what God has ordained.* I internalized my vows deeply. *I will do this because I love God.* My sense of obeying God was crucial to my being able to be at peace with myself, so I had accepted that this was God's will. Hansen had sealed my commitment to him by appealing to my inner enthusiasm for devotion to God. I had bonded with my captor, and was happy.

Hansen seemed just as happy. He said that he wouldn't have to worry anymore about my not loving him, or that I would leave him. My taking the vows had given him closure in trusting me to be faithful to him.

I expected that we would float along in this happy state indefinitely, but it only took a couple of weeks before the bottom fell out.

When answering the phone one morning, he sounded distressed and panicky.

"I've been up all night. I've been struggling with Satan. He's been telling me that you are leaving me. You're going to break your vows," he said, nearly crying. "I don't know how I'm going to be able to preach this morning in church."

I felt obligated to rescue him from his pain, reassure him, and shore him up. "No, really, I love you. I don't know what you're talking about. I'm keeping my vows completely." I reassured him over and over. I was fearful that he might arouse suspicion at church if he wasn't able to preach in his usual dynamic style.

For several days he seemed depressed and morose. I went to pay phones in between classes to listen to him and bolster his mood. I was exhausted emotionally and physically. I confessed every minor fault I could think of, wondering if somehow I might have caused this tension. His solution to "putting Satan down" was for us to begin fasting, a Christian practice usually accompanying a time of deep prayer and seeking God's wisdom.

"Maybe we should end the relationship," he sounded completely whipped. His reasoning was not that he had launched an improper relationship in the first place, but that I wasn't going to be strong enough to keep my vows, or do God's will, or live up to my calling. The focus was always on *me*. The fault was always *mine*. Was *I* devoted enough? He'd said he'd rather be let down now, than be strung along and have me ditch him later.

My response was to feel terrified to end the relationship. I hated it when he made me out as the guilty one. I felt that I couldn't stand this and I'd fall into begging him to have more faith in me.

Deep inside, but suppressed by fear and confusion, I didn't want to be left alone to figure out what had happened between us. I didn't want to admit that he was an evil person or that God wasn't in the relationship. I was now a full participant. *I willingly married him, didn't I?* I wouldn't want to be guilty of something that was against God. I was now emotionally invested in proving to myself that I should be where I was. To face our relationship as corrupt would be to admit that I was deceived. I still wanted him to be good.

While these were the actual issues which wove the powerful web of fear deep within me, I couldn't articulate them. Even if I could have formed my fears into thoughts, they were still too terrifying to vocalize. Overlaid with layers of confusion, they were almost inaccessible to rational thought. I was swept along in the tyranny of the daily emotional conflicts.

I had no objectivity. I was now predictably responding to his moods by placating him, conceding to every emotional attack from him, and becoming increasingly more compliant. I had no remaining psychological boundaries. He had pushed his way through each layer. When I felt helpless and gave in out of fear, I was reinforcing the cycle of sickness between us. He would temporarily let up the emotional pressure, and I learned it paid to just act helpless and never challenge him. We were destined to repeat this cycle hundreds of times.

The truth did try to break through my psyche occasionally. I would have periods of anxiety, but I shoved it down, keeping it under the lock and key of denial. I renamed my anxiety by saying, "Satan is bothering me, too." The result was to pray more, asking God to give me strength to live more faithfully for Hansen.

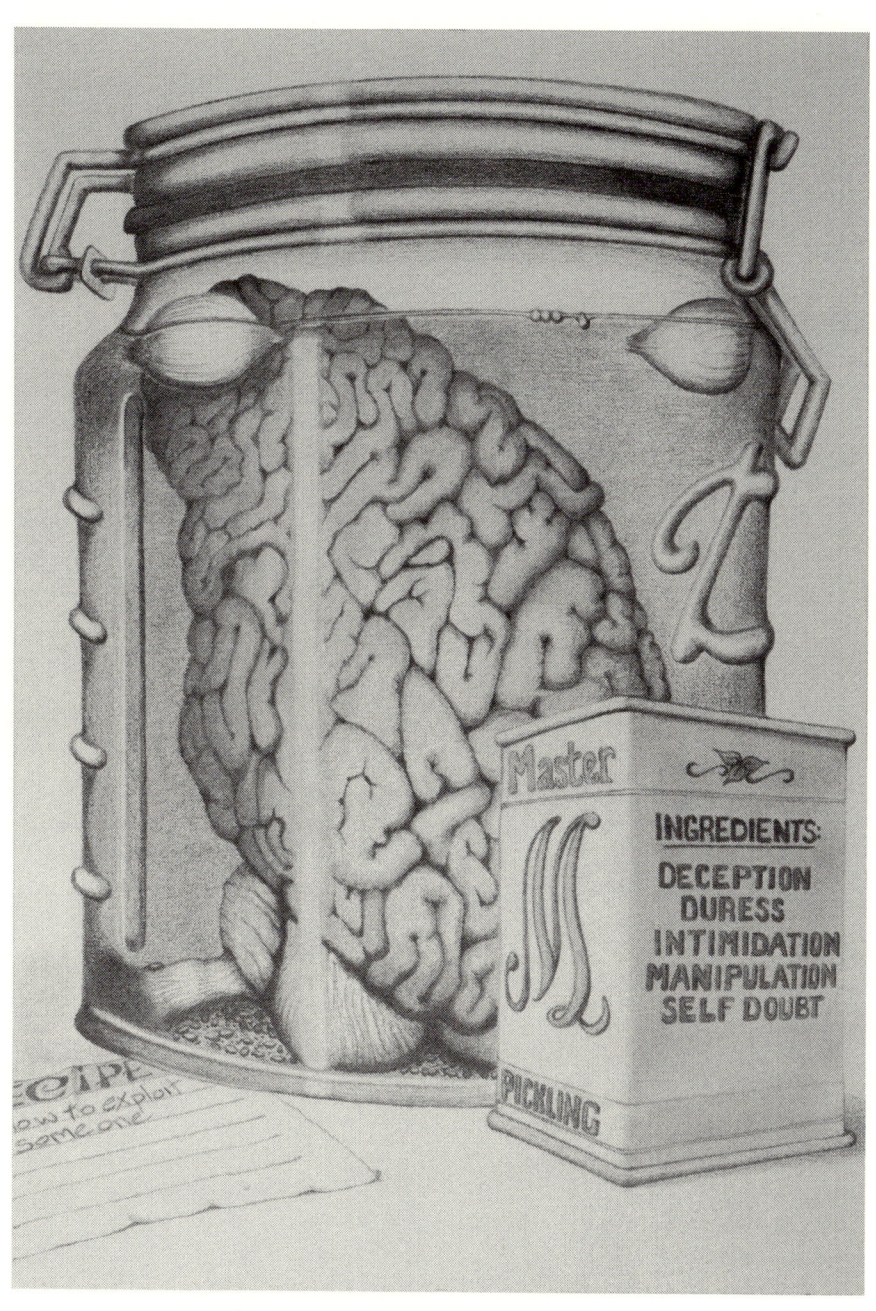

Indoctrinated and emotionally undermined,
my brain was now fully pickled.

Rather than bailing out of the relationship, there was less immediate pain in continuing it. I was in too deep. Since I'd taken the vows, I was even more likely to deny any doubts that tried to leak through.

I took a job as a housekeeper for a Tulsa couple in their fifties. It was a way to get more money for my expensive phone bills. The couple appreciated the good job I did on their house, and offered me the use of their car for a few hours weekly so I could go shopping or run errands.

Driving to a local park one afternoon, I felt overwhelmed with anxiety. *What is happening to me, Lord? I am so scared. I feel I am losing my mind.* I walked through a wooded area in the park and saw a grassy ditch where I could lie down. My emotions were similar to those I had the afternoon my mother found me crying at home. It seemed I would explode.

I lay in the ditch for quite a while crying loudly, half praying, half moaning. *This is so hard. I'm so torn.* Finally, the real dilemma found its way out of my mouth. *I don't want to sin, Lord. I don't want to sin. Am I sinning? Please, God, I don't want to sin.* This was the crux of my pain. My prayer revealed that I really wasn't convinced the vows I'd taken were approved by God. I didn't want to hurt God. I didn't want to sin.

I cried so loudly and so long that I completely exhausted myself. Finally, I was aware of a strange numbness, or at least a cessation of emotional pain. *This must be peace I'm feeling. This must mean that I'm okay, that everything is really okay.* Believing anything else carried too many threatening repercussions I felt helpless to face.

Hansen never spoke of having anxiety about living a double life. I didn't initiate the topic because I feared insinuations from him that I was doubting our relationship, followed by lengthy reproofs. He occasionally made comments about hiding phone calls from Blanche, but otherwise seemed to have little anxiety about the discrepancies in his public and private life and the relationship he had with me. He was carrying on his typical duties as a pastor: studying and preparing sermons, giving counsel to church members, praying for those with concerns, and preaching three times a week. He still appeared outwardly normal to those in his congregation and the community.

Meanwhile I invested myself in several girlfriends on campus. Helping them with their problems seemed a way to connect with a part of myself that felt more normal. I was good at giving advice about problems and encouraging others. They validated me as a devoted Christian who loved the Lord. I knew that this was a part of me that was true, and I turned my attention to helping several students who were socially awkward or struggling academically. I worked hard at being a good friend to them and caring about their problems.

When I talked to my parents on the phone, I reported the positive aspects of college life that I really did like: the professors were engaging, the student athletic center was state-of-the-art, and I enjoyed talking with the international students. I worked hard at masking anything negative, and they seemed confident that I was fine. I hardly felt guilty at all about being deceptive with them. *They, like everybody else, wouldn't understand this relationship as being from God.*

When possible, I engaged in college life everywhere I could, provided it wouldn't threaten Hansen's sense that I was being faithful to him. When a graduate student asked for volunteers for physiology research, I volunteered (after checking to see that the student I'd be working with was a female). During part of the research, this woman used instruments and formulas to measure body muscle and fat.

There were no such instruments to measure Hansen's gripping of my mind.

> **Whenever a victim of abuse or manipulation appears to "side with" or "join" her abuser, she is usually doing so out of gripping fear, and is subconsciously seeking a way to reduce the intense threat which she feels.**

Dr. George Bach has coined the term "crazymaking" to
describe power plays in a master/slave relationship.
The master controls the slave by "crazymaking,"
demanding complete and instant obedience,
while giving conflicting or unclear commands.
No matter how the slave responds,
it is impossible for him to avoid a reprimand
or at the very least, feeling guilty
for not being an adequate and good slave.
The master assumes a position of being sincere and perfect.
And since he could not give an imperfect command,
any misunderstanding must be the fault of the slave.

Adrian and Anne Greek
Mind Abuse by Cults and Others
Positive Action Center, 1985

CHAPTER 9
My Double Life

My genuine love for God, which I'd had since I was twelve, was unchanged by Hansen's brainwashing. In college chapel services I relished the beautiful praise times when everyone sang. I prayed and related to God in simple things the way I always had. I prayed for help in getting through a tough exam. I prayed for people in need. I was concerned for world evangelism. I volunteered for a service project. I attended a prayer conference.

Desiring to grow in my walk with God, I took Hansen's suggestion that I memorize some Scripture. He suggested a particularly complex passage, the second chapter of Ephesians. I remembered that it was one of his favorites, and one he'd often preached about. I typed up the verses on note cards and went about reviewing them. During that year I memorized the entire book of Ephesians consisting of six chapters. It felt good to be mulling over Scripture, and I felt it drew me closer to God.

I convinced Hansen to allow me to go on a weekend retreat with my women's dorm at a dude ranch (since no guys would be present). On the last day of the weekend I went for a horseback ride. As I was returning to the barn, my horse ran away with me. He ran very close to a telephone pole, with my head narrowly missing the guide wire on one side and the pole on the other. With terror I realized the wire could have caught me by the neck. It was a close call! Later that day I rode back to campus in a car with several female students. Just as we were crossing some railroad tracks, we caught a glimpse of an oncoming train nearly upon us. The train whistle blasted at us and we barely cleared the tracks as the train flew by. We were all so stunned that the driver pulled over so we could collect ourselves. Several of us cried.

Later that day Hansen called. He was breathless when I answered it. "Are you all right?" he sounded alarmed.

"Well, yes, I'm OK, but I've had two close calls today." I related what had happened while riding the horse and the near miss by the train.

"Well, I've been praying fervently for you. God told me that Satan was going to try and take your life today," he said with conviction. "Thank God you're alive." His response felt genuine to me, and I was grateful for his concern and prayers.

As with many situations that transpired between us, each was interpreted according to the understanding of the relationship. Everything was interpreted to fit the belief system. I concluded that this was just one more proof that I belonged to Hansen and that he had special knowledge about me. Instances of fulfilled prophecies and special knowledge happened regularly, and seemed to "give life" to the idea that he knew everything about me. This played into the belief that

God had indeed brought us together. Hansen seemed to be protecting me with his prayers and had intervened to save my life.

As the rest of my freshman year played out, my grades were good, and to most everyone I appeared to be a happy college student. I showed Hansen the emotions he wanted to see. I worked hard at being happy, being grateful for my blessings, and being helpful to others.

As the summer approached, we wondered what I should do. Hansen actually suggested that I not return to Louisiana for the summer, because my parents would be "watching us." After searching for a summer job, I eventually settled on selling books door-to-door for a company that hired college students in the summer. After sales training, I was assigned to a sales territory in Florida. Midway through the summer I flew to see him one weekend.

"I guess we're not going to be together as soon as we thought," he said. "We're going to have to be patient."

I felt some relief. His driving belief that we would be married soon had only added to my anxiety. Obviously, Christmas was long past and along with it his first deadline for marrying me. Blanche was still alive. Now he was vague and admitted that he didn't know when we'd be together. We'd just have to "trust God."

I returned to college for my sophomore year. I had signed up to live in a different girl's dorm known to plan fewer activities with male students. My refusal to engage in co-ed activities would be less noticeable. Becky and I had grown distant, and we awkwardly agreed that we needed different roommates. She had grown tired of my secretive ways, my irrational explanations about why I wouldn't participate in some activities, and the way I avoided honest sharing with her. My new roommate, Ramona, had a steady boyfriend and would be too involved with him to take much notice of me.

Hansen and I continued our relationship without interruption. I was careful to play by the rules of being his wife and tried not to do anything that a wife wouldn't do. Every decision, every thought was related to the idea that I had taken vows with him to be his secret wife. I devotedly measured all my actions against the standard, "Would a wife do this in these circumstances?" The bondage of the vows pervaded everything.

I was relieved that he was getting angry at me less often. This was largely because I had honed my skills in appeasing him. When he did get angry, I immediately felt guilty. *Who was I to argue when he bellowed, "God said…!"* I didn't want to question something that was a mandate from God. Occasionally he shamed me by his piercing "I thought you loved me" speeches. I quickly apologized and told him that I needed to be more humble and try harder. He accepted my over-played gestures of guilt, repentance, and self-deprecation.

If I told myself that his anger was my fault, then the problem would be in my control. My unspoken task became to control him by trying harder not to make him angry. I took responsibility for every difficult moment in our relationship.

I played out the role so regularly that it felt normal. My extreme submission had grown out of my extreme fear. I feared his shaming speeches, his anger, and his spells of self-pity. I had no defenses for them. They left me exhausted and wounded.

My sophomore year passed with less intensity. I had accepted our relationship and my role in it. My anxiety was carefully locked away, and if it did surface, I had renamed it as "a spiritual attack from Satan." I sought to eradicate any doubts by detaching from them. I knew he'd be questioning me each week to see if I was having doubts, and it wasn't emotionally safe to have doubts. I felt that he knew all my thoughts, and I worked hard at not thinking anything that would contradict him.

As the school year ended, my family was preparing to gather at the Air Force Academy for my brother, Sam's, graduation. Hansen felt particularly threatened over the possibility that someone might want to fix me up for a date to the cadet graduation dances, and he was sulky and depressed. I twisted myself into every emotional direction I could, trying to relieve his distress over it. During the graduation week, my father passed by a hotel pay phone where I was crying on the phone with Hansen. Later I played it off as a misunderstanding I had with a girlfriend on the phone. Another close call, I thought, when my parents might have suspected something.

I spent several days after Sam's graduation in a buoyant mood. I stayed with my college friend, Marisa, and her parents at their home in Colorado Springs. I couldn't remember laughing so much or having so much fun in a long time. I played their piano and told jokes and savored their family humor. I had learned to compartmentalize my relationship with Hansen and still experience some good times. Living a double life had become second nature, and it felt like the real me. It had become my reality.

After enduring any type of abuse over a period of time, the victim loses objectivity. She is no longer shocked by the abuse, she may adapt to it by mentally compartmentalizing it, and she may even come to see it as "normal."

Your Anger

I've mastered hypervigilance.
    I scan your face, looking for cues.
    I interpret each inflection of your voice
    to see if you are bordering on anger.

My defining question, in my every contact with you, has become:
    "Are you angry with me today?"

Fear of anger.

Fear of anger.

I repeat this feeling often.
    This is the state of being with which I have become most familiar.

I never know when I'll be ambushed.
    Your sarcasm pierces me.
    I feel defenseless.
    Intimidated.
    Reduced to tears.

I am caught in the cycle of yielding my dignity and absorbing your anger, begging you again, "*Please* don't be mad at me."

Being very nice to you.
Hiding my deep wounds.
Lying to myself that I am okay.

Unaware I *do* have anger, and that I am stuffing it inside myself
    into a
        very deep,
            black,
                emotional hole.

                        JoAnn Nishimoto

CHAPTER 10
Fear and Obedience

I needed to attend summer school before my junior year of college, so I enrolled in a small state college in Monroe, Louisiana, about 70 miles from our town. I came home every weekend to my parents' house and lived in the dorm during the week. I secured a job as a waitress on weekend nights at a local family restaurant. Being home on the weekend gave me the opportunity to attend Hansen's church and to meet him secretly. I planned to go back to Oklahoma in the fall.

A new friend at college suggested that I try attending a church in Monroe, and told me about their excellent pastor. She said that he was divorced, but he was not considered the guilty party in the divorce. He was now single again, about age 30, and quite a good Bible teacher. Hansen approved my attending that church on Sunday nights, since I would have had to drive back too late if I stayed for the Sunday night service with him.

Sitting in the Monroe church, I found myself focusing on this young pastor. He was quite a good-looking guy, and his personality was warm. In a flash I thought of this pastor and myself. *What would it be like to be married to someone near my age?* Almost as swiftly as it occurred to me, I censored my thoughts. *I'm married. I can't think like that. Lord, I'm sorry!*

The next day I made my confession to Hansen. I had been disloyal in my thoughts. I dreaded the lengthy retaliation. I'd been through it before. His speeches ranged from anger to self-pity. Once again, he suggested that we fast so that I could spend time in introspection about what was in my heart. I felt a sense of shame and failure when he said we should consider ending the relationship, based on *my* inability to keep God's mandate to me and my wandering thoughts of other men. Although I knew that he was exaggerating the severity of my "crimes," I regretted having thought of the young pastor romantically, and it contributed to a strong sense of personal guilt.

My summer roommate had quit school unexpectedly and left, so I had the room to myself. I stayed in the room for four days, praying and searching myself. I left the room only to attend class for a few hours a day. I had fasted nearly four days, was getting weak, and had reviewed my guilt forward and backward. It was no surprise that my level of fear merely drove me deeper into professing what Hansen expected me to say. I even distorted a passage of Scripture to say that God wanted me to intensify my obedience to Hansen.

Once again, I had not come close to any honest review of the relationship. Despite my fasting and prayer, the bondage was too deep. I felt so threatened by the power he had over me that I had merely replayed another exercise in twisting myself to pacify and appease him. Again I would show him how sorry I was for what I'd put him through. I only hoped to end the immediate agony I felt when he turned on me and to return to the equilibrium of our everyday master-slave relationship.

Whenever he suggested that I "take an honest look to see whether I wanted to end the relationship," his underlying message was "see if you are willing to fail God by leaving me." This subtle technique of twisting my mind was effective. He knew my sincere commitment to follow God, and he was using this as glue to hold me in the relationship. Not once was I able to transcend this manipulative technique or see it for what it was. Oddly, I returned from these times of "reflection and prayer" with even more intense affirmations of my commitment to him.

When I met him in the woods one Friday afternoon, I was shaking with fear. It was the first time I'd seen him since my "disobedience" in thinking about the young pastor, and I didn't know what he'd do or say. Feeling in grave psychological danger, I felt that I'd do anything to know I had his forgiveness. I knew the familiar pattern of yielding and complying, and I was prepared to carry it out.

Standing outside the cars, he spoke: "I don't know if I'll ever be able to trust you again. I thought you loved me, but after this week, I can see that you don't."

"But I do love you and I'm really, really sorry that I hurt you." I was frightened and groping. "Please forgive me. Will you please forgive me?" I begged.

He stood in silence. He seemed so powerful. I felt like a small child. He looked away, as if denying my request.

"Please, please, I'm so sorry." I was crying, trying to get him to acknowledge me.

"I guess I'll be going. I've got to get back to the house." His voice sounded bored, as if he had more important things to do.

"Don't reject me. I'm sorry. I'm sorry. Please don't be angry with me." I felt I would die without him forgiving me. As a last resort I lay face down on the ground in front of him. I grabbed some sand and put it on my head in a self-debasing gesture. I thought that I could not stand it if he would not relent and say he forgave me.

"Okay. Get up. Call me later, I've got to be going." He denied me the dignity of making eye contact. He got in his car and left.

If there was any remaining dignity left in me after the previous two years, it was gone now. I felt hollow. It was a new level of brokenness. The humiliating effect of the previous four days had drained me of my last remnants of dignity. More than ever, I battened down the hatches of my mind so that I'd never have any more betraying thoughts about other men. I had become his obedient puppet, testifying against myself for any unfaithful thoughts, and giving up even more of my mind to him.

He had eroded so much of my dignity that there was little hope I'd ever allow myself to consider leaving him. Once again he had reinforced the fact that my vows to him were, in effect, equal to obeying God. The subduing effect of this particular incident lasted several months. I was now more quietly submissive than ever. The crisis had passed.

Several months later Hansen began talking about a money-making idea, a pyramid marketing plan to sell a gasoline additive. A man we knew wanted to recruit Hansen, and then he'd recruit others for a percentage profit on their sales. I'd be down line under Hansen and this would benefit us, he said.

I had some anxiety about the venture. I'd heard some friends caution about these sorts of pyramid business plans. Having a business degree had also sensitized me to sound financial ideas. I wanted to warn Hansen that this might be a waste of money and effort.

Trying to be diplomatic, I'd learned I needed to tiptoe, spoon-feeding him so as not to trigger his knee-jerk rejections when he thought I was questioning him. Proceeding cautiously, I brought up the topic over coffee at his kitchen table. I'd already worked out the wording in my mind. First, I soft-pedaled it with disclaimers.

"I'm probably wrong about this, but I was wondering if we shouldn't re-think the gasoline additive business," I ventured with as friendly a tone as possible. He was silent and his face seemed neutral. *I think he's going to listen.* He got up from the table for more coffee. With his back turned, I tiptoed further. "There might be a better way that we could make money."

He poured his coffee and turned. An evil glare came over his face as he sat down. He looked at me like an enemy, someone who'd been mistreating him for years.

"You're the most skeptical person I ever knew!" he snapped. He grimaced as if I had offended and disgusted him. Once again his exaggerated retorts were an emotional stun gun that sent me reeling. It had the same startling effect as if I'd been slapped. He proceeded to belittle me with comments about my thinking being inferior to his.

Later at home I felt like I'd been handed an emotional block of ice that froze me cold. I felt staggered and pierced by an iciness I couldn't name; it was outside my vocabulary. I kept running into this wall. *I can't make him love me. I can't make him trust me.* These two bitter truths were the heart of what dumbfounded me. *I don't understand this. I've worked so hard to make him love me. Why does he attack me with such cruelty?* These weren't the rules I'd learned in my family. I believed in love, fairness, and respect. I naively believed that when he told me he loved me that he was playing by the same definitions and rules that I did. I'd used up all the ways to make him believe in me.

I feel helpless to make him love me. After four years in the relationship, I thought he'd trust me by now. I can't get love from him. I obsessed about this idea for weeks.

Victims of abuse may become so stripped of dignity and broken in spirit that they feel powerless to protect themselves or even hope for deliverance. Instead, they may robotically try again and again to earn their abuser's love.

The term "codependency" describes
a lack of objectivity and a distorted sense
of responsibility (in relationships).
Codependents lose themselves
in others or they take responsibility for
the actions of others.
Codependents may identify so strongly with
those who abuse them that
they lose their own identities.

Cindy Kubetin Littlefield
Shelter from the Storm:
Hope for Survivors of Sexual Abuse
Search Resources, 1995

CHAPTER 11
The Lost Decade

By the end of the summer, Hansen had decided that I didn't need to return to college in Tulsa. We had become used to seeing each other every weekend. I had settled in at the small state college in Louisiana. Being at college in Monroe did hold a particular enjoyment. I met two Vietnamese sisters who were new in their faith and eager to grow. They were recent refugees from Vietnam. I became their suitemate, and enjoyed teaching them the Bible and helping them. In return, they were good friends, and due to their lack of understanding of American culture, they weren't quick to suspect me of anything unusual. I also led a Bible study in my dorm and felt some pleasure in helping others spiritually. I had learned not to feel odd about my dual life.

Upon graduating from college with a business degree, I went to work for Hansen as a secretary for the church. My folks felt a lot of distress over this, and said so, but I defended Hansen and said that the Lord was leading me to work at the church. My parents knew that he held some sort of powerful influence over me, but the depth of it was unknown to them. If they had put any pressure on me, I would just have lied more. I was so indoctrinated that I would have only withdrawn from them. They resigned themselves to keeping our lines of communication open in the areas they could. I continued celebrating holidays with them and participated with them in the care of my four aging grandparents, whom I loved. They knew that they could get nowhere discussing my job or relationship with Hansen.

My parents and I never spoke of the past regarding Hansen. We had adopted the dysfunctional "no talk rule" about the incident in high school when I'd revealed to my mother that Hansen had kissed and touched me. They continued to attend the church after that, but I understood on an unspoken level that they disliked him strongly after that.

Meanwhile, Hansen's behavior was declining at church. He had become sarcastic in a few of his sermons. People had begun to wonder if this was the same man they had once admired so much.

Once while Hansen was preaching, he bragged about himself in an obvious exaggeration. I felt immediate shame, knowing everyone in the service was shocked. I was so emotionally enmeshed with him that I was feeling all his feelings for him. He had also become more publicly defensive, while in private he was telling me how prideful and resistant many in the church had become. I was disturbed at the crude remarks he made about church members, but listened meekly. I wouldn't have dared to contradict him.

In the summer of 1980, after I'd graduated from college, Hansen resigned from the church and announced that he would be starting an independent ministry called The Great Commission. About a fourth of the congregation left with him, and he started a small house church with them. He felt happy to be getting out from under any accountability to the church elders. His public behavior had deteriorated to the point that it was probably only a matter of time before he would have been asked to resign.

Hansen and Blanche moved to a nearby town and bought a modest house. I had purchased a small mobile home after college, and then lived about three miles from them. During the next four years, I helped Hansen start a small mail-order ministry for his sermon tapes. I adopted a white German shepherd puppy, Elsa, and I threw myself into loving and caring for her. I channeled a lot of love into Elsa, and she was a solace for my deep emotional wounds. I lived on a small stipend Hansen paid me each month, plus money my brother, Sam, contributed to the ministry toward my salary. Sam was a generous contributor to many Christian ministries, and in good faith decided to partially support me each month so that I could do the ministry work with Hansen. Of course, he knew nothing of the true nature of our relationship.

During the post-college "slump years" (as I call them) of 1980-1984, I remained under-developed and under-stimulated. My natural gifts and talents were largely dormant, and if I did anything that could be considered an achievement, I quickly had to give Hansen credit for helping me accomplish it. Needing a challenge, I built a deck on my mobile home out of scrap wood and factory crates. I walked Elsa every morning and evening. The one highlight of my week was attending an inter-denominational women's Bible study at the home of a lovely woman named Roberta. Roberta was an excellent teacher, and I slowly began to absorb her honesty about life. The women from the study filled a void. Occasionally, I met one of them for lunch, and I grew to be a part of the group. I truly loved these women. Everyone seemed to respect this unusual ministry I had with the "retired pastor" and saw me as a devoted Christian.

My relationship with Hansen had settled into a kind of equilibrium. I learned to focus on the positive parts of the relationship. I enjoyed it when he gave me compliments. I offered him my complete allegiance. Blindly trusting him had become a bargaining chip to earn his acceptance, please him, and avoid conflict. I kept convincing myself that I was happy. Although to keep a "happy" atmosphere, I had to lay aside my needs and be his emotional caretaker.

Whenever someone inquired about my work with Hansen, I responded almost robotically, "God has called me to it." I even told one woman that I would probably continue as long as Hansen was alive. There were times when I felt others were suspicious. They may have noticed that I repeated the clichés about being "called by God" a bit too rigidly or overstated myself defensively, a tip-off to how hard I was working at keeping myself from slipping.

During 1982, Hansen received an invitation to preach weekly at a nearby Louisiana medium-security prison. Every Wednesday night I led the song service, Blanche played the piano, and Hansen preached. I had a strict policy of never giving my address or phone number out to any of the inmates, and Hansen relaxed his vigilance and didn't seem to mind when the inmates talked to me after the service. I began playing my guitar for the inmates. This gave me a creative outlet, practicing songs and making cakes to take to the prison each Wednesday. Over the next seven years, we would visit the prison more than 300 times.

Our relationship stabilized to a détente-like calm, having little exposure to many outside threats. I spent a lot of time by myself and with Elsa, who was a comforting companion. Walking in the woods with Elsa was a solace for me. Sam took me on two very nice cross-country trips with him, one in 1983 and the other in 1985. Although I had to call Hansen and "report in" during the trips, I reveled in the small independence of traveling with Sam. Although Sam and I often spoke honestly about many areas of life, I carefully compartmentalized my relationship with Hansen, and I never risked disclosing to Sam even one hint of the real nature of it. I continued to hold the same rigid view of my relationship with Hansen. I believed I was "spiritually married" to him, and there were no conscious thoughts of leaving the relationship.

In 1984, I went to see the Barbra Streisand movie *Yentl*. In the movie she plays a young girl disguised as a boy so that she can study at the Jewish University. Her dishonesty plays out in an ever-thickening web. Finally she reveals her deception and comes clean. In an emotional ending she tells who she is.

When the movie ended I sat in the theater stunned. The movie had connected with something deep inside of me that I wasn't admitting to myself. Perhaps I identified with her life of deception and the complicated duplicity she worked so hard at playing out. I felt so impressed with the movie that I immediately went out and bought the soundtrack, something I rarely did. I sat on my bed at home during the next few weeks, playing the music and singing the songs. Still I had no conscious awareness of how this movie reflected my own life, or the duality of my own existence. My blindness was profound. I only knew that I really liked the movie, nothing more.

Hansen was convinced that God was leading him to build a retreat center where people could come for counseling. Again, he was on his soapbox, saying that he had never been able to do the things he had always dreamed of doing. People had always thwarted him. The retreat center would become well known, he said, and help a lot of people. It would probably be the crowning achievement of his ministry.

In the spring of 1984, I moved my mobile home to 28 acres of wooded land in a secluded area outside of Minden. This was where we planned to build the retreat center, to be called Victory Haven. My parents had given me the property when I was only fifteen, thinking that one day I could sell it and use the money as a down payment on a house. It was no surprise that Hansen had seen it as "the Lord's leading" that I use my own property for his project.

Meanwhile, I had become increasingly interested in carpentry. After building a porch on my mobile home, I built some rustic furniture. My natural optimism coming to the fore, I began to think that perhaps I could build my own house. I had been intrigued by several log homes being built in the area, and had stopped by the building sites to ask questions. After studying the process for more than a year, I announced that I wanted to build a log home on my property at Victory Haven. After several months of hearing about my ideas, Mom and Dad offered to lend me money for the project.

Building the house began a series of events that changed my life. While working on the house with me, Hansen cut off part of his thumb in a table saw. As a result, he stopped coming out to the work site daily. This began a time of personal growth for me as I faced the challenge of building the house alone. Hansen was also aging and declining in his ability to monitor my every move. Although we still saw our relationship the same way, it was less intense. I focused my attention on the house, and we continued our weekly services at the prison.

After a year of building my house, we decided to build a camp guest lodge with five motel-style rooms. With bunk beds in each room, we could sleep more than 20 guests. This was another step in establishing the camp property as a retreat center. Early in 1986 I told Hansen that I wanted to hold a summer girls' camp for a week during July. My plan was to recruit a volunteer staff and have 25 campers. It would be a ministry to low income girls and also model the program that I had loved so much at the camp in North Carolina. I believed in Christian camping and this challenge seemed to capture my eager desire to do something positive.

During 1986 and 1987 I held the girls' camps for several weeks each summer. Being director of the camp gave me a lot of joy. I was awakening my gifts of service and leadership which had been so underdeveloped. There was a genuine satisfaction in giving to others and helping the girls. The irony was that I did, at times, help others with their problems while being in complete denial about my own. The camps gave me some measure of fulfillment apart from just doing what Hansen told me to do. Meanwhile, I continued going to the prison and attending Roberta's Bible study.

Something was slowly changing in me that I couldn't put my finger on. I was coming of age in my late 20's, while Hansen was showing some obvious signs of aging. I had learned to tell myself that Hansen and I would probably never really be legally or openly married, but that God had His reasons for giving us the relationship. I had begun to think that he would eventually die, and this would be the only way the relationship would end. I was resigned to the finality of my commitment. I concluded that maybe one day I would tell a future husband-to-be about it, but other than that, I planned to live out my life never telling anyone. Both building the house and leading the girls' camps had given me a sense of fulfillment and direction. I still walked on eggshells around Hansen and would have cowered at his anger, but he was not angry as often. A small distance was growing between us. I had even risked having some of my own thoughts.

During the summer of 1987, just after the girls' camps were over, I made a startling announcement to Hansen. I told him that I didn't think we should have any more sexual or physical contact until we were legally married. I didn't know how I managed to propose this, but it changed the dynamic between us. The balance of power was beginning to shift, if ever so slightly. My sense of having some personal power was just beginning to emerge. This was another small boost in my making a few boundaries for myself and beginning some small separations from his control. Despite the fact that I'd told myself that I didn't have guilt over our sexual touching, I felt an immediate relief when I finally stopped it. Surprisingly, there wasn't much of a backlash from him.

A few of my own thoughts were surfacing. My friend, Betsy, twenty years older than me, had been honest with me about some of her life struggles, and I was surprised to hear myself risk telling her, "Hansen is hard on me." Although this was a gross understatement, it was a beginning. It was the first negative thing I had shared with anyone about him in nearly eleven years. Meanwhile, the stone fell out of my "engagement ring," and I made no plans to have it repaired. Hansen overlooked this, and I didn't mention it again.

Late in 1987, as I was walking through the living room in my log house, I thought about an inmate at the prison, Wayne Thomas, who was respected for his authentic spiritual commitment. I had begun talking to Wayne for a few minutes at the service each week. My friend, Betsy, and her husband, Jim, had helped Wayne to find Christ two years earlier. He would be released from prison soon and was going to live with them and get a job.

In a brief flash of thought, I imagined Wayne sleeping on the couch in my house, the way any man might do on a lazy Sunday afternoon. I let myself wonder what it would be like to be married to him. Quickly, I caught myself and redirected my thoughts back to my work. I was aware that I had "betrayed" Hansen in my thoughts, but contrary to my usual inner responses, I didn't feel much guilt.

I quickly decided that I wasn't going to tell Hansen about it. I remembered the incident ten years before with the pastor in Monroe. I resolved that I didn't deserve to go through that again. I didn't deserve to be punished or put through the mill. I would keep the thought about Wayne to myself.

It was the first real act of defiance in nearly twelve years.

Once the abusive relationship has been rigidly established, the patterns of behavior and fear become fully ingrained. Objectivity is lost. The relationship can endure for years.

For the Word of God is living,
and active,
and sharper than any two-edged sword,
piercing as far as the division of soul and spirit,
of both joints and marrow,
and
able to judge the thoughts and intentions of the heart.

Hebrews 4:12 (NASB)

CHAPTER 12
The Fall of Denial

I felt excited as I drove to northwest Arkansas that weekend. I'd be speaking at a youth retreat for high school kids. Several of the girls who attended camp had invited me to speak at their home church. It felt great to be getting away. The trees were bare along famous Highway 7, which just made the features of the beautiful mountain foothills more obvious.

Driving along, it seemed a good time to review some of the scripture I'd memorized, so I started repeating the book of Ephesians to myself. I wanted to prepare myself for the weekend challenges, and I hoped to inspire the kids to follow the Lord. Occasionally I glanced down at my Bible on the seat beside me if I was stuck and couldn't remember the next verse. I'd first learned these passages during my freshman year at college, eleven years before.

Getting into Ephesians chapter 5, I began to repeat verses 7-11:

> Therefore do not be partakers with them; for you were formerly darkness, but now you are Light in the Lord; walk as children of Light, (for the fruit of the Light consists in all goodness and righteousness and truth), trying to learn what is pleasing to the Lord.
>
> Do not participate in the unfruitful deeds of darkness, but instead even expose them; for it is disgraceful even to speak of the things which are done by them in secret.
>
> But all things become visible when they are exposed by the light, for everything that becomes visible is light. (NASB)

The phrases began rolling around in my head. *Children of Light...the fruit of the Light is truth...the things done by them in secret...everything that becomes visible...* I went over it several times. Although I had reviewed this verse many times when memorizing it, and probably 20 times in the last five years alone, it suddenly gripped me. I began to look at each phrase, meditating on it.

This says that if we are children of Light, we should walk in openness, not in secrets. We should expose those things in our lives that are darkness. If something was permitted to be made visible, it would be a validation that it was "Light" or good; if something was kept secret, it would be evidence that it was darkness.

The conclusions seemed to come to me. *Since what I am doing with Hansen has been operating in secret, it must be darkness. Either what I have been telling myself about Hansen all these years is true, or God's Word is true, but they both can't be. One excludes the other.*

I felt the point of decision in front of me. This scripture demanded a decision. I knew I couldn't deny it. God's Word had to be the one that was true.

I drove toward my destination, a strange stillness around me. I turned off my praise music. There was something holy about the moment. I wanted to be quiet.

That evening when I stood up to speak at the retreat, there were 30 teenagers listening. I put aside most of my prepared talk, and I found myself speaking about the verses I'd read in the car.

"There's a certain way you can tell if what you are doing is approved by the Lord or not," I told them. "If you have to keep it a secret, or try to prevent anyone from knowing it, that's a red flag that you shouldn't be doing it." As I spoke, my mind was further digesting the truth, almost as if I was preaching to myself. "When you decide to follow God's word as the truth, you have to get truthful about your life."

Later that evening I called Hansen. "When I get home, I have some things to tell you." I felt a strength to speak up to him.

"What is it?" His voice was guarded.

"I've got to get truthful about my life." I was vague, but he must have sensed some tenacity in my voice. "I'll tell you more when I get home." It wasn't like me to be telling him anything on *my* terms, rather than his, and my frankness surprised me.

During the two days before he came, I thought more clearly about the truth that was coming to me. It was true, I had denied what God's Word said and had let a man tell me what he wanted me to believe. I had committed the very sin that I preached to others about. I had betrayed God's Word. I had rationalized my actions. I had put a man's word above God's Word.

That afternoon I knelt in my bedroom by my sitting chair and ottoman. I had to tell God I was sorry. *Lord, I really don't know how I did this, or why I couldn't see it before. I know that I really wasn't married to Hansen and that You didn't tell him that I belonged to him. It was all a lie. I didn't marry him because You weren't in any of that. I renounce those vows. It was all a hoax. I'm really sorry, Lord. I'm not going to continue in any secret relationship with Hansen. Please, please forgive me.*

My voice was steady and there were no tears. It was a confession on an intellectual level, and very definitely a repentance of my will. I meant it. Still, my emotions were carefully locked away.

After delaying our meeting for several days, Hansen arrived. I asked him to sit down. I felt some fear in how to address my new convictions. "I need to tell you that I don't believe that I'm married to you or that I ever was," I began. "I don't believe any more that God was telling us that."

I held his hand as I told him, almost feeling sorry to let him down. He looked at the floor and didn't say much. I continued, "I'm going to continue working for you and doing the ministry, but I'm not going to believe that I'm married to you anymore."

Hansen was strangely silent. He hardly made eye contact with me. He seemed detached, and I was surprised that he wasn't angry. "Well, I can see you've been doing some thinking. I guess you've made your decision..." his voice trailed off. An awkward silence hung between us. Finally he got up and walked out.

After Hansen left, I felt relieved. I was surprised that he hadn't attacked me emotionally. Things seemed strangely quiet. I went about my day's work.

The next day we went to the prison service as usual. I spoke to the inmates about the same topic of "no secrets" that I had used at the youth retreat. This time I was doing it in front of Hansen. While making casual conversation after the service, Hansen took the opportunity to take a sarcastic jab at me.

"Well, I see you are on a little righteousness kick," he mocked. I didn't respond. I felt hurt by the sarcasm but didn't buckle or recant. I turned and walked away. Nothing else was said about my new convictions.

A few days later, I began to think about Wayne Thomas again. I knew that he was now living at Betsy and Jim's house. He had called me twice during the last six weeks since he had gotten out of prison. I had refused both his invitation to go to the theater and also a church party. I suddenly felt free to call him and, hardly admitting my eagerness to myself, I dialed his number.

Wayne was surprised to hear my voice on the phone. "Hey, I was wondering if I could take you up on your invitation to play some racquetball," I stated.

I could almost hear him smiling on the phone. "Great, how about Tuesday night?" he asked.

We arranged to meet at a church racquetball court. I wondered how it would go when I told Hansen that I would be playing racquetball with Wayne on Tuesday. I was afraid he'd launch an emotional attack. When I told him, he was quiet, detached, offered no challenge, and changed the subject.

"We'd better look into getting the road fixed at Victory Haven before that retreat group comes next month." He was sticking to safe topics and keeping the conversation to business.

When Wayne and I finished playing racquetball, we went to Burger King for a Coke. For two hours Wayne told me all about his life, how he'd gotten into drugs, been convicted of distribution and possession of narcotics, and the various places he'd been incarcerated. He was 35 years old, had never been married, and had been in jail a total of twelve years. He had decided to put all his cards on the table. He made it clear that he'd like to date me, and that he'd been hoping for some time that I'd change my mind and give him a chance. He wanted me to know all about him so that if I couldn't handle his past life, I could back out now. The good news was that he had been sober for more than three years and had been working hard on himself.

I appreciated his honesty. He certainly had faced up to the terrible pain he had caused himself and his family. We ended the evening on a mutually satisfied note. We were clearly attracted to each other, and we both knew it.

During the remainder of the week I continued to check in with Hansen with daily phone calls. For years this had been so much a part of my routine. We discussed the Sunday morning house church which would be at my home that weekend. I monitored his voice to see if he were about to challenge me, but everything was strangely quiet. Other than my saying that I had played racquetball with Wayne and we talked afterwards at Burger King, nothing else was mentioned.

It seemed that Hansen had accepted my new position on our relationship. I didn't allow myself to question the future too deeply. I avoided the looming questions of how we'd actually have some kind of normal working relationship, given our history. For now I was focusing on the awareness that I had accepted the real truth about my relationship to Hansen and that I had asked God to forgive me for compromising His Word. It was enough to ponder. I didn't question what would happen next. I did feel in a sort of limbo with Hansen, waiting to see what the fallout would be.

On Saturday morning, Wayne called unexpectedly. He had been scheduled to attend a men's conference with Ken, his mentor friend, over the weekend, but Ken's father had died and the trip was called off. "How about if I come up to your house, and we'll do something today?" Wayne asked optimistically.

"Okay, come on, and we'll figure out what to do when you get here." I was excited. It was February 20th, and we were having one of the first preview days of Louisiana springtime. The sun was bright and the temperature would be rising to 60 degrees.

When Wayne arrived we decided to go canoeing down Dorcheat Bayou, as he'd never been canoeing. I had made this canoe trip several times, and knew that the Bayou would be beautiful in the sunshine. I was eager to show him the cypress trees hanging with Spanish moss.

As we canoed down the bayou, Wayne didn't hide his exhilaration. "The sun's so beautiful! The water is so pretty!" His Mississippi accent seemed even richer than I'd noticed before. He seemed as happy as a child. His delight over nature's simple beauty, after being in prison the past seven years, was fun to watch.

As we floated along, it was my turn to tell him about my life. I told him the version I would have told anyone during the past twelve years. I stuck to the facts. I went to camp growing up. I was a majorette. I went to college. Then I went to work for Hansen. Then I built a house. Then I led the girls' camps. I filled in the details as Wayne asked questions. I kept to the safe facts, of course not mentioning the secret relationship with Hansen.

While we were loading the canoe back on the car, Wayne asked me to eat supper with him before we parted. I declined, not because I wanted to, but because I felt fearful. In the back of my mind I knew that my dates with Wayne were going to eventually cause a blowup with Hansen. Intuitively, I knew Hansen was cooking with resentment, and a showdown was coming. I was automatically defaulting to my ingrained patterns of fear. I needed to get home.

Since I'd be passing Hansen's house on the way home, I decided that I should just stop by in person. I was used to reporting in. I had, because of habit, called him and told him that Wayne and I would be canoeing and I knew he'd be waiting for a report afterwards. As I pulled into his driveway, a sense of dread was surfacing in me. I went in and found him sitting in his study.

"Well, did you have a good time?" his voice was sarcastic. "Tell me about it."

I stuck to the facts of the beautiful day and that Wayne had never canoed before. I could feel the tension between us. He looked at me as if he were going to interrogate me.

"Well, have you slept with him yet?" Hansen feigned detachment and glanced down at his books. I felt repulsed by his exaggerated accusation and deeply insulted.

"I can't believe you'd say that. I haven't even held his hand," my voice had firmness.

We sat in silence, staring at each other. Rather than cowering, I felt something livid rising in me. I looked at Hansen. *He's a lunatic! He's a madman! I hate him! I am disgusted by him!*

If he was reading my thoughts, I didn't care. It was my first moment of face-to-face defiance with him. I wasn't about to apologize for having a good time with Wayne.

Hansen couldn't hold back his insane jealousy anymore. "Well, you just go right ahead and have fun with your little friend," his voice dripped with sarcasm. He cocked his head in a scoffing gesture.

Instantaneously, I felt like I would explode with anger. It was as though scales fell off my eyes. For the first time, I could see who he really was.

My thoughts flooded in: *He's evil! I hate him! I hate him! I cannot ever be in his presence again!* I left without a word.

Driving the thirteen miles to my house, I let myself scream in the car. "I hate him! I hate him! He's a lunatic!" I screamed it out loud. I was crying hysterically, and my eyes and nose were dripping profusely. I kept on screaming. "Leave me alone! I hate you! You're disgusting! You always hurt me!"

At home, I realized that I was at a crossroads. I could not even work for Hansen anymore. I could never trust him. He was crazy.

I began to think about running away. I couldn't stay here. Hansen had once threatened that if I ever resigned from the ministry, he would have full control at Victory Haven. I still believed him. If I left, I'd be giving it all to him. I'd be leaving my log home that I loved, since it was a part of the camp facility.

I passed the rest of the evening in restless confusion. The delightful day with Wayne had quickly faded into a life crisis. *What was I going to do?* I walked Elsa and her puppy, Gabriel, in the woods and tried to think. *I can run away to Dallas and come clean with Sam. I can tell him everything. I can ask for help. I can be honest. I can't live this way anymore. I can't stand it. I have to run away from Hansen. I don't care if I lose everything. There is no price too high to be free!*

Before I lost my courage, I called Sam. I asked him to drive to meet me tomorrow afternoon, on Sunday. If I drove west on Interstate 20 and he drove east, we'd meet somewhere near Tyler, Texas. We agreed on a time and an exit where we'd rendezvous.

"Can you just tell me what this is about?" Sam was mystified.

"I can't tell you now. Please just meet me tomorrow." The urgency in my voice convinced him that something serious was up.

The next morning, twelve people arrived for the morning service at my house. I went through the motions of the service, singing the songs and listening to Hansen's sermon. Hansen and I hardly made eye contact.

As everyone was leaving, I made an announcement. "I'm going to Dallas to see Sam for a while." I was matter of fact.

"When are you coming back?" Hansen tried to sound detached.

"I don't know."

I loaded my suitcase and my two German Shepherds in the car. I hadn't planned what to do with the dogs. I drove to the vet's office, hoping someone would be there to take them in for boarding. Thankfully, the assistant was there, feeding and tending to the animals. The dogs dropped off, I got on the interstate.

As I drove west I still didn't know how I'd be able to tell Sam about Hansen. I tried not to worry about it. Somehow I'd do it. The drive seemed to drag on and on. I looked at my watch. I still had at least another hour. A sense of dread was coming over me.

Maybe I should turn back. I can't tell this stuff. It's too awful. Turn the car around and go home. Sam will be so disappointed in me. It seemed like I was struggling against an oppressive presence. I worked hard to keep my eyes ahead on the road. I tried to mentally coach myself. *For now, just don't think. Just get to Sam.*

Important note: No woman should try to leave an abusive relationship without seeking professional help. There are many factors to consider, and one's safety is paramount. This is the most dangerous time in the relationship, and an abuser may become more controlling, angry, or violent.

If you want to leave your abuser, first try to make contact with a therapist, women's shelter, or domestic violence program. A professional can offer you emotional support and help you assess the potential for harm. She can also help you find legal resources so that you can obtain a restraining order if needed. Most communities have access to safe houses for women and children, legal support, and volunteers who will help you with this process.

Although I wasn't harmed by my abuser when I left, at the time I did not know that this would have been an important precaution for me.

"It was facing myself
that I feared the most.
I knew I was going to have
to pass my own
personal challenge.
I had been humbled,
exposed.
I finally saw
what I had become."

Richard Dortch
(After the collapse of the PTL Ministries)
Integrity: How I Lost It and My Journey Back
New Leaf Press, 1992

CHAPTER 13
The Dam Breaks

"Just what do you need to tell me?" Sam was puzzled. We were sitting in a hotel room. We decided that we needed a private place to talk and had checked in.

I hardly knew where to start. My fear level was sky high. "I don't know how to tell you all the things that have happened. It's real ugly." I got on the bed and curled up. I wanted to hide.

"There's some bad stuff that's been happening...with me and Brother Hansen." Even being vague was bringing on tremendous emotional pain. "I've been believing...that I was...uhhh...married...to Hansen for some years." I began crying and stuttering. It sounded terrible to say that out loud.

Sam looked shocked and skeptical.

During the next two hours I tried to unload the facts of the situation. I related that Hansen had started telling me he loved me when I was in high school, that we were called together by God, and that we had taken vows together during my freshman year in college. Each statement felt like lead coming out of my mouth. There were long pauses where I cried and sat silent. I pulled a few stories out of my memory, but they weren't in order and hardly made sense to me. I'd never made a sequential or coherent narrative of it. It all felt muddled.

Sam was stumped. He was kind and reassuring, but he didn't hide his own confusion. After talking for a couple of hours I asked him if he believed me.

"I think I do, but it's hard," he stated honestly. "Why didn't I know or suspect this?" I understood his caution. It all sounded surreal to hear myself tell it. I could only imagine the shock of someone being hit with all of it at once.

I was beginning an emotional meltdown. Flooded with pain and shame, I could hardly stop crying. Sam was faced with trying to decide what to do for me. At first, he saw my situation as a serious personal conflict with Hansen, but one that could be negotiated and end positively. Sam thought that maybe I could go back and work for Hansen, but with accountability to others in place. He had never encountered this level of pathology before in a pastor; he didn't have a category for it. Always willing to consult with wise individuals, he called some friends who were mature therapists. He described the crux of my situation to them on the phone.

"Get her out of there," they told Sam firmly. "She's been under a kind of cult-like influence. She doesn't have any skills to stand up to him. Don't let him get to her." When he hung up the phone the reality hit him. He was starting to realize that he'd been naïve in his interpretation, and under-responding to the breakdown I was having.

"You're going back to Dallas with me," he said.

Later, Sam called Hansen on the phone. "JoAnn is with me, and she's told me everything," his voice was firm. "You are not to try to contact her ever again.

I'll be calling you later. There will be some things to settle." (He was referring to some money Hansen had borrowed when I had cosigned a note with him.) Knowing that Sam was intervening as my advocate gave me some relief from fear and a sense of emotional safety.

Sam told me Hansen had been quiet on the phone. "Please don't release this to the newspapers," was all he said.

We stayed at the hotel two nights contemplating my crisis, then headed to Dallas. Because Sam lived in a men's dormitory, I couldn't stay with him. Sam arranged for me to stay with a single woman who was a secretary at the Bible college he attended. Shirley was a lovely 55-year-old woman with a soft, motherly appearance. I instantly felt safe in her apartment.

Meanwhile, my emotional dike had completely broken. I collapsed into a black emotional hole. I stayed in bed for a week, barely able to function. Sam came by the apartment twice a day to check on me and talk. I could hardly eat. Mostly I cried and thought about how ashamed I felt and how stupid I was. I could barely explain anything.

One evening Shirley sat by the bed and offered me some food. I declined again to eat. "Well, you're going to have to try," she said lovingly but firmly. Then she began feeding me yogurt from a spoon. It was hard to eat in between crying and blowing my nose. I couldn't make sense of my thoughts. I couldn't articulate who I was or how I got where I'd been. I was emotionally and mentally disorganized. Only a few months before I had been confidently leading a girls' camp and was feeling more fulfilled than I had in years. Now someone had to feed me. This felt shameful. I could not remember ever feeling so broken.

In the silence of Shirley's apartment, waves of emotional trauma rolled over me. Little by little I remembered incidents from my past with Hansen. There were so many times when he'd mistreated me, times when I'd lied to defend him, times when I pretended our relationship was above board and wholesome. The explanations I'd used to rationalize our relationship crumbled as I recalled events. The truth of what had happened was starting to emerge.

At times the shame and pain were so great that I held myself and rocked back and forth, attempting to manage the erupting anxiety. I was not yet able to feel any anger toward Hansen, just shame over having been so messed up. I thought about taking the vows with him. *I'd agreed to that, hadn't I?* Although I began to remember many events historically, I had little insight into the abuse they actually represented. I remembered telling him so many times that I loved him and how happy I was to be his. I felt nauseous. *How could I have thought I was married to an old man? When others hear it was him, they will be repulsed. I am so embarrassed. I must be a defective and unworthy person.* The brutal self-evaluations felt like truth to me.

There were feelings of freedom at times, but more often of shame and fear. *What will I do now? Hansen will be taking over everything. I can't go back to the camp or my house.* I thought that I'd have to start a new life somewhere else.

I was thrilled to be free from Hansen, but still filled with fear. *How will I tell my parents?* I knew that I'd have to level with them. I owed them that. They had remained supportive and patient over the years though they had hated my working for Hansen. I was filled with self-hatred over the years of deceiving them and others. *How could I have believed all that? I've led a double life for twelve years. I have deceived everyone who knew me. I don't deserve to ever be respected by them. Was I even sincere about loving God? Was I just a hypocrite like those in ministry who got involved in immoral relationships?* Everything in my life seemed up for grabs.

I prayed brief prayers of humility: *God, I'm sorry. I love You. Help me.* It was all I could get out. At times I felt rushes of gratefulness to God that I was delivered. But in a moment, I would return to anguish and pain again.

Meanwhile, Sam called our parents and told them that I was in Dallas with him, that I'd made decisions about not working for Hansen anymore, and that we'd be telling them more soon. They had a sense that bad news was coming. They were at once both alarmed and relieved.

During that week, Sam arranged for me to meet with one of his professors whom he deeply respected. We went together, and I told the professor my story. It was hard to know what parts to tell, there was so much that had happened over twelve years. I felt mentally scattered. I wasn't sure it sounded believable. As I talked, I watched his face. Rather than being shocked and disgusted, as I feared, he was nodding in understanding, his face compassionate. He had heard similar stories before.

"I know it's hard to believe, but in the past I always thought Hansen was a godly man," I stumbled to sum up my story.

"He's not a *godly* man, he's an *evil* man." The professor's tone of finality was blunt. The word "evil" was a word I had never applied to Hansen. I had hardly been able to articulate that Hansen had violated me, much less looked at the truth of who he was. It had a startling effect on me, shattering more denial.

The truth had unearthed another layer of pain for me: *had I wasted twelve years of my life with an evil man?* I returned to Shirley's apartment both validated and burdened with another round of grief. There was so much loss.

As the first week of my freedom ended, I was faced with gargantuan emotional tasks. I had decided to tell several of my friends what had happened. I knew I would need their emotional support, and I didn't want to lie to them about why I was quitting my job and leaving Victory Haven. If I sold my house and moved, they deserved to know the truth. They had all been real with me about their lives. Now it was my turn.

Sam and I would be driving back for the weekend. I phoned ahead and asked seven close friends to come to my log home for a meeting. I also included Wayne in the group. Only two weeks before he'd told me about his life and all the messes he'd gotten into. I wanted to continue a friendship with him, but it would have to be on completely honest terms.

Telling others first was a way of getting up my courage to tell my parents. I felt so ashamed to admit I had gone back to Hansen against their wishes. I knew they had sensed something was wrong and tried to get through to me, but I had rejected them. Now I'd have no credibility with them. I also felt more guilt about the ways I'd followed Hansen in criticizing them. *They'll be so shocked and ashamed of me. Nobody in my family has ever failed like this.* Although the thought of telling them brought on dread, I knew I'd have to. I wanted back the honesty I'd once had with them.

I didn't yet understand my own actions over the years or how Hansen had manipulated me. *How had I believed so many lies from him?* I was a long way from forming any answers. I was only beginning to form the questions.

> **It is very difficult for someone to shatter the grip of mind control and to leave a life-dominating cult or abusive relationship. Victims are often deeply broken, bewildered, and suffer from mental, emotional, and spiritual disorganization.**

Buy the **truth,** and sell it not;

    also wisdom,
        and instruction,
            and understanding.

Proverbs 23:23 (KJV)

CHAPTER 14

The Healing Begins

Looking around the room, I felt some sense of comfort in my friends who were gathered. It took an hour to tell the basics of my story. Having told it twice now, I could be a little more organized in relating it. Wayne sat frozen on the couch, and I couldn't read his expression. He, like the others, had to be in shock. I wasn't the innocent Christian young woman he had watched for the past two years at the prison.

"I guess it's like Hansen raped...my mind," I surprised myself by blurting it out that way, but when I said it, it felt true.

At the end of my story, everyone gathered around to hug me and pray for me. Betsy and Jim, Tom and Dorothy, Wayne, Cherry (one of my camp counselor friends), Thomas (a friend who'd helped me a lot with camp), and Sam. I had wanted Roberta and her husband to come, but they were out of town. I felt everyone's love and compassion. I had asked them to forgive me for deceiving them. For a few minutes their support relieved the heavy anxiety I'd been struggling under for the last week.

After the meeting, Sam and two of the men planned to confront Hansen. They would require him to resign from his position over Victory Haven and to release me from any financial obligations he'd put me under. It was a relief knowing they would deal with Hansen. I certainly didn't want to ever see him again. The idea of being in his presence evoked extreme fear.

As Wayne was starting to leave for the evening, he asked if he could see me outside alone. As we stepped into the cool air on the back porch, he looked red-faced and flushed with emotion. It seemed he was fighting back tears.

"I don't understand what's happened to you," his voice halted and he paused, searching for words, "but I'll pray for you."

I felt embarrassed. As each new person heard my story, I felt like a fake and a heel. If Wayne had turned and run, I wouldn't have blamed him.

"I'm sorry you had to hear all this trash. It's so ugly," I said. I had worried how Wayne would take it when he heard the truth about Hansen. He had, like so many others, experienced Hansen as a good Bible teacher at the prison.

"Well, you could start your life over with me," Wayne said through a haze of tears. Surprised by his sincerity, I realized he had feelings for me. I was too emotionally exhausted to respond. He left with the others and I spent the rest of the evening with Sam. Now that I was coming out of the initial shock phase, I was able to answer a few more of his questions.

Telling the truth to others had given me a bit more strength to do the most difficult thing...to talk to my parents. Yet the next day, driving to my parents' house with Sam, I could hardly put down the near panic feelings that were rising in me. I could hardly breathe. *This is definitely the hardest thing I have ever done.* As we sat with them, I got through an abbreviated version of the story. I didn't think they could stand hearing more. I felt flooded with shame buffered only by a bit of relief that I'd made it through the confession.

"I should get a gun and kill him," my dad said angrily. While I could have seen my dad's words as a healthy emotional reaction of protection for his daughter, in my present frame of mind I could only feel fear.

My mother cried and looked bewildered. "I'm just so glad that you're out."

Everyone's pain was enormous. They expressed forgiveness for my duplicity and relief that it was over. Although I had never felt more defeated, my parents' unconditional love was tangible. They had suspected that I was a sort of "captive" to Hansen, but had never dreamed the relationship could have been so sick.

After their initial comments, an awkward silence set in. No one knew what to do next. We quickly looked for a diversion from the emotional intensity and went to the kitchen to prepare some food. The appalling disclosure hung over us while we ate a near silent meal. I felt responsible for causing the pain we were all in. There was nothing I could do to control it. It just had to be faced.

As I arrived home that evening, a huge burden was lifted. I had made it through telling my friends and parents. The worst of the disclosures was over. I'd drive to North Carolina in the next few weeks to tell my sister and her husband.

The phone rang and it was Wayne, wanting to know if I'd like to go to his church with him that evening. Later, sitting beside Wayne, I thought how good it was to be there. Although others couldn't see it, I knew that I was a different person. *God, thank You that I'm free. Thank you.* The pastor's sermon that night was on a "repentance that was real." He talked about the honesty needed to begin fresh. It seemed the message was just for me.

During the last week I had experienced a complete crash of my identity. I didn't know at the time that this was one of the most difficult things a human being can experience. Everything from the past twelve years had to be reviewed in the light of truth, with new honesty, and with emotional independence to make my own interpretations. I was no longer Hansen's emotional hostage nor was I emotionally blackmailed to see things his way.

I was a strange mixture of depression, hope, fear, and relief. I never knew how many times a day I would cycle through each emotion. In some ways it was just as emotionally wrenching as the first identity crisis when Hansen had broken and then re-defined me.

Sam took me back to Dallas for another week. This time I could eat and my mind was beginning to clear somewhat. I continued to have anxiety attacks, usually brought on by memories of events with Hansen. One afternoon Sam arrived after class to find me crying on the couch.

"Hansen spent about $500 of the ministry funds on his personal bills the last few years," I reported to Sam. I had been fixated on this since I first thought of it that morning. "He always said he would pay it back, but he didn't. Should I earn the money to pay back the funds?"

I was willing to do anything I needed to live honestly. I felt guilty by association. There were hundreds of events during the twelve years when I might have intervened to stop Hansen from being devious, mean, or manipulative of others. *Was I just an evil person, too?* It was hard to figure out. I didn't want to excuse myself if I was also guilty. It seemed easier to blame myself for nearly everything. *I'm so confused!*

I felt like I had committed some sort of treason…not against my country, but against myself. I had collaborated with the enemy. I thought of people during World War II who had been duped into fighting for Hitler. *What did they do when they "woke up" after the war and realized they'd been fighting for the evil side? How did they live with themselves?* I felt like I had spent twelve years supporting and collaborating with an evil person. *It's sickening. I'm so stupid. I'm the stupidest Christian who ever lived.* This seemed the most truthful way to view my life.

I had little insight into Hansen's early attacks on my mind. I had suppressed thoughts about his manipulative tactics and lived so long in deception. Understanding was slow to seep through. I wavered between seeing myself as a victim *(he's responsible for it all)* and seeing myself as an atrocious sinner *(I'm responsible for it all)*. I carried my brokenness and sense of humiliation everywhere I went. I wasn't sure if I deserved anyone's compassion. *I have hurt the body of Christ. If the girls who had attended my summer camps knew this, they might be permanently turned off about God.* When these thoughts came I felt terrible dread about anyone knowing about Hansen's and my relationship. *I hate myself for failing Christ.* Shame seemed to roll over me in waves. I had discredited the God I loved. My sense of loving Him, of serving Him for years, was shattered. *I don't know who I am.*

Meanwhile, Sam, Tom, and Jim had confronted Hansen and he signed their prepared statement, resigning from Victory Haven and designating me as the President of the non-profit organization. The statement also released me from a bank debt I'd signed with Hansen two years earlier. I was relieved that Hansen had resigned quietly, and that I wouldn't have to sell my home and move. However, I didn't know what the future held. It would have to evolve as I slowly got well. I returned from Dallas to a sense of security in my own home.

Being with Wayne relieved my private torture of mental shame, and we began to spend more time together. It felt so good to be with someone my age. After all the deprivation of the last twelve years when I'd never had a date and never even gone out to dinner with a man, I reveled in every hour with him. He became my personal confidant as I mucked through recalling the hundreds of events with Hansen and the pain that went with them. I cried at some point during *every* date.

"I remember crying daily when I became a Christian three years ago," Wayne said. "I used to walk around the track at the prison, crying and praying. It went on for several months. I went outside to pray so the other inmates wouldn't see me crying. There was so much pain to grieve. I was a long time forgiving myself even though I knew God had forgiven me."

"Yeah, but you weren't a Christian when you did all that drug stuff." I envied the fact that he didn't have to say he was a "messed-up Christian." The insanity of his drug-littered past had occurred while he was ignorant of God.

"My sin is worse," I stated. "I lived a lie. I knew better than to believe that a person could supersede the Bible with his own word. I don't know how I could have given in to that." I was insistent about my guilt. I never missed an opportunity to berate myself.

"Well, we both have to live in the new light of who we are now." Wayne was matter-of-fact and hopeful. "I think you're going to heal from this and be fine."

When Wayne talked that way I could see a little hope.

"Come on," he said. "Let's go walk the dogs. The stars are beautiful tonight." Wayne handed me his handkerchief, and I blew my nose, seemingly for the hundredth time.

As Wayne and I walked down the country highway near my log home, I felt we were psychologically equal. No top-dog/under-dog relationship here. He had become a true friend. He had a lot to say about starting life over. It seemed we had a lot in common.

We had both been in prison for twelve years.

You're only as sick as the secrets you keep. The courage to break bad secrets and tell the truth about yourself may be the most profound courage you could ever exercise.

For more understanding of the issues at stake when turning your life around, see Essay #3: Do I Really Want to Get Well, Essay #4: Put Your Hand to the Plow, and Essay #5: When I Kept Silent.

What do I pray for?

    Pray for courage.
*Courage. Not for daring feats
like facing lions or bears...
Courage. Not for meeting foes or
staring down their stares.*

*But courage needed for the job
I've dreaded and run from...
Courage, Lord, to look within
to see what I've become.*

    Pray for strength.
*Strength. Not for keeping up
the secret games I played...
Strength. Not for guarding tight
the house of cards I've made.*

*But strength to start my life anew
on truths that really last...
Strength to overcome the pain
that constitutes my past.*

    Pray for hope.
*Hope. Not just that I'll be fine
tomorrow when I wake...
Hope. Not for some quick fix
to make me feel real great.*

*But hope that somehow since I've told
the truth and gotten real...
That hope and peace will multiply
and heal the grief I feel.*

JoAnn Nishimoto

CHAPTER 15
The Fight To Accept and Value Myself

During the first months of freedom from Hansen, I struggled with trusting myself. Fortunately, I was still able to trust my friends and family who had shown themselves faithful over the years. I knew my parents and friends were going to stick with me. This gave me a foundation on which to stand against the grief and self-rejection I felt. I knew that others loved me even though I didn't feel worthy. I reached for their love, but I constantly struggled with despising myself.

I tried to think ahead to the future of Victory Haven. Sam and others had agreed with me that I was in no shape to be planning summer girls' camps that year. I was too depressed and confused about my past. The camp facility would remain closed down for now. I felt guilt over being a "fallen spiritual leader." *I wonder whether I'll ever be used by the Lord again. Maybe I never was used by Him. I can't understand myself. What's happened to me? I have destroyed all my opportunities for leadership. No one will ever respect me again. How would anyone ever believe me? I have no credibility.*

I viewed myself as sorting through a demolished house after a tornado. I'd seen pictures like that on TV. The owner slowly steps through the rubbish, lifting broken furniture and belongings, wondering if she will find anything to save, anything to bring forward into the "new life." I thought back on the previous twelve years. *What could be saved?* I didn't have answers. Everything seemed tainted by my past relationship with Hansen.

Sam continued to send me money each month until I found work. My self-esteem was so low that I felt terrified to look for a job. Nearly every day I found myself struggling against fear. *Why am I so afraid? It doesn't make sense. I'm free from Hansen now. Why can't I be happy or relaxed?* I didn't want to tell anyone how depressed I was. It only heightened my sense of failure.

Wayne and I continued to date. He was working as a maintenance man in an apartment complex in nearby Shreveport and we began to see each other several times a week. He was living with Jim and Betsy, the couple who had ministered to him in prison and helped him to find God three years earlier. Wayne and I often laughed about the nature of our dating relationship. Other couples might be working hard at impressing each other in the early stages of a relationship...putting the best foot forward. Wayne and I were struggling through gut-level issues related to my recovery, my self-hatred, and confusion over my past. Occasionally we found humor in it.

"Everyone thinks you're such a lucky guy, getting to date me," I said. "They're thinking, 'That poor guy, Wayne, must feel so lost after getting out of prison. He needs her.' They don't know that *you're* the stable one in this relationship, and I'm leaning on you!" We had a good laugh about it.

"I remember how embarrassed I used to feel about all of my past," Wayne said thoughtfully. Looking at his boyish face, it was hard to envision him being a convicted felon. "I just know that it took me a while to understand myself. You're being honest, JoAnn, and that's the foundation. God will build on that."

As he turned to make eye contact with me, I saw that his eyes were an even more brilliant blue than I'd previously noticed.

"You're right, I'm sure." I decided to borrow on his hope. My depression felt suddenly lighter. *Is it the sensible things Wayne is saying or my sudden recognition of how gorgeous his blue eyes are? Maybe a combination of the two?*

As planned, I drove to North Carolina to disclose my past to my sister, Helen, and her husband, Steve. I felt compassion for others and shame for myself whenever I knew someone had to cope with hearing my story. *It has to be terrible for them. It's so ugly. I wouldn't blame them for thinking I'm stupid.* They were, like everyone else, overwhelmed to hear my story. Their children were ages ten, eight, and four, and I only told them that I was "changing jobs." Later, my brother-in-law told me that he was so distressed over my story that he went to a professional therapist to try and sort out his thoughts. He found it hard to believe that I could have actually been so controlled by a man.

Wayne had been saying that he wanted to marry me, and while I was in North Carolina he wrote me several persuasive letters. I also talked to Helen about my growing attraction for him. She had mixed feelings. On the one hand she knew I was vulnerable and in a chaotic emotional state. On the other hand, she was delighted to see me attracted to someone and my excitement about it.

After returning from North Carolina, my friend, Cherry, contacted me. She had been present the night I "came clean" at my home. Her church in Arkansas had been making a $50 gift per month to Victory Haven for the past year. Several girls from the church had attended my summer camp and Cherry had been a counselor. The pastor had received glowing reports after the camps and the church had voted to give the camp a regular monthly gift as a part of their outreach giving. I had been using it to pay part of the camp's liability insurance. Although Hansen was out of the picture, I was still left with the responsibility of the camp expenses.

"JoAnn, I hate to tell you, but my church is suspending their monthly check to Victory Haven," Cherry was apologetic. "I told the pastor briefly about what happened with you and Pastor Hansen. He feels that given the situation, the church should not be supporting the camp anymore."

I felt inwardly devastated. I managed to be gracious.

"I understand. It's okay." I couldn't say anything else. I felt so fragile and weak, any emotional blow seemed to usher in more fear.

I hung up the phone and waves of shame rolled over me, flooding me to a level that felt like paralysis. *I was afraid this would happen when people find out.* I felt rejected and hurt, yet I understood their position. My fears were confirmed. *Others see me as a fraud. How will I ever convince anyone that I thought I was obeying God?* Again, I spent hours lost in depression. *Will everyone withdraw from me when they find out the truth?* I felt hopeless about it.

During the previous month, the well-known southern evangelist, Jimmy Swaggart, had been caught seeing a prostitute. It had caused a huge public response, and the media had a feeding frenzy over the whole incident. The Christian community had also endured a serious blow during the PTL Ministry scandal the previous year. It had been the largest and most far-reaching breach of trust by a religious ministry in anyone's memory. Now, with Swaggart's hypocrisy exposed, it seemed that immoral Christians were center stage in the media again. I couldn't watch TV or see a newspaper without confronting the issues of those in ministry who had been "caught" in sexual scandals. *Will others think I was just one of them?* I could think of no defense for myself. If I reasoned that my circumstances were different and Hansen had pushed me into things, I felt condemned about trying to justify myself. No matter how I tried to reason, I still felt like a creep.

I made an appointment with a professional counselor to begin talking about my past. It was grueling to tell my story, and it left me emotionally hollow and exhausted. The male counselor was supportive, but in hindsight I don't think he'd encountered anyone in my category of severe abuse before. I also wanted to talk to him about Wayne, but he cut to the chase quickly.

"If you had a friend who had just come out of twelve years in an abusive relationship," the therapist said, "what would you tell her about jumping into a new relationship so soon?" He was justified in worrying that I wasn't managing the pace of my relationship with Wayne.

"I'd tell her that it was too soon to be thinking that you were in love with someone else," I admitted to him.

"Well, can you take your own advice?" the therapist was gentle, but direct.

"I know you're right. I should go slow with Wayne."

When I left the therapist's office I lapsed into fear. The goal-oriented approach of this particular male therapist was a mismatch for my inner confusion. He seemed to be leaping to goals that I couldn't even envision. He underestimated my emotional capacity, and told me that he wanted to transition me to another therapist whom he thought could help me more. After two sessions with him, I couldn't imagine starting over with another therapist. In my fragile state this frightened me.

I also felt guilty that my mother was paying for the sessions, and I saw this as even more proof of my failure. Instead of pursuing another therapist, I turned to Dorothy and Betsy, my two stable and mature friends, for informal counseling. They had credentials in pain, if not formal degrees, and an honesty about life and themselves.

My resolve to "go slow" with Wayne lasted only a few days. The joy I felt when I was with Wayne was compelling. It was the only place I felt hopeful about the future. My relationship with him felt like the one area of my life where I *didn't* have self-doubt. Within weeks I wanted to marry him. I knew all the cautions, but they were not enough to override the desire. We both felt the past deprivation, the desire to be married, and the longing for someone to love.

We had spent nine weeks sharing our deepest agonies and our worst failures. I knew we shared a mutual commitment to live honestly before God. *Yes! I want to make a decision for myself. I want to make a choice. I want to marry Wayne.*

It seemed Wayne was in my life to give me a new start...a future. Wayne's love seemed to be slowly helping to restore my self-esteem. Our relationship had a nurturing quality. Together we were starting our lives over, and we felt compatible. Although I felt that God was giving Wayne to me, I found it hard to say that to anyone. I found it nearly impossible to say, "I think God is leading me to marry Wayne," because who would believe me or trust me that *I* knew what God was doing? I believed I had no credibility to voice that, because I had often told people in the past that "God was leading me to work for Hansen." The legacy of my screwed-up past remained.

During the two months since I had "gotten honest," as I called it, I had struggled to make sense of my past. I found it hard to read the Bible, because a lot of my Bible knowledge came from Hansen's sermons. I felt everything I believed had to be reviewed in the light of my new honesty. I listened carefully to every sermon at Wayne's church, trying to see if I had distorted the Scriptures in some way. I remembered the times when Hansen had twisted the Bible for his own ends, and I was finally beginning to feel a little anger toward him.

"There is an Old Testament Scripture that says, 'If you make a vow and break it, you will be cursed by the Lord,'" I related another incident to Wayne. Hansen had mentioned that verse to emphasize the vows I had made to him and why I should keep them. Now I was beginning to see Hansen's manipulation more clearly.

Even so, my spiritual life didn't seem to make sense. I had been the kid in high school who committed my life to God and wanted to be godly. Now I seemed to have turned out worse, or more messed-up than others who didn't really seek to walk with God. I had been the teen who didn't want to lie to my parents. Now I was sure that I'd turned out to be the queen of lies.

My thoughts kept returning to the beginning of the relationship with Hansen, trying to remember the tactics and pressure he had used. He had convinced me for so long that the relationship had begun mutually. I remembered how he had pushed me to use "we" language: "*we* love each other" and "*we* know that *we* have to keep it a secret." It wasn't always easy to figure out just how and when the small deceptions had grown into big ones.

As the weeks went by I discussed a lot of these questions with Dorothy and Betsy. Although they weren't professional therapists, they encouraged me with thoughtful listening and emotional support. Both of them had weathered difficult first marriages and valued honesty in addressing life. They weren't afraid of emotional pain and their wisdom helped steady me during the difficult days. They seemed to be able to stand my confusion and tears.

I remembered my initial feeling that it was wrong for Hansen to say he was in love with me. *How had I let him convince me that God was for it?* If I pondered it too much I only felt more depressed. I still didn't understand how I had lost my "eye for truth." I began to refer to myself as "the blind one." Hansen had messed with my mind. Somehow I had ended up thinking that I was suffering according to the will of God, and that God wanted me to be with Hansen. Now I knew that I was only being manipulated in an evil scheme.

I understood that when women were physically raped, they felt shamed and invaded. When I thought about my past with Hansen, I also felt shamed from all the mental invasion. It was like he had taken power over my mind. I had always seen myself as being smart. *This doesn't happen to smart people. I must be stupid.*

My parents were shocked when I told them I was going to marry Wayne. They were both alarmed that I was making a decision too fast. They liked Wayne, but knew he had a past history of abusing drugs and prison convictions. They urged me to wait at least a year before getting married.

Wayne was assertive in pressing his position when we were alone. "We know we're going to be all right," he said, "why should we wait?"

Not wanting to disappoint him, and being emotionally needy, I agreed.

We set the wedding date for July 30th. By then we would have been dating five months. My parents struggled with my decision, but decided to offer their support. They didn't want to put me in the position of "proving" to them that I should marry Wayne, and they reluctantly gave their blessing on the marriage.

A month before the wedding, Wayne and I attended a marriage conference. Listening to wisdom on all the different aspects of marriage, we felt confident that we had a sound basis for our relationship. We knew what it would take to build a successful marriage. We believed in the same principles, and we would be intentional about developing our relationship. We felt hopeful about our future.

Things looked good for us. Wayne planned to go back to college to finish his degree, but first he had been accepted into a six-month jewelry program at a vocational school. He wanted to enhance the skills gained during the previous three years in prison as an apprentice to a goldsmith. After completing the course, we planned to live in my log home at Victory Haven and re-open the camp as a retreat center. My mother had offered me a job in her tax accounting business as her receptionist. Everything seemed to be coming together.

My engagement ring had a special significance. Wayne had designed it and cast it himself. When I looked at it I felt joy.

> The supporting church had mistakenly put my situation into the simplistic category of adultery, rather than the category of spiritual, emotional, and sexual abuse by a pathological narcissist. An appropriate response would have been to make a personal contact to ask how to help and to express compassion for my victimization. Cutting off fellowship or support to the victim heightens the victim's sense of shame and penalizes the victim rather than the offender.
>
> For more understanding of how to resolve spiritual confusion, see Essay #7: The Preservation of Personal Dignity.

My 23rd Psalm

The Lord causes me to see truth,
I shall not fall back into blindness.

He puts me in new situations
And causes me to learn and grow.

I trust that I shall always be led
And never forsaken or rejected.

I may suffer regrets or setbacks
And temptations to fear and shrink back,

But the Lord gives me His security
Filling the places where I'm not sure of myself.

Surely my life will please Him
since I'm willing to walk toward the pain.

JoAnn Nishimoto

CHAPTER 16

Vows Made Freely

The previous month had been a flurry of wedding parties and showers. Support had been poured out by so many friends and family, and Wayne and I felt very loved. Wayne had never been to a wedding before, although he was 35 years old. Sometimes he felt self-conscious about all the attention we were getting. Not me! I savored each display of love. It helped in small ways to heal my woundedness.

At this same time Sam was getting married to his fiancée, Mary, whom he met in Oklahoma while he was in the Air Force. Our weddings were going to take place only two weeks apart, mine in Louisiana and Sam's wedding in Oklahoma. Mom and Dad's church planned a delightful party for both engaged couples. During the party we played the "Newlywed Game." Mom and Dad, Sam and Mary, and Wayne and I were all vying against each other for points. It was a hilarious time.

As I looked around the room I saw many faces I loved. *Although this is the church where Hansen used to be, they are totally unaware of all the evil he did to me. They are such good people. I don't want my story to "get out." I'm afraid they wouldn't understand me.*

July 30, 1988, dawned hot and muggy in the Louisiana summer heat, but I was riding on a cloud of joy. We'd be getting married in a church in Minden. As Wayne and I took our vows before 150 people, I had to restrain myself from laughing out loud. Joy and love seemed to be bubbling up from my soul! In contrast to the manipulated "false" vows with Hansen, my vows with Wayne were intentional, freely made, and witnessed by family and friends. No one there could have possibly imagined what this meant to me.

After spending our wedding night at our log house, we set out for a three-day honeymoon in Hot Springs, Arkansas. As we drove, our conversation turned to the self-doubt I'd struggled with since getting out of the abuse. I'd been so distracted the last few weeks with the wedding preparations and fun that I'd stuffed down any negative feelings that had tried to surface.

By the time we arrived in Hot Springs, my emotions were feeling raw. I realized I would have to immediately share with Wayne more of the painful events with Hansen that had been coming to the surface and needed to be dealt with. I had found that only by talking about these events was I able to get past the pain and shame about them. If I didn't unload the stories and the pain, I'd be battling the shame for days until I did talk. The only way to decrease the anxiety was to talk about it.

I felt angry. *I don't want to be discussing my past while I'm on my honeymoon! Ugh! Sometimes I feel stalked by it. Can't I just forget it for a while? After all, Wayne and I are on the way to the hotel, and we've got things to do! When will I ever get to the end of talking about this mess?*

Reluctantly, I told Wayne that I needed to talk. Finding the local mall, we parked our car and began walking the perimeter of the parking lot as the sun was setting. I began unloading more stories about Hansen. I seemed to have an unending stream of them that I hadn't yet told anyone. Given the fact that I lived at least two painful incidents with Hansen each week (where he'd emotionally manipulated or hurt me), or 100 incidents a year, that meant I had 1,200 incidents to process. Now an incident could be faced with the freedom to feel my real feelings, discuss it, hold my own view, and work out any pain or low self-worth it fueled. I was starting to see more clearly how Hansen had used his age and pastoral office to intimidate me.

Within minutes of talking with Wayne, the tears were streaming down my face. Hand in hand, we kept walking. The hot July breeze was humid, but Wayne didn't complain. Two hours passed. Wayne listened thoughtfully while I tried to sort out my feelings. I unloaded everything that I'd been stuffing during the past month while I'd been distracted with wedding plans. As usual, when I cried hard, I got a painful headache.

"Oh, great. Now I've even ruined our honeymoon. I'm sorry that I had to bring up this trash," I apologized. "I feel guilty for even having to talk about this." I didn't want my past pain with Hansen contaminating my new life with Wayne.

"There you go again, feeling automatically guilty," Wayne pointed out.

He was right. Feeling guilty for nearly everything had been reinforced with Hansen over twelve years. Now I was identifying the old, learned patterns of behavior and trying to break them. In small ways I was making gains in my ability to critique myself. I could usually tell when I was acting like the "old me," but at times the shameful feelings won out.

"Right now, all I can say is that I've only been married 24 hours, and I already feel like a bad wife. I didn't want to tell you this, and part of me knows it's not true, but I was afraid that you'd wake up this morning and tell me that you had made a mistake and didn't want to be married to me." I mustered courage to tell him what I really feared.

"What?" Wayne was incredulous. He made a startled face and shook his head in disbelief at my comment. Sometimes the depth of my low self-esteem stumped him.

"I'm fighting it as best as I know how, but over and over my shame drags me down," I tried to explain myself. "I want to trust that you'll love me, but I'm afraid I'm unlovable."

Wayne stopped in his tracks. He pulled me around so I'd have to look him in the face. He could see how my self-deprecating attitude was going to hinder our relationship.

"Well, I *do* love you." His voice was firm. "When I woke up today I thought I was the luckiest man in the world to be married to you. And I'm going to keep on telling you this until I get it through your *thick head*!"

I managed a little laugh at his exasperation with me.

"Can we just go on to the hotel? My head is killing me, and I want to take some Tylenol," I said.

After nearly three hours of talking and processing my feelings, I felt lighter emotionally and a little less guilty. My anxiety level had gone back down again. Talking about my past initially brought on more emotional pain, but the pain resolved if I would push through and talk it out. However, I usually felt like a wrung-out rag after a three-hour session like this one.

"Let's just go to the hotel and go to sleep," Wayne said. "Tomorrow we'll start our honeymoon again." I could tell he was as exhausted as I was. No doubt he was trying to process it himself. He gave my hand a little squeeze.

That night Wayne slept more than I did. I lay beside him and threw one leg over his. I felt some security this way. In the dark room it seemed like there was still a deep emotional crevice waiting to swallow me up. With one leg draped over his, it seemed I could keep from falling into this imaginary black hole.

I prayed off and on during periods of wakefulness in the night. *Lord, heal my brokenness. Help me not to hate myself.*

I felt defective that my pain had intruded on our honeymoon. I wanted to be emotionally strong and feel good about myself. Instead I had ruined the evening. I remembered what Wayne had said about being the luckiest man in the world. It helped me to hear him say that. I believed it *now*, but I had begun to see that when my pain overwhelmed me, I could lose the feeling of being loved in an instant. I could regress to fear at the drop of a hat.

I should be over this by now. I didn't know that getting well was going to be this hard. Will I ever get to the bottom of the damage Hansen has done?

The five factors in emotional healing are: radical honesty, relationships that affirm you, right thinking (denying the lies and embracing the truth), the Holy Spirit's healing, and time.

People throughout history have been subjected to "brain-washing," and there are many documented accounts of this following the Communist takeover of China in 1948. The following is Lifton's account of Vechten, a Catholic priest, reflecting on the shame and irrational guilt the priest felt after having "given in" to the Communists' "re-education" and thought reform indoctrinations:

> ....his sense of shame and guilt could not be stilled. He kept thinking that if he had been physically tortured, as some other priests had, his concessions might have been justified.
>
> "But I had not been tortured. Why have I come to such deeds?"
>
> During this early period, it was almost impossible for him to talk about his prison experiences. He did, on one occasion, tell a colleague a few of the things he confessed; but when the latter gave evidence of surprise, Vechten felt deeply upset. He could find no relief from his suffering, despite considerate, and often psychologically sensitive attitudes on the part of his fellow-priests.

Robert J. Lifton
The Psychology of Totalism: A Study of Brainwashing in China
University of North Carolina Press, 1989

CHAPTER 17
Positive Growth for Wayne

During the first months of our marriage I realized that Wayne was growing, too. He was savoring every bit of his first year of freedom. He applied himself to the six-month jewelry course at the vocational school. I could see that he was feeling creative and confident about the gold casting work that he was doing, and friends were commissioning him to do projects. He was taking his place as a talented jewelry craftsman.

Our church in Shreveport had been a real source of encouragement to Wayne. Because Jim, Betsy, and others from the church held a weekly service for the inmates, Wayne already knew about 20 people before he got out of prison. Once released, he had a ready-made church family that welcomed him. Wayne felt completely accepted there. The congregation of 200 knew about his prison experience and accepted him unconditionally. I felt accepted too, but I was thankful they didn't know about my past. I liked attending where I could be the "new me." I still couldn't imagine how I'd cope with these people knowing my story.

Occasionally I challenged Wayne in his growth, too. We were planning to have friends over for supper one weekend, and Wayne reminded me that I should call and invite them.

"Why do you always ask me to make the phone calls?" I said.

"Because you're a better talker than me," he said. "I freeze up when I'm on the phone. During all those years in prison, I never talked on the phone to anyone, and I guess I just feel awkward about it."

"Then shouldn't you practice it, instead of avoiding it?" I ventured a challenge.

Wayne put down his jewelry project and looked at me. He realized that I was switching roles and asking *him* to grow a little. "I don't know what to say when I'm on the phone."

"Well, you tell them that we'd like to invite them over for supper next Saturday, and you're wondering if that would be a good date for them."

"What if they can't come?"

"Then you ask them to suggest another date when they are free, or let them know that we'll ask them again next month." I had always been confident about my social skills.

"You're a real slave driver." His voice was half-playful and half-irritated.

"You wouldn't want to be a hypocrite by pushing me to give up *my* fears when you aren't willing to work on *yours*, would you?" I realized I had the teacher's role for once, and I was enjoying playing the upper hand.

Wayne went to the phone and made the call. As he hung up, I shot him a mischievous look. Baiting him to chase me, I ran out of the house laughing. Our two German Shepherds, Ellie Mae and Gabriel, picked up the cue that fun was at hand. They jumped up off the porch and began prancing around me, panting and wagging their tails.

"I'll get you for making me do that!" He pretended to be mad, chasing me and the dogs.

These moments of playful silliness felt wonderful. Although there was still a lot of heaviness about my past, there were now stretches of time when I could feel playful and joyful too. My twenties had been lost to the oppression of Hansen, and it felt wonderful to be carefree in my early thirties. We were both growing into our new lives.

Wayne had accepted several speaking engagements in local high schools where he and other ex-felons shared about the damage of drug abuse. He was honest and open about the eighteen years that he had used drugs. Except for the last three years since he'd made a decision to follow Christ, he had used drugs nearly continuously, from ages 14 to 32, even while in prison. During two particularly terrible years when living in Houston, he had even abused heroin extensively.

"I was little more than an animal during that time," he told the students. "I never had any hope of being free from drugs until I began hearing that God could forgive me and help me lay down the drugs." Wayne always included his spiritual growth as a part of his presentation.

Watching him speak, I thought about how much I loved him. It took a lot of courage to be honest about a painful past, something I still struggled with daily.

That night, we were walking down our country road. Our nighttime walks had become a ritual, and the quietness and solitude were beautiful. It wasn't unusual to see a shooting star at least once a week during summer. It was so quiet that we could hear an occasional car approaching from a mile away. Usually we walked down the middle of the highway. The dogs romped along, enjoying the woodsy smells along the tree line and returning often to us for pats and affection.

"You know, when you were sharing today at the high school, everyone could see how drug use leads to predictable patterns," I said aloud as I formed my ideas.

"You are a good example," I continued. "You got hooked on drugs. Then you lied about it. Then you started stealing to keep up your habit. Then you ran so you wouldn't get caught. Eventually you did get caught and went to prison. It doesn't take a rocket scientist to understand that."

"Okay, but what's your point?" Wayne was wondering where I was going with this.

"Well, it's so much easier to explain *your* life than the complexity of *my* situation. I'm still trying to understand for myself how Hansen messed up my mind. I know I can't explain it yet to anyone else. No one wants to discuss sexual misconduct by pastors, but everybody knows how to talk about drug abuse."

I kept on, sounding like an attorney laying out a case. "People don't always realize the power men can wield over women; many men wouldn't believe my story. Then there's the weird part about how I betrayed myself and became 'addicted' to my own abuser, without an outside substance like narcotics that I can point to as the culprit. It's all so hard to explain."

The sky was clear tonight. We walked on in silence, studying the stars.

"It *is* really hard to understand your story sometimes, I have to admit."

Wayne let a bit of his own struggle out.

"You're lucky," I stated with a tone of self-pity. "You were only a drug addict."

> **Emotional healing is a "two steps forward, one step backward" process. Positive feelings eventually come, although setbacks are common.**
>
> **For more understanding of the fear of facing negative judgments by others, see Essay #10: The Fear of Others.**

In coming to grips with what has happened to an ex-cultist, it is quite helpful to employ the victim or trauma model.*

According to this model, victimization and the resulting distress are due to the shattering of three basic assumptions the victim held about the world and himself. These assumptions are:

1) the belief in personal invulnerability (*these things can't happen to me; I would never fall for something like that*)
2) the perception of the world as meaningful (*things operate logically for a purpose*)
3) and the perception of oneself as positive (*I have control of my own life and know what is best for me*)

The victim has been traumatized, deceived, conned, used, and often emotionally and mentally abused while serving the group and/or leader of the group.

Paul Martin, PhD
Cult-Proofing Your Kids
Zondervan Publishing, 1993
(Words in italics added by JoAnn)

*Because I was a victim of cult-like mind control, I have found healing in literature which deals with ex-cult members and their emotional issues. Although I wasn't an actual member of a cult, many of the same dynamics were in effect.

CHAPTER 18
I Respect You

I'd always trusted Roberta for the eight years that I had known her. During my relationship with Hansen I had attended her home Bible studies. It was a secret reprieve, a weekly place I went to be with other women. There was something so appealing about her honesty, her vulnerability to others, and her non-judgmental attitude. I knew she loved me. She and her husband, Graydon, were leading a couples' study on the topic of prayer. I told Wayne that I wanted us to attend their twelve-week session.

"Isn't that study for younger Christians? I think you already know lots of scriptures on prayer, don't you?" Wayne couldn't see why I wanted to go back to a basic prayer course.

"I still can hardly pray," I said. "Ever since I got out of the abuse, I've been trying to find my spiritual footing. I'm still afraid to read the Bible because everything reminds me of Hansen and how he used to distort certain Scriptures. I still feel confused. I just want to rethink everything from the ground up. I think it will help me."

Hansen hadn't shattered my basic belief in God, because I knew Him even before the abuse started. I wasn't tempted to make a wholesale rejection of faith because of one impostor; I'd known too many authentic people. However, I longed to be confident again spiritually.

Yet I was only beginning to figure out my new spiritual life. Ever since my "crash," my sense of following God was very threatened. I felt I was still in a spiritual crisis. I couldn't feel God's love. I could barely pray. I was timidly beginning to ask the hard questions within me: *How could God have let this happen? Why didn't He rescue me?*

Wayne didn't "get it," but he reluctantly agreed to attend the study.

At the first meeting, I felt some immediate encouragement. We'd be doing homework that would help me conquer my fear of getting back in the Bible. It felt comforting to be with Roberta. I hadn't yet told her my entire story, but she knew that something huge had happened.

The format of the study group was that one person would share their testimony each week. It was a way of sharing our own journeys and being real with each other. In previous years I would have been one of the first people to volunteer. Now, however, it terrified me. *What will I say? Will everyone pull back from me? How will they take it?* I remembered the reaction from Cherry's church; I had a sick feeling in my stomach.

As the weeks went by, I started to dread the time for my testimony. Each week Graydon would ask for a volunteer for the next session. I tried to avoid making eye contact with him. Wayne took his turn. Finally, it was the last week of the course, and there was no one left but me.

"I don't know how to tell you my story," I began tentatively. I began to cry. A wave of shame came over me. Other than Wayne, everyone's story in the group had been relatively tame.

"Well, I've been living a...uhhh...double life. It's real mixed up. I've been blind." I had to pause to get my composure. There was a noticeable pain in my throat.

I couldn't seem to even make a brief synopsis of my story. Wayne was sitting beside me. He reached over in his familiar way and rubbed the back of my neck. It was a way he tried to comfort me when I found myself in places of emotional agony. After pausing a while I spoke a few more words.

"Well, I finally got truthful. And I'm trying to start my life over." I uttered the last sentence with some conviction and my voice signaled that I was done talking. That was it. That was my testimony. In six complete sentences.

Everyone sat quietly, as if trying to figure out the ambiguous nature of my statements. Suddenly Roberta stood up, walked over to my chair, and knelt in front of me, putting her hands on my knees.

"JoAnn, I want you to know that I deeply respect you." Her voice was earnest.

Roberta's love brought my tears quickly to the surface. She hugged me.

I couldn't speak. *Respect me? Something in me yearns for that, but something in me says that I am not worthy of respect.*

Roberta's affirmation that she respected me was a building block. One more step in trying to rebuild my life. An important moment in healing.

As 1989 started, Wayne finished jewelry school and we both began new jobs. Wayne went to work as a technician in a hospital chemical dependency treatment unit. This was a great way for him to build on his four years of sobriety. He would continue his jewelry work part-time at home. I began working for my mother as a receptionist in her income tax accounting practice. It was a step forward for both of us, as we'd both been vocationally under-developed. Our jobs were positive growth areas for us and brought a lot of satisfaction. Wayne also decided to work further on his college degree, and began a video correspondence course at home.

There was no doubt that I was making strides in my emotional recovery with each month that passed, but it was "two steps forward, one step backward." The pattern of being too hard on myself for even the slightest error still remained. Any mistake, no matter how small, seemed to knock down my shaky self-confidence.

One night at supper, Wayne told me that the food I'd served him was cold. I felt an instant, pervading sense of failure. I was keenly oversensitive to any cue that I had made even a small mistake.

"I'm sorry, honey. I'll fix it." My voice had that "stupid me" tone of self-disgust. I jumped up to put his food in the microwave.

"Hey, don't take it so seriously," he said. "Your face looks like I told you something terrible. All I said is that my food was cold." His comment had come from a place of male objectivity and was not meant as criticism.

My face flushed and I teared up immediately. The shame feelings flooded over me, igniting fear, defensiveness and emotional pain.

"It's just that I'm always doing something stupid." My voice went shaky immediately, and that familiar sense of feeling stupid and defective took on irrational proportions. "I'm just stupid, that's all."

"When are you going to stop saying that *ungodly* stuff to yourself?" Wayne was irritated now.

I didn't know what Wayne was talking about. I felt offended by his use of the word "ungodly." In my opinion, "ungodly" applied to sins like lying and stealing. *What does that have to do with me calling myself "stupid?"*

During the next several days I replayed the scene at the dinner table. I thought about the word "ungodly." Did it refer to anything that was "*un*-God?" Anything that God wouldn't do or think? I began to see a little of what the problem was. I was saying something to myself that God wouldn't say to me. I knew God had compassion and love for me. God didn't see me as stupid, and He wouldn't be calling me "stupid." I *was* doing something God wouldn't do… so I *was* being *un*-godly.

This revelation shook me up. *Maybe I am hindering my own emotional stability by reciting this negative message in my head.* For nearly two years I had reflected on my embarrassment and shame over being trapped in the emotional bondage to Hansen. I felt I should have been able to resist it. *I should have been stronger.* I had been constantly repeating to myself, *"I'm the stupidest Christian that ever lived."* Now I was seeing another side to this. *Maybe I should play a role in stopping these negative self-statements. Chiding and berating myself isn't going to lead to my healing.*

The aftermath of the sexual, emotional, mental, and spiritual abuse by Hansen had been a deep presence of inner shame. I had become preoccupied and painfully aware of myself and over-sensitive to others' perceptions of me. My own voice had become a mocking echo in my head, always telling me how uniquely stupid I was. My shame had taken on a chronic life of its own, and I had grown used to my habit of self-attack. I was passive and accepted it as inevitable.

Previously, I had no awareness that I could or should change this. Through Hansen's abuse I had internalized a deep loss of dignity. Now, even in his absence, I continued to humiliate myself. It helped that others, like my friend, Roberta, gave me permission to respect myself. But even that didn't reach to the foundation of the shame. The "permission" ultimately had to come from myself. *I give myself permission to respect myself.* In that core internal world where victories are born and nurtured, I had to give myself permission to stop the self-attacks.

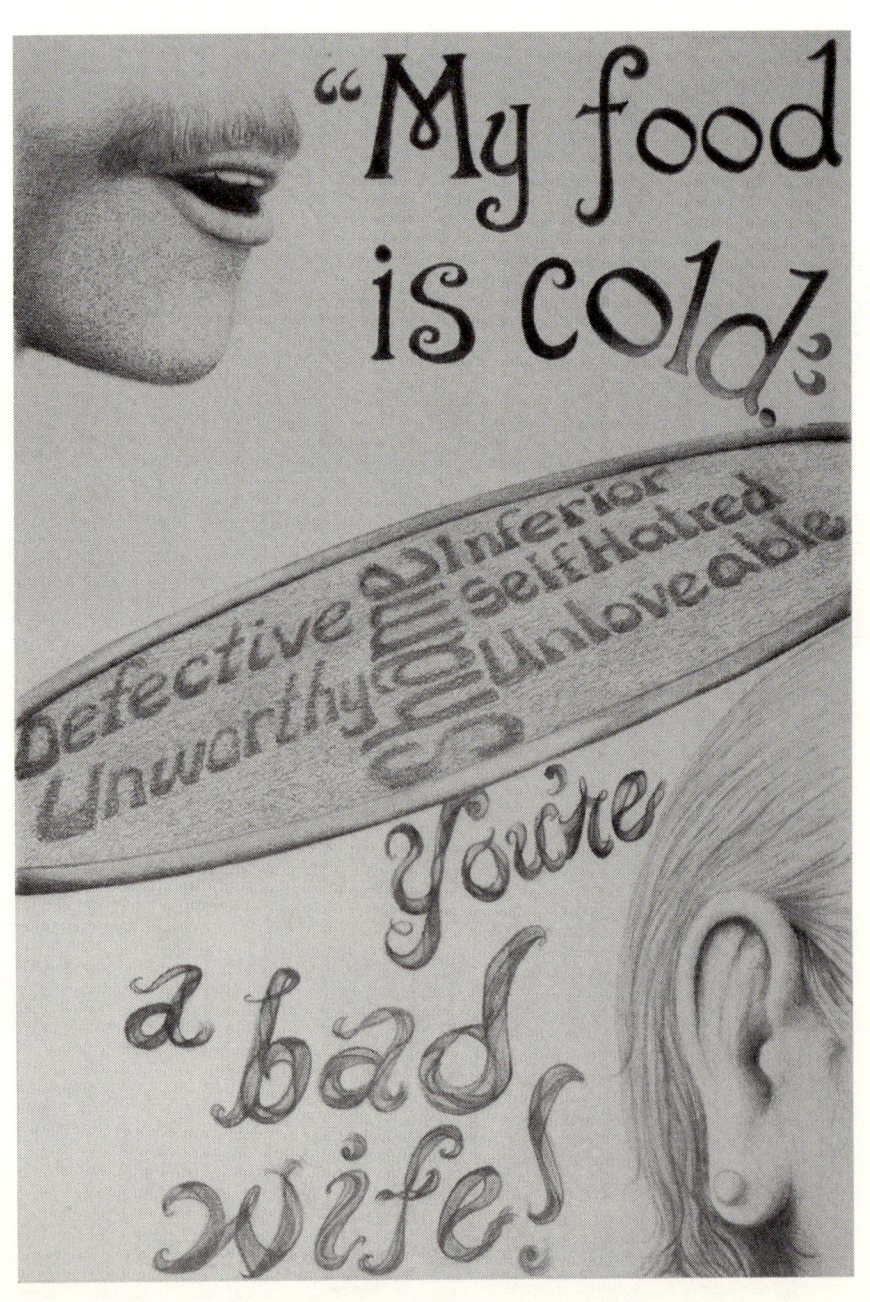

Wayne's comment, passing through my
low-self-worth filter, felt like an accusation.

The battle played out a few days later at the office. Suddenly realizing I had made some trivial mistake, I defaulted to the "I'm so stupid" line in my head. For the first time I realized that I would have to confront myself about it. Wayne was right: I *was* being ungodly.

I closed my eyes at the typewriter. A part of me still wanted to insist "I'm stupid." I felt like I was trying to change the direction of a spinning merry-go-round that had tremendous momentum. I remembered the large metal merry-go-round at our public park. It was as though I had grabbed the word "stupid," but it had so much power that it was still spinning and dragging me, much like trying to stop the inertia of the merry-go-round. I gripped the typewriter. The power of my mental struggle felt physical. It was going to take all my will power to say this.

I whispered the words under my breath. *I'm not going to say that anymore. I'm NOT stupid. God doesn't say that about me. God loves me. He understands all about how I got trapped.*

Saying these positive words felt like the moment when you try to grab the merry-go-round and change its direction, dragging it to a stop and reversing it. It's heavy and hard to do. Push! Push!

I'm NOT stupid. I did the best I could. It took an enormous amount of determination to say it. I felt a fatigue from it, like the energy was going out of me as I fought against the inertia of self-rejection. I was pushing my thoughts in the opposite direction. *Oh, this is so hard to do! Lord, help me!*

During the next few weeks I forced myself to stop the way I had been berating myself. I wasn't sure how much I *believed* that I wasn't stupid, but a first step was to start affirming that I had done the best I could. Gradually the positive self-statements seemed more real and started to take hold in my mind.

The next time Wayne and I talked about my abuse, we reflected on how intensely Hansen had worked on me and what a master he was at exploiting me.

"I think I did the best I could...with the maturity I had at the time." I was almost surprised to hear it come out of my mouth. It was a step forward. I hadn't automatically reverted to the "I'm stupid" line. The truth was beginning to take a hold.

"Congratulations," Wayne said. "You're starting to say it like it was."

I thought of Roberta's loving affirmation, "I respect you." Maybe I was beginning to plant the seeds of respecting myself.

Every survivor must give up the notion that there were inner resources which she failed to draw upon to prevent the abuse: *I should have known better. I should have been stronger.* Those who previously saw themselves as brave or independent often struggle with this the most.

Recovery involves confronting one's irrational self-statements with the truth: *I am highly prized by God, deeply loved by Him, and understood for my humanity. I did the best I could with the maturity I had at the time.*

For more understanding of the critical process of shame recovery, see Essay #1: The Arch Enemies: Shame and Grace, Essay #2: The Compulsion to Hate My Own Life, and Essay #6: Chase the Robbers.

Shame is learned interpersonally.
We take in information about ourselves based on
how we perceive others regard us. Learning to
anticipate other's attacks on our worthiness may not be a happy
way to live, but it usually functions to keep us safe at the time.
Unlearning the habit of self-attack must initiate
within the victim, but can only grow and develop in
the healing space of safe relationships.

Elizabeth A. Horst
Recovering the Lost Self:
Shame Healing for Victims of Clergy Sexual Abuse
Liturgical Press, 1998

CHAPTER 19
The Marriage Lab

As we approached our first anniversary, I was beginning to feel the momentum of making progress in my healing. Occasionally I noticed that I was really relaxed. When I reflected on it, I couldn't remember feeling this way in a long time. *Wasn't this the way I used to be before Hansen?*

I remembered that as a teenager I was easy-going and spontaneous most of the time. It seemed that this was coming back. With Hansen I had learned to over-monitor every cue to see where I stood with him. I always watched his facial expressions for clues as to whether he was angry or happy with me because my emotional safety was at stake. I could never relax because he often emotionally ambushed me, surprising me with accusations or anger. I had learned to maintain a kind of emotional hypervigilance. I had done this for so long that I had learned to experience this as normal. Being fearful of his anger had been the rule. Monitoring him for potential rage had become a survival skill.

Now I had new tasks. I was stripping off the unhealthy ways I had adapted to a sick relationship with Hansen and learning more authentic ways of relating in a healthy relationship with Wayne. I didn't want to perpetuate the poor emotional patterns from my past. Those patterns hindered my intimacy with Wayne. This wasn't as easy as it sounds. First, I had to become aware of what I was doing.

I could tell that I was "working" too hard to be sure that Wayne was happy with me. This was a perspective grounded in fear and insecurity. I knew that it was healthier to relate to him from an assumption of confidence in his love. I didn't have to work for his acceptance. Instead I could rest in it. I had grown up with the unconditional love of my parents, and during childhood this had been my anchor. But Hansen's abuse had damaged me in this area. I had every reason to believe that Wayne loved me, but a sense of insecurity was always interrupting my experience of this. My marriage with Wayne seemed to have become a lab where I worked out these issues.

One day Wayne was changing the oil in my car, but it wasn't going well. He'd been in and out of the house searching for various tools, muttering something about the oil filter being stuck. It seemed the last time we'd had it changed at a station they had put it on too tight. I could tell he was getting more and more angry.

Meanwhile, I had made several trips to the car, loading our household trash. Every week we had to make a run to the dumpster because there was no garbage service in our rural area. I quietly put each bag in the rear, nearly tiptoeing because I knew he was under the car struggling with the oil filter.

Wayne appeared in the door with oil on his hands. The filter had split apart while he was trying to loosen it. I could see he was boiling.

"Bring me some more rags." Wayne's voice was sharp.

I scurried to bring the rags. I offered to help.

"Stay in the house." Wayne spoke in a flat command.

My fear level was building equally with his anger level. I watched meekly from the window.

Wayne came out from under the car, and just as I was hoping things were better, he suddenly exploded with anger. Our 90-pound male dog, Gabriel, had climbed into the car on top of the garbage sacks, hoping for a recreational ride to the dumpster with us. Wayne saw that he had split several of the plastic garbage bags, and wet kitchen trash and other garbage had spilled in the car.

"Gabriel! Get out of the car right now!" Wayne was livid. He rarely swore, so I knew he was furious.

Hearing Wayne's tone of voice, I wanted to hide. I knew he wasn't mad at me, but being around someone who was angry still filled me with anxiety. As Wayne stormed back in the house, I quickly pretended I had to go to the bathroom and went to hide.

During the next several days I realized that I had lost my sense of security and had returned to being afraid. The sound of Wayne's anger had triggered me back to that hyper-vigilant, watch-everything-for-danger state. I'd been over-accommodating Wayne in little things. The insecurity was back.

"You know, when you're angry your forehead tenses up and your eyebrows sort of move together," I tentatively broached the topic at supper. I tried to stir the soup nonchalantly in my bowl.

"What? What makes you bring that up?" Wayne's mind was a hundred miles away.

"Well, it makes me scared when your eyebrows go together." There, I finally said it.

"I'm sorry, but could you clue me in on what we're talking about?" Wayne wasn't finding the topic intuitive.

"I'm trying to figure out what I should do when you're angry and your eyebrows go together."

"You don't need to *do* anything. Who said I was angry with *you*?"

"Well, I'm trying to understand how I could help you be less angry....you know, how I could fix it."

"Maybe I *don't want* you to *fix* it. Maybe you should just let me be angry," Wayne had that factual tone. He went back to eating the soup.

I didn't like Wayne's suggestion. If I didn't *do* something, I couldn't have any control over his anger. If I couldn't control his anger, I couldn't manage the sense of insecurity and fear I felt. I *wanted* to fix it. My control and fear seemed like cousins who went everywhere together.

I was good at trying to fix people who were angry. I had been born with a peace-making temperament and had never liked anger anyway. When someone was upset, I usually tried to control their anger by being overly nice. My inability to separate myself from Hansen's rage had led to my absorbing it and suffering incredibly. It seemed I had developed an emotional "catcher's mitt" with which I felt I had to catch every angry pitch thrown within earshot. I didn't have the foggiest idea how to dodge misdirected or unfair anger.

I decided to admit the insecurity I'd been carrying for several days.

"When you were so mad at the car and at Gabriel the other day, I got really scared. I hid in the bathroom for a while."

Wayne put down his spoon and sighed. His face had a faint expression of "here we go again." I felt worse knowing that my emotional struggles wearied him.

"I *have* noticed that when you think I'm mad, you start over-apologizing and acting fearful," he said, "like you want to appease me."

I was surprised that Wayne could put it so succinctly. These were the same behaviors I had used for years with Hansen. They were second nature to me. An angry person was very intimidating. Also, I had never known how to express my own anger. If I was angry I usually just swallowed it.

"I know that I over-apologize a lot," I conceded.

"Yeah, and when you do that, I think it's really unattractive." Wayne emphasized "unattractive" and was not apologetic for his honesty.

I felt instantly threatened. I wasn't secure enough for Wayne to be telling me that something about me was unattractive. Instantaneously, the old emotional ache flared inside me. At times like this I felt that I'd never get past these kind of struggles.

"So what am I supposed to do?" I felt bewildered. I was trying not to cry or look afraid about this topic. I didn't want to be unattractive!

"Just be honest with me, and tell me if you're mad at me. I'm not going to bite your head off or anything. I hate it when I see you acting like you're afraid."

"I know you love me," I said, "but I have a hard time resting in your love."

In the weeks that followed I made a conscious effort not to over-apologize. Wayne was asking me to trust his love by showing more of my real feelings toward him. This felt like a big risk. I couldn't seem to stop fearing. I remembered how, in my relationship with Hansen, I had learned to appease him and had always walked on eggshells to avoid making him angry. These old patterns were now interfering in my marriage.

One evening, I arrived home to find that Wayne had completely emptied the antique oak cabinet where I kept mementos and personal items. A hundred or more items were in stacks on the floor. He said that he'd been wanting me to clean it out and thought he'd empty it for me.

"You can sort through it all while you put it back in," he remarked, half-distracted by the football game.

I swallowed hard. I was furious. I felt tightness in my throat. *Why hadn't he just asked me to clean out the cabinet if it was bothering him?* I had kept those things in there for several years. I saw it as my personal space. To top it all off, our friends,

Tom and Dorothy, were coming to eat supper with us shortly, and I had to get dinner ready. The piles were right near the dining table. It was bad timing.

I didn't say anything, but disappeared into the bedroom to change clothes. Then I remembered the healthier behaviors I was trying to learn.

"There's something I need to say." I came out, mustered some courage, and faced Wayne. My voice was tentative.

"I'm angry with you." It was the first time I had uttered those words, probably in my whole life.

"Then why are you saying it with a smile?" Wayne was firm, crossing his arms. He stepped toward me to raise the emotional stakes.

"Because I don't know how to *look* mad," I blurted. His comment exasperated me. I ventured my opinion with real emotion behind it. "You shouldn't have taken that stuff out of the cabinet without asking me. I would have cleaned it up if you had asked me to." I spoke firmly, rather than politely. I expressed my anger in the tone of my voice...something I wasn't used to doing.

"But it's been a mess for a long time." Now Wayne was getting angry and defensive. His eyebrows went together.

"Hey, I'm supposed to be the one showing my anger, not you!" I jabbed.

"You're watching my eyebrows again, aren't you?"

"No, I'm not!" I broke the intensity by walking away. He followed me into the bedroom.

"Yes, you are. I saw you looking at my eyebrows!"

"You're being unfair! I don't go in your stuff without asking. That was bad timing to take the stuff out when we had company coming." I was actually starting to *look* as well as *sound* mad.

Our fight was interrupted by the arrival of our friends. We cooled down and ended up having a nice evening. After they left, we continued our discussion.

"Congratulations, you managed to act mad at me." Wayne's voice was a bit teasing.

"I know, but I didn't *like* it." This was a serious issue with me and I didn't think it was funny. I felt pouty.

"Well, you were honest. And I think I respect that more than when you're over-nice about everything. I get tired of that."

I turned from washing the dishes and faced Wayne. We stood staring at each other. It was a moment when the truth was laid out plainly.

"I guess I did make some progress," I said. "When your eyebrows went together I didn't back off."

"See, I told you," Wayne playfully savored his little victory, "You *were* looking at my eyebrows!" He danced around the kitchen, twirling the dish towel. I grabbed another towel and we playfully tried to snap each other.

Sometimes I woke up at night and thought about these interchanges. I had risked showing that I was mad at Wayne and he didn't punish me for it like Hansen would have. Instead, he said he respected me for it. There it was again, that word "respect." I wanted Wayne's respect. It felt wonderful that he encouraged me to be honest and then offered me respect for standing up to him. I was respecting myself a little more for my honesty. I was learning to relax a little more in Wayne's love. My hypervigilance was calming down.

My emotional "black hole" was shrinking.

> **Negative patterns from previous relationships can contaminate present relationships and must be confronted. New insights must be gained, so new behavior patterns can take root.**

For most of us, the experience of healing
comes not in one dramatic incident,
but in many small experiences.

Elizabeth A. Horst
Recovering the Lost Self:
Shame Healing for Victims of Clergy Sexual Abuse
Liturgical Press, 1998

CHAPTER 20
Test of Growth

Our first anniversary came and went with quiet joy. The year had been a mixture of agony and hope. My marriage to Wayne had certainly given me a sense of optimism. He had been my partner in healing, my sounding board, and my own personal therapist. I had struggled against tremendous grief about my past, an exhausting battle against self-condemning thoughts, and nearly daily confrontations with fear. But there was progress. I could see it and feel it. I wasn't healed yet, by any means, but I was gaining ground. A year and a half of hard work in talking, processing, and grieving was yielding fruit.

During the fall of 1989, Wayne and I attended an alcohol counselor training seminar in Dallas as a part of Wayne's job. It was targeted for substance abuse counselors to strengthen their counseling skills and encourage their own growth. Like Wayne, many people in chemical dependency counseling jobs were recovering addicts and alcoholics themselves.

At the workshop I was stunned to see how much of the recovery training applied to me, even though I hadn't been chemically dependent. I had more in common with addicts and the recovery process than I'd thought!

The most useful concept I learned was the idea of codependency. Codependency referred to the patterns of behavior used in trying to manage or control the sick person (often the substance abuser). I had fallen into many of these same behaviors with Hansen, who was the sick and power-abusing person in my life. I had allowed myself to be intimidated and defined by him. I had covered for him, enabled him, and been controlled by his anger. I had absorbed his feelings, feared him, and adapted to his pathology. I had much in common with other abused women. I had given up my dignity and believed I was helpless to change. I had become so beaten down that I came to see my circumstances as normal. It was comforting to hear that the recovery process I'd been going through was very predictable.

During the course of the three weekends we traveled to the Dallas training, I continued to vigorously process the material between trips. Wayne saw how deeply I was working on things.

"You ought to be a counselor yourself," Wayne offered.

I thought he must be kidding. My self-esteem wasn't at the level where I could believe something like that. His suggestion morphed into a perceived criticism.

"Don't kid me about something like that," I said. "It isn't funny."

"Who said I was kidding?" he said. "You could help a lot of people."

Although I didn't believe him then, a seed was planted. Later I enrolled in several psychology courses and began to think about pursuing a master's degree in counseling. However, at this point the primary incentive was to help heal myself.

During our second year of marriage, Wayne and I continued to work for Victory Haven. Once a month we hosted a church retreat, maintaining the facility and preparing the meals. With work, camp activities, church, and friends, life was busy and full.

Our marriage, too, had an overall positive quality. We frequently exchanged the affirmation "I'm so blessed to have you" with one another. If one of us was hurt or angry, we didn't run from it, but addressed it. We had fairly good communication patterns. We had both kept our end of the bargain. We had been *intentional* about cultivating our marriage. We hadn't left it to chance. It felt good.

The only negative curve we'd been thrown was that Wayne had begun having periodic migraine headaches. It was hard to watch him vomit and lie incapacitated in bed. After five or six headaches, he received a prescription of pain medication from a doctor. We were both grateful that he could have a little relief when the headaches struck. At the time we had no fear that Wayne couldn't handle a few pain pills. He was vibrant about his recovery and stalwart about not abusing drugs. His sense of freedom from his past felt so real to him, and I never worried about his taking medication for a legitimate medical need. After all, he wasn't trying to get high.

In March of 1990 Wayne was involved in a traffic accident when another car ran a stop sign and broadsided his car. He was checked out at the hospital and released with some bruises and a case of moderate whiplash. Within hours, a serious headache set in.

In the next few weeks he struggled with more headaches and I began to see that he was acting erratic. Several times he had been unusually sharp and impatient with me. He became demanding about my taking him to the doctor for more medication and defensive if I asked him how many pain pills he had left. One evening I discovered that he had taken four or five pain pills at once.

"I can't get pain relief from only one or two pills," he said defensively.

I wanted to give him the benefit of the doubt. I knew he had a high tolerance for narcotics due to the years he had abused them. *Maybe it did take more medication to give him relief.*

"I'm worried. You're not acting like yourself," I tried to reason with him.

"I'm okay. Don't worry. You know I'm not going to take them if I don't need them."

It sounded reasonable enough. Weeks went by and the headaches were still coming several times a week. One day I found a pill bottle in the car from a doctor I'd never heard of.

"Why did you go to another doctor without telling me?" I confronted him.

"Our doctor wouldn't renew my prescription," he said, "and I had to get another one. You don't know what it's like to have these headaches. You don't want me to suffer, do you?" He sounded annoyed.

His logic was convincing. I felt uneasy, but I didn't know what to say. Later that night he was suffering another headache and vomiting again.

We arrived at a hospital emergency room for treatment. After a shot of Demerol, a strong narcotic, Wayne was calm. I felt relieved to see him out of pain, but within a week we were back at the emergency room again.

One day, while following him home from town in my car, I could see his car swerving from side to side on the road ahead of me. I was terrified. When I confronted him at home about being on too many pills, he lashed out at me with an uncharacteristic meanness.

"Stop telling me what I should and shouldn't take," he barked. "I can handle my own medication."

I backed off. His defensiveness was intimidating, and I didn't know what to say.

That night I heard a crash. Wayne had fallen. He'd taken so many pills that he couldn't walk. My fears were confirmed. He was out of control with the pain pills. Now the look I'd seen in Wayne's eyes made sense. It wasn't just sleepiness or confusion. It had a name, and its name was "addiction."

Though I'd never been around someone who was abusing drugs, I realized that he was really getting strung out. Using so many pills caused vomiting and headaches, for which he took more pills! I could see that the cycle had become full blown in the six weeks since the car wreck.

I called Jim and Betsy. They had been close to Wayne for five years now. When they came to the house they agreed he wasn't himself. After talking privately with them I knew what had to be done, but I dreaded taking a bold stand against him.

"Wayne, you've got to go to treatment. You can't stop yourself." I focused on using an intentional tone of voice.

"I'm NOT going to any hospital. Those treatment programs don't help anybody. They never helped me before. Besides, I can stop by myself." Wayne really believed what he was saying. This was the symptom of denial I'd been hearing about at the chemical dependency training we attended.

Since he refused my personal request for treatment, I knew that I'd have to get some reinforcements to help me leverage Wayne to the hospital. I called our pastor and asked him if he could come and bring several men from the church. I was sure that, in the presence of several of our close friends, Wayne would cooperate. I didn't know how staunchly addicts would fight for their drugs.

When our pastor and friends arrived together in a van, Wayne stubbornly refused to go to treatment. When the pastor insisted, Wayne got ugly. Finally, they "manhandled" him into the van. It wasn't pretty.

I was deeply shaken. *What is happening? Wayne is acting like a wild man. This isn't the man I married.* I avoided looking him in the eye as he waited in the van, but I kept my resolve. *I know I'm not overreacting. Wayne needs help!*

Arriving at the hospital, I had an interview with the admitting physician for the substance abuse program. I told him about the chaos of the last six weeks. In that timeframe, Wayne had been uncharacteristically rude and angry with me. I was suspicious that he had lied to me and been to several additional doctors seeking pills. He'd driven dangerously with too many narcotics in him. His addiction was obviously accelerating.

Hearing about Wayne's behavior, the doctor agreed that he was a threat to himself and others and should be committed for 72 hours of mandatory treatment. Hopefully by that time we would have won his cooperation to stay in the hospital longer. The doctor called Wayne into the room and informed him that he was being involuntarily committed.

Wayne turned viciously on me. "If you leave me here, you'll never see me again!" His voice had a hostile quality I had never heard before. "It will prove to me that you don't love me."

It seemed my blood froze. Suddenly I felt as though I would be sick to my stomach. Wayne was wielding the powerful emotional sword of intimidation. Threatened by losing his drugs, he abandoned emotional loyalty to me and quickly sent me the message that *I* was betraying *him*. Implicit in his accusation was "I won't be able to trust you again."

Deep within myself I knew that Wayne's future hung on my decision. A part of me knew he was out of control. With his drug history, he might be tempted to buy street narcotics and could be arrested again. Another part of me felt devastated that he would make such a vicious accusation about my not loving him. I greatly feared that I might be making a mistake that would end up embarrassing him. *Maybe he really can stop by himself and I over-reacted? Maybe it will jeopardize his job at the hospital treatment program if we make it public that he relapsed?*

You could have cut the tension in the room with a knife. Wayne leaned forward in his chair and glared at me.

I took a breath and prayed for courage. "You have to stay," I said and broke eye contact with him. I walked out of the room.

I felt no sense of satisfaction from getting him to the hospital. Wayne's ultimatum hung over me like death. *Does this mean he was leaving me?* I choked back the tears. Our friends' insistence that I'd done the right thing didn't relieve my deep anguish.

That night, alone in our home, I was visited with panic and then depression. Wayne had said that if I left him there I'd never see him again. I believed him. A morbid sense of defeat came over me like a cloud. *Oh, God! How could this happen? Wayne and I were so close. I can't picture living without him. After all I've been through, this is happening? I thought life was going to make sense now. I don't want to go on...*

I puttered around the house, obsessing with fear and unable to shake the dread of Wayne leaving me. His manipulative statements had made me feel crazy. My previous experiences with Hansen's manipulation empowered this present crisis. A kind of déjà vu set in. I had a subconscious memory for this kind of situation, a built-in terror. Being in a position of extreme intimidation had triggered panic feelings in me, a replay of my past trauma. The present feelings were doubly powerful because of my abuse history. There was an echo of the cruelty of Hansen putting extreme pressure on me. In the past I had placated Hansen when that happened, and a part of me wanted to call Wayne and beg to be reassured that he loved me. But I knew I didn't dare. He'd only try to manipulate me to get him released from the hospital.

The next morning I called to talk to one of the counselors. Wayne had been up all night, vomiting and pacing the floor. Finally he had collapsed on his bed. I agreed with the counselor that I wouldn't visit for several days. He was in withdrawal and the process of detoxing from drugs was all-consuming. Besides, I worried that he might verbally attack me again. I feared the worst. *Would he be leaving me?*

On the third day Betsy and I visited the hospital. Betsy went in to visit Wayne first and came out to say that he was calm and asking for me. She assured me that he seemed humble.

When I sat down on the bed beside him, he began crying. He grabbed me and hugged me so tightly that it hurt. Relief flooded me. He still loved me.

"I don't know what I've done," he spurted through his tears. "I can't remember the past couple of weeks." The overload of narcotics made him amnesic to his behavior.

I started filling him in on his actions. I didn't spare him anything. He'd abused me verbally and lied about the pills he took. He had been swerving in the road and could have killed someone. He'd fallen in the house, crashing against a glass-front cabinet that could have shattered. He'd consumed so many narcotics that he couldn't remember much of anything. I told him about the ugly ultimatum he'd made when I left him at the hospital. I surprised myself by not softening my report. I let him feel the pain of the truth.

"I don't remember that," he kept crying. "I know it hurt you."

Seeing his brokenness, I was both relieved and worried. Addiction now loomed as a threat to our life together, yet it was something I had been so sure Wayne had conquered. I was thankful that I'd made him stay at the hospital, but resisting his manipulation had taken every bit of the emotional growth I'd gained during the last two years.

Ironically, it was Wayne who had helped me build the self-esteem and tenacity to overcome the fear of confronting others. I had finally broken my pattern of giving in under intimidation…the only pattern I had known during the dark years with Hansen. Now I couldn't just swallow my feelings or act polite. I had a lot of fear when I committed Wayne at the hospital, but there was something else rising in me…*courage.*

"The counselor told me that when you threatened to leave me, it was just the 'pills' talking," I told him. "But I still worried like crazy that you meant it."

Wayne's eyes were swollen from crying, but they were clear again, not glazed over with narcotics. I could see that he felt humiliated that he'd fallen under the power of drugs again.

We embraced for a long time.

"I never thought I'd relapse," he was crying again. "I had been sober for five years."

I reflected on a phrase I'd heard the night before at the hospital's family support meeting: "Alcohol and drugs are cunning and powerful." I had now seen it up close.

In a desperate effort to protect his addiction, the addict will attack. "You don't love me" is a powerful emotional arrow shot at family members in an effort to manipulate them away from taking action and setting boundaries.

For more understanding of the concept of codependency, see Essay #8: Am I Codependent, and Essay #9: Wise as Serpents.

Letting go means
that I can't do it for you,
it's not in my control,
and I might just have to watch you fail.

It seems easier to believe
the fantasy that I can
rescue and save you
if only I try hard enough.

                                              JoAnn Nishimoto

CHAPTER 21
The Real Confrontation

Following Wayne's relapse we struggled through the emotional aftermath. His self-esteem had suffered enormously. He felt embarrassed by his behavior and bewildered that he'd abused the narcotic prescriptions. Our church friends had been supportive and understanding, but he assumed that they'd lost confidence in him, despite their reassurance. I found myself coaching him in his self-esteem.

He completed only a small part of the hospital's treatment program, but agreed to return to an Alcoholics Anonymous (AA) group to think through the issues that had led to his relapse. The headaches continued, and he tried a number of non-narcotic medications to try and reduce their number and severity. It took several months before he felt better. Whenever he began to have a headache I felt anxious. I hoped he wouldn't rationalize taking narcotics again. Other medications usually didn't work, and it was hard to see him in pain and vomiting again when a migraine came on.

After several months it seemed that Wayne stabilized. We had so many positive things going for us. It seemed we were growing even closer. I was also excited about starting a Master's program in counseling from Liberty University. It was a program I intended to complete in three years by taking courses at home and going to Virginia for intensive modular courses once a year. The program included a one semester internship which I would complete locally.

One of my Liberty University courses was going to be held in Dallas, TX. Knowing that I'd be in Dallas for a week, my sister suggested I look up a friend of hers who was a counselor and see what insights she could offer me in understanding my abusive relationship with Hansen.

I met Sheila in a Dallas restaurant for what was supposed to be a quick lunch. I told her the brief version of my story with Hansen. After two years of healing, I was finally able to discuss the vows I had taken with Hansen, something I had always found too shameful to discuss with others.

"Once I'd taken the vows, it seemed that I was sealed, in some type of mind-control. I could never go back and rethink the big questions, such as 'Could this man be bad?'"

"He broke you." Sheila was quick to respond.

"I thought I was obeying God. I hate even saying that now because it's embarrassing."

"Your story reminds me of one I heard about in California," she said. My ears perked up immediately. I didn't know anyone else whose story paralleled mine.

"A pastor seduced several young, single women in his church by telling them the same 'God has given you to me' line. None of them knew about the others. He compelled each of them to take a vow to be his concubine," she related. "He was exposed when one of the young women eventually confided in her mother who took the pastor to task."

"How old were they?" I was very curious about this.

"I think they were in their 20's, probably 24-27 or so," she stated.

"I always thought that I should have been able to resist Hansen's persuasion because I was seventeen," I reflected. "I wasn't a child."

The look on Sheila's face told me she didn't agree.

"Listen, JoAnn, people who are masterful manipulators can trick and deceive just about anyone at any age. You're being unrealistic about the amount of power you had in comparison to Hansen," Sheila said. "As you get older you'll become more objective about how little you knew at seventeen!"

"I've been so unsure about what was or wasn't my fault. I don't know what parts of it I caused." My mind quickly defaulted to my over-responsible mindset. I had been so slow to understand that I didn't "cause" anything.

We continued discussing many parts of my story. The time with Sheila was very helpful, more so than with the other therapist I had tried to see immediately after getting out of the abuse. After talking for four hours, I felt such relief. Something had changed inside me. This conversation helped chip away at my burden of shame.

I called Wayne from a pay phone. "I'll be later than I thought getting home. I've been talking to Helen's friend for four hours. I have good news. I found out about someone like me!"

Thank you, Lord, for letting me find out about other women. I'm not the only one. I'm not alone. As I drove back toward the Texas-Louisiana line, I was able to play some of my favorite music and sing along.

Several weeks went by and I noticed that I was beginning to think about just how angry I was at Hansen. The anger had begun to emerge months ago as the fear began to subside. Confronting Wayne had helped me to make steps in standing up to someone when I needed to. I was allowing more of my real feelings to surface. I was finding more courage and dignity.

One day I'd been thinking of a past incident with Hansen and felt the anger rising in me. I was headed to the closet to grab a sweater when suddenly the pain and anger hit me like a bomb. My eyes swelled up with tears and I wanted to kick something. I closed the closet door behind me, trying to control my feelings. I didn't want Wayne to see me crying. I usually cried openly in front of him, but I felt that I'd probably worn him out and it was time to keep some of it to myself. I didn't know how much more he could stand.

"What are you doing in the closet?" Wayne had come into the room and discovered I was there.

"I am just being angry about Hansen," I said as I gritted my teeth. My neck felt hot with the anger I was trying to contain. "I could get a gun and go kill him." I hadn't said that out loud before, but it felt good. Tears welled up, but this time it was because of anger, not shame.

"Hansen robbed me of so much. I trusted him and he only used me for his selfish, screwed-up needs. I hate him! I lost the whole decade of my twenties to his manipulation!"

Saying these things was a point of healing for me. I was only now really able to get angry about my abuse. It had taken two and a half years to reach this point. I was angry enough to stand up for myself. The ability to be angry meant that I had reclaimed the dignity that Hansen had shattered. Anger was definitely a healthier response to the abuse than the fear I'd been carrying for so long.

About a year prior, I had been shopping in a local store when I rounded the aisle to find Hansen was standing there. I had frozen with fear. I pivoted quickly, found Wayne, and insisted we leave immediately. Now I was feeling a decided shift away from that kind of fear.

"I think I want to confront Hansen," I stated. "I'd like to stand in his presence for once and not be afraid."

"I'll support you," Wayne affirmed me.

For the next two hours I passionately discussed what I wanted to say to Hansen, how I might do it, and what his reaction might be. Finally, I wound down.

"Could we go eat now?" Wayne said. I guess he had a point. We had talked through suppertime and I was still standing in the closet with him at the door.

I had heard that Hansen had a mild stroke and was in a local nursing home. He was now 83 years old. I didn't know anything about his mental state, and I didn't care. This confrontation would be about what *I* needed, not what *he* needed. I mentally rehearsed things I wanted to say to him. This began to occupy my mind more and more.

I thought back to the earliest days when he had begun his high-pressure "grooming" of me, when I worried so much that I'd hurt him by confronting him. I had wanted to protect him and his ministry. To give him chance upon chance. Often he'd told me he would die if I didn't love him. I had bought into his coercion and felt responsible for keeping him alive.

When it came time to confront him, I expected him to "pay me back" by dying on the spot in front of me, trying to make me feel guilty for killing him. But I saw through all those lies now. If he wanted to die when I confronted him that would be fine. It wasn't my fault. It would be *his* choice. I was learning to discern what I was and wasn't responsible for in life.

One day I was home alone. Suddenly it came to me that I wanted to write a "List of Crimes" committed by Hansen against me. I'd stand in front of him and read them. I'd state my case. Getting a pen and paper, I began composing the list:

You defrauded me of my innocence.
You were supposed to be my spiritual leader and you betrayed my trust.
You played on my respect for you and manipulated my feelings.
You coerced me to take "fake" marriage vows to you.
You abused me with anger and enjoyed the fear you engendered in me.
You twisted God's Word to get power over me.

After an hour I had developed an extensive and articulate list of 25 items. Saying them out loud gave me such a sense of dignity that I began marching around my living room, reading it out loud with a confident and forceful voice. I savored the feeling of being a prosecuting attorney, ready to nail the defendant in the courtroom.

"Listen to this," I stated confidently when Wayne came home. I read him my list. "I'm ready to do it tomorrow."

When we arrived at the nursing home I was determined and single-minded. Nothing could have diverted me from my mission. When I entered Hansen's room I immediately saw him sitting in a geriatric chair with a tray across his chest. I hadn't anticipated that he might have a roommate, but there was an alert-looking old man in the other bed who was being visited by a middle-aged woman. No matter. I was resolute. I didn't care who heard my confrontation. I wasn't worried about protecting Hansen's reputation. If the others didn't want to hear it, they could leave.

Hansen lifted his head. He had been slumped over asleep on the tray. He looked like he'd aged ten years since I'd seen him in the store just twelve months earlier.

"Do you know who I am?" My voice was confident and firm. I wasn't without some anxiety, but my determination was stalwart.

Hansen squinted a bit. "Yes, yes, I know." His voice sounded weak, "You are JoAnn."

"Well, I've got some things I want to say to you. I don't want you to speak while I am speaking. I want you to look at me."

I was calling the shots here. I was glad my voice wasn't shaky, even though I had some anxiety rising inside me.

Hansen sat silent, his eyes fixed on me.

"This is a list of crimes you committed against me." I cleared my throat.

"First, you defrauded me of my innocence. You betrayed my trust when you were my spiritual leader. You used me for your selfish needs. You twisted God's word to make it sound like I should obey you...."

Hansen's voice broke in, "I'm sorry...I'm sorry."

I felt instant anger. I didn't want him butting in. I kept on.

"You pushed me to have sexual contact with you for your egotistical, selfish needs." My voice was becoming more forceful. I didn't care about the strangers in the room. So what if they were getting an earful! The lady pulled the curtain between the beds, removing them from view.

I started in again. "You must bear sole responsibility for using your pastoral authority to manipulate me." I could feel the power of my own tenacious voice.

Hansen broke in again, interrupting my list. "I'm so sorry. Please forgive me. I'm so sorry." He started drooling and lowered his head pitifully onto his arms.

I felt repulsion and anger. I wanted him to stand up to me, not cower and wimp out. I didn't want his apology. *Who could apologize for twelve years of sexual, emotional and spiritual abuse? Just shut up and listen to me!* For once I felt the strength to nail him, and I didn't feel afraid in his presence. I was determined he would hear my whole list. I started in with the next item, but he broke in again, whining.

I stopped and stared at Hansen. I knew he wasn't making *real* amends. He had never understood the depth of his evil twisting of my life. Knowing his warped mind, I knew he was interrupting as a manipulative tactic to make me stop the confrontation. There was no point in continuing. I dropped the list to my side. I looked at Wayne and nodded toward the door. I was ready to leave.

"I'm leaving now." My last words to Hansen were terse.

Hansen leaned forward and reached out as if to grab my hand. I dodged his reach immediately so he couldn't touch me. There had been so many times when he'd touched me without my permission. Touching had always been his call, on his terms. This time it was going to be on mine. In support of my hard-won dignity, I wasn't going to feel sorry for him, or touch him when I didn't want to.

As we drove home I told Wayne I was disappointed. "He was such a blubbering old fool. I was ready, for once, to stand up to him. I could have held my own. Instead, he wimped out and kept interrupting me. I was hoping I'd face the man who used to abuse me but he was just a shell. He played that whiny role to avoid having to face me."

Nevertheless, it was a real victory for me. I shed a lot of shame and gained a lot of dignity by confronting Hansen. It may not have played out like I had anticipated, but I found my voice in a powerful way.

When victims are finally able to get angry, it is usually a milestone of healing. Healthy anger can mobilize and cleanse, and give one the energy to combat depression and fear.

A confrontation is most helpful when it is a victim's statement of her own dignity and does not depend on the abuser's response, which she cannot control. Every victim deserves the right to confront her abuser, if she wishes. However, most perpetrators are firmly entrenched in their denial, and will not accept the responsibility for their damaging acts.

Many victims are encouraged to forgive their abusers before they've even had time to appropriately feel the betrayal and anger. This is premature and can cause more harm. For perspective on what appropriate forgiveness looks like, see Essay #12: Forgiveness is a Messy Thing.

Hansen:

You can die now if you want to.

There are some things that I haven't said to you; there are some things that you need to hear. I'm ready to confront you now. I'm not afraid of you anymore. I can look you in the eyes now. You cannot take advantage of me. You no longer have power over me. I am not going to feel sorry for you ever again!

You were my pastor whom I trusted. You selfishly took advantage of me. You said you loved me, but you only loved yourself. You continually lied to me and to yourself. I think you are so good at lying that you no longer can tell what is true. You were supposed to be a good leader of others, but secretly you led a trusting child into a trap. You held me as a psychological prisoner. I felt powerless to know how to break your grip on me.

When I tell you this, you will probably get sick and die and try to make me feel guilty for confronting you. But I am only telling you the things YOU did. You chose these actions.

Go ahead and die now. It's your choice. It won't be my fault.

JoAnn Nishimoto
October 2, 1990
(Written after 2 ½ years of healing)

CHAPTER 22
I Won't Tell You

During the three years that Wayne and I had been married, he had been a model listening partner. Our marriage had an atmosphere of comfort and healing. My recovery had been a central issue that came up several times a week, and I used Wayne as a sounding board to work on my fears, insecurities, and shame. I was intentional about giving him "time off" from hearing my stuff, and tried to focus on the many positive things I had going on in my life.

At times my emotional neediness created a sort of vacuum in which I needed reassurance from Wayne that he loved me. Although he expressed his love affectionately and often, in my brokenness I always craved more. The emotional pain I struggled against was so deep that I often looked for more and more reassurance from him, hoping to quell the fear that would rise in me.

It seemed to help, at least momentarily, for him to say, "I love you, JoAnn." It would shore up my wavering self-esteem. I longed to hear it over and over, especially if I was feeling insecure. I had developed a silly little ritual of coping with insecurity and of getting him to tell me he loved me. I'd say in a matter-of-fact voice, "You love me so much," to which he was supposed to respond, "Yes, I love you so much." By leading him to voice his love, I was hedging against my inner feelings of insecurity. For the most part, he humored me in this. I don't think he understood just how much I depended on this quick fix when I felt low.

Sometimes I felt that I had overcome a particular issue, only to have fear or insecurity raise its ugly head again. I was learning that the depth of my woundedness meant that things rarely were settled just because I talked about them once or twice.

During one week I seemed fixated on the shame I had over Hansen invading my mind. When I thought of the intense mental programming he'd used on me, I felt violated and used, and then I felt inadequate for not having been able to stop it. *I should have been strong emotionally and been able to tell Hansen, "You're wrong! Stop telling me these things!"* I had a good knowledge of Scripture. *Why hadn't I been able to just tell him, "I'm sorry if you don't like it. I won't believe that God told you to marry me. You're already married. You're violating the Scripture, regardless of what you say. Stay away from me!"* It seemed so easy to blame myself for not standing up to his pressure. I could think of the perfect responses now. I had 20/20 hindsight, something like Monday morning quarterbacking. I understood now that it was more difficult to say "no" when my pastor came on to me sexually than if, say, a same-aged peer had, particularly since Hansen had moral authority and leadership status as my pastor. Being "brainwashed" to believe I was married to Hansen was the single most shameful part of my past. I knew others might never understand it. I feared facing judgment from others that I could have or should have stopped it.

"I've had a bad day today," I reported to Wayne on the way home in the car. "I've been wondering again why I wasn't strong enough to refuse Hansen." Wayne knew we'd been over this one several times already. He was quiet for a minute. The car headlights illuminated the next curve in the road.

"Remember, you did the best you could with the maturity you had at the time," he repeated the affirmation I was beginning to use. It was getting late and I thought he probably hoped we weren't going to delve into anything tonight.

"I believe it...sort of. It just makes me so bewildered to think how he twisted my mind. He could talk faster than I could think. I couldn't see the process of how he was sucking me in." I was talking to myself out loud as much as talking to Wayne.

Again, the feelings of grief over the abuse I'd been through rose inside me. Although the strength of the grief had lessened month by month, I could still have a "wave" of it. I decided to go for the quick fix that Wayne's words always gave me.

"At least I know that you love me so much," I presented my familiar lead-in line. Now it was his turn.

Wayne kept driving in silence. This time my invitation felt like a game that he'd grown tired of. He didn't respond.

"I said...at least I know you love me so much." I put my invitation out there once again, insecurity showing in my voice.

"JoAnn, I won't tell you that right now." Wayne's voice was factual and blunt. "You're going to have to fill that emotional hole with something deeper than I can give you with one 'I love you.'"

We rode on in silence. I was hurt and angry. *How dare he deprive me of that!* I felt a little panic. I used his "I love you's" as something to steady myself with. *It feels mean for him to refuse me.* I was hoping that he wasn't going to mess up the coping system I had worked out!

As we got in bed that night he finished his thought. "You're going to have to find out how to fix that pain in yourself. You can't always be trying to suck it from me."

I felt sorry for myself because he hadn't nurtured me. But I knew there was truth in what he said. I knew that there was only one source that could reach the deepest parts of my pain. It would have to be God. I knew that I was loved by God...but I needed to cast myself on Him and not use Wayne as a substitute. Although Wayne loved me, I knew I couldn't make him solely responsible for my emotional support. It was too much to require of a human. Wayne was tired of my low self-worth taking its toll on our relationship.

I was beginning to feel more stable spiritually, but it had been an uphill climb.

I now saw myself as very human and very frail. Capable of being deceived. Capable of deceiving myself. Even though I wasn't responsible for getting into the abuse, I'd adapted to the deception of it. During the abuse years, I had become so accustomed to lying for Hansen that at the time I had no guilt about it. I had seared my conscience. I saw my own sinfulness in this.

I thought back to high school when I had perceived myself as being spiritual. I had such a zeal and love for God then. At that time I saw myself as belonging to Him. I was glad that I'd known God before all the abuse started. Now that I was out of it, I no longer had any trouble confusing Hansen's abuse with the God who would never abuse me. I had met several abuse victims who had been turned off to God because of their abuse. It was clear to me that Jesus had warned there would be wolves among the sheep.

Now my walk with God was so different. I was seeing that He loved me through all the failures. He loved me through the lies. He'd never left me. He had even given me many blessings during the years when I was sunk in deception. I realized that if He waited until we were perfect in order to bless us, none of us would ever be blessed.

It was dawning on me that God wasn't surprised at my humanity. Maybe now I was coming to peace with it myself. It was becoming easier to admit that I'd been majorly screwed-up. I stopped seeing myself as an enigma, or a unique failure as a person. Maybe the qualities of honesty and authenticity I now possessed were going to be used by God. There wasn't much false pride or judgmentalism left in me. I was repentant of having rationalized His Word, though I had first fallen into this solely from Hansen's pressure. *Maybe God doesn't think I am "finished" or washed-up. In fact, from God's perspective, maybe I am in a wonderful place. He isn't disgusted with me. In fact, He has a plan to redeem all this for His purposes.*

I thought of Psalm 126:5: *Those who go forth weeping, bearing precious seeds, will doubtless come again, bringing their sheaves with them.* I had certainly gone forth weeping. I had done a mountain of crying during the past three years. I had been planting a lot of precious seeds, which I figuratively saw as repentance, surrender, honesty, humility, and willingness to grow. Now came the last part of the scripture promise. I would doubtless (without a doubt) "come again" with some kind of harvest (the sheaves, or the harvested wheat). It wasn't all for nothing. I've heard, "God doesn't waste your sorrows." *God must have a way of making good out of all this pain.* My faith had been growing that God was bigger than my abuse and that maybe He could use it. *Couldn't He redeem the wasted years?* I was beginning to embrace this.

I thought of Joseph's story in the book of Genesis, the Biblical model for those who have been unfairly abused. Joseph's abuse came from his own brothers who had thrown him in a well, then sold him into slavery. Ending up in Egypt, he was unjustly betrayed again and thrown in prison. God did not forsake him, however, and he later rose to power in Egypt and ultimately saved the same brothers from starvation. *What they meant for evil, God meant for good.* I was beginning to trust God that He could do something good with my years of abuse.

The belief that God was bigger than my abuse slowly began to seep through me and bring me hope. When I looked to Him for this I found something far more sustaining than in just getting Wayne to tell me that he loved me.

Hope had become an important word to me. My marriage to Wayne had been a hopeful path. He had been my companion and partner in healing. Now I was beginning to have a deeper hope that God would use the abuse in some way to show His greatness.

> **Although the love of others is important to our healing, even those who love us deeply cannot put us back together and fix our deep brokenness. A relationship with God is the key to healing.**

The cultic experience often results in a crisis of faith:
> *"How could God allow this to happen to me?"*
> *"I must be a horrible person since I failed God and His plan for my life."*

The ex-cultist's belief in a "just world" is shattered. He can no longer say, *"It won't happen to me."* A need for meaning among these people is paramount. The victim must be helped to regain a belief in self and the world that allows room for "bad things happening to good people."

He or she may also need to talk out and relive the trauma again and again, as do the victims of other types of crises. Victims need to be freed from the view that they were somehow solely responsible for their plight.

Paul Martin, PhD
Dispelling the Myths:
The Psychological Consequences of Cultic Involvement
Christian Research Journal, Winter/Spring 1989

CHAPTER 23

Hope Arrives

Looking out over the 40 women present, I finished reading my presentation. I'd been invited to share my testimony at a Methodist women's retreat, and had typewritten a 45-minute testimony which covered the basic story of my abuse. The women seemed to have been glued to my talk. Sharing with this group had been "safe." No one here knew me personally. I was 70 miles away from my hometown. It was a step in testing the waters. *What would the response be?*

Wayne was sitting in the back row. A few months before he had felt reluctant for me to tell my story publicly. We had both wondered: *Would others see me as too strange?* But now I had convinced him that the time had come to share the healing that I had. Of course, I was still working on it, but I had begun to develop the courage to speak out.

I wrapped up my testimony to the ladies. "I'm happy to end my talk with some good news," I ventured. "I'm six weeks pregnant!"

Wayne beamed from the back row and everyone clapped.

Afterwards seven or eight women gravitated to the front to speak to me. One woman's daughter was in an abusive relationship. Another woman said that I had given her courage to seek counseling. Still others related to specific topics I had touched on: abuse of power, fear, codependency in relationships, shame over one's past, and resting in God's love and forgiveness. I saw that although my story was unusual, many women felt helped by my honesty and openness.

On the way home I didn't need to bug Wayne for an "I love you." I was feeling the strength of my four years of healing. God had opened a door for me to share, and I had walked through it. In my growth I had transitioned from *victim* to *survivor*. Now I was having the first taste of what it could mean to live as a *thriver*.

As a couple, Wayne and I were celebrating. A baby was on the way. We were eager and ready. Other things were going well also. Wayne had changed his college major to nursing and had been accepted into an RN program. He wanted to become a nurse on a substance abuse treatment unit similar to the one where he worked as a technician. This seemed an optimal way for him to use his own sobriety to help others. He was doing well since his relapse, and we felt we had recovered from it and learned a great deal.

I had begun counselor training at the YWCA in Shreveport. This was the hands-on part of my master's degree requirements. At the YWCA I led group therapy for women who had been through sexual abuse as children or sexual assault as adults. Although my abuse happened in a different context, there were many overlapping topics which I understood. As I talked over their cases with my counseling supervisor, I was also fine-tuning my own healing. As I completed each one of my graduate courses, I was applying the principles of healing to others and to myself. It all seemed to be coming together.

Tom called one day with news. He heard that Hansen had died in the nursing home. Although Wayne and I paused to discuss it, it didn't have much emotional impact on me. Later, I fantasized that I would go to the cemetery with a can of spray paint and write ABUSER across his headstone. A part of me knew I wouldn't really do this, but I enjoyed thinking about it. Feeling a bit powerful was a healthy state after all the years I'd felt intimidated.

In June of 1992, I was six months pregnant. The previous months had been the happiest in our marriage. After all the hard work and honesty I'd put into my healing, I was emotionally grounded and fairly stable. We were enjoying the benefits and joy of my progress, and this had spilled over into our marriage. I didn't see it coming. Wayne relapsed again.

Following the same pattern as before, he had gone back to medicating his migraine headaches with pain pills and narcotics. He'd lost control. This time I caught on sooner. With much less resistance to treatment this time, he agreed to go to the hospital. He stayed for three weeks in a spiritually-based treatment program in Houston called Rapha.

It was still a shattering setback. It had been more than two years since the first relapse. Everything had felt so solidly secure. Now the bottom had fallen out again. This time I was angrier with him. I didn't think, as I had the first time, that the relapse had taken him by surprise. I felt he had known what he was doing, but had taken the pills anyway. During four weeks of relapse, he'd run up several thousand dollars of bills for emergency room visits, seeking Demerol shots while already overloaded with narcotics. Although we had insurance for the hospital charges, the deductible and other expenses were a blow. At a time when I'd wanted to use our extra money to prepare for the baby, every extra dollar had to go toward relapse expenses.

When Wayne came home I tried to see things in a positive light. He seemed to have faced more of his issues and become more honest. The Christian program had helped him to work on the spiritual issues he had struggled with after his relapse. These were familiar to me as well: *Have I ruined my Christian testimony? How can I forgive myself?* This time we reached a deeper level of talking about his addiction, and weren't as quick to gloss over it.

"If you relapse, you're at risk for doing some really stupid things like buying street narcotics when you're 'high' and don't know what you're doing," I said. I had gotten more direct when we talked about drugs.

"The last judge who sentenced me told me that if I ever got another drug conviction, I'd get a life sentence," Wayne had told me once.

"I don't want you bringing our child to see me in prison," Wayne said soberly.

That was a very terrifying thought.

When Wayne returned from Rapha, there were only three months until the baby's arrival. We signed up for childbirth classes, Wayne resumed his school schedule, and we began collecting baby furniture. Amid the excitement over the baby, we tried to work through the issues surrounding the relapse. Wayne would be on probation for his nursing program. They would let him continue, but he would not have another chance if he relapsed again.

As the baby's arrival was getting closer, we were given several baby showers. My parents' church showed their love to us by planning a shower and celebrating this milestone. Everyone knew that Wayne had just weathered another relapse, but they openly declared their love to us. Other gifts and displays of love came in day by day.

As I was leaving the fourth baby shower, I had my first labor pain. By 8 p.m. the next evening I delivered a beautiful baby girl. Wayne stayed with me through the whole labor and the emergency Caesarian. We had agreed on the baby's name weeks before. It seemed natural for us to name our child after a word that had become very important to both of us: Hope. In honor of my mother, her middle name would be Lillian.

We brought Hope home from the hospital and celebrated God's goodness to us.

Wayne, Hope and me in front of our log home

> Doing the hard work of recovery eventually has its rewards: increasing freedom from shame, reaching out to others, and positive feelings about life, God and self.

The only way we can overcome the fear of rejection
is to value the constant approval of God
over the conditional approval of people.

> Robert S. McGee
> *Search For Significance*
> Search Resources, 1992

CHAPTER 24
Another Blow

Being a mother felt like one of the easiest job assignments I'd ever been given. Although I knew little about baby care and infants, learning the tricks of the trade was fun. I was determined to breast feed, and despite some problems and infections, Hope and I figured it out. I had that deeply internalized sense of confidence about parenting that comes from being raised in a secure home. *I can be a good parent and mother. I know how to do this.* At age 34, I was ready to be a mother, and I'd been looking forward to the time when Wayne and I could have children.

On the other hand, Wayne's lack of parenting confidence reflected the insecurity from his own family of origin. His dad had been deeply lost in alcoholism while he was growing up. His parents divorced when he was nine. His mother had difficulty parenting him. Without a father, Wayne had manipulated his mother when he was a teenager. Coming from a chaotic family background, Wayne didn't have the same assumptions of confidence about parenting. He had to grow into it, little by little. He was happy to be a father, but he required reassurance along the way that he was doing fine. He'd have to gradually cultivate his security in parenting. It wasn't a given for him.

As the calendar turned to 1993, we seemed to be on a positive path. We were only a year and a half away from Wayne graduating with his nursing degree. During the income tax preparation season (January – May), I'd be working full time for my mother in her business again. I'd taken several tax preparation courses and had advanced my skills. My dad, who had retired, took on the role of being Hope's full-time babysitter during those months. He rolled up his sleeves and became quite adept at baby care. Occasionally he called the office, "Can you leave work early and come nurse Hope? I just can't settle her down this afternoon." At times like that, it was convenient that my employer was also my mother. I did have a bit of an inside connection!

Our relationship with my parents was solid. They were supportive, but not controlling. We enjoyed their involvement with Hope. They were wonderful and doting grandparents. Meanwhile, my brother Sam and his wife, Mary, had their third child. Although they now lived in Saudi Arabia, their trips home to Louisiana were cherished times when my parents' house was filled with small children and family fun. I loved seeing my brother's young family and knowing that Wayne and I were launching our own. Sometimes I reflected on the present openness and joy I felt about my life. When thoughts of the past came to me, especially compared to my present life, I could only shake my head with disbelief that I'd once lived so differently. *This peace I have now is what my life was supposed to be. I've healed so much.*

Wayne's migraines continued, but he was reluctant to pursue preventative strategies. Several doctors suggested that he stop drinking caffeine. He had been drinking more and more of it in the past several years. However, he wouldn't agree to a trial period off of caffeine.

"Look, why don't you quit caffeine for six months, and if you don't have fewer headaches, then go back to it if you want. At least you would have ruled it out." I had waited until I thought he was open to talking about it, then offered my best suggestions. I tried to help him see a rational approach to reducing his headaches.

"I don't think it will do any good," he rebutted my suggestions without giving them serious consideration. I felt angry that he wouldn't try.

Wayne had developed a cynical attitude toward the inevitability of having migraines, and seemed unwilling to work on it. This was very frightening to me since I knew the migraines brought on a sense of victimization in him... his attitude was "I'm suffering and I'm not allowed to have the relief (narcotics) that others can take when they hurt." In turn this fed self-pity in him which I had learned was very dangerous to addicts. Self-pity leads to compromising one's sobriety...a sort of "I deserve better" attitude, "I deserve pain-relief like others are allowed to have."

His migraines were also followed by several days of depression, a typical aftermath for many migraine sufferers. A migraine usually meant terrible pain and vomiting for at least 24 hours, followed by several days of depression. It was scary to see him depressed. It was taking a toll on his morale. The headaches and depression were happening several times a month, and frequently interrupted our plans and work.

I offered to cut out a number of other suspect foods, but he declined. He didn't seem to have patience for dietary interventions. Occasionally he tried a medication, such as an anti-depressant, which reduces the frequency of migraines in some patients, but he was never consistent with the medication. He tried Lithium for a time, and felt some help from it after several months, so I was alarmed when one day he announced that he'd stopped the Lithium several weeks previously without telling me.

"Lithium was giving me a funny feeling in my head, and I didn't like it," Wayne reported. I felt exasperated that he had ditched another potentially helpful medication without giving it a full trial.

I was starting to recognize a pattern in Wayne that I'd read about in some of the recovery literature. Drug addicts are used to controlling their own medications, experimenting with drugs, and "prescribing" for themselves. They tend to be resistant to letting someone else, such as a doctor, dictate their medication, and they impulsively abandon potentially helpful medications if they don't deliver quick results. Even Wayne admitted that he was impulsive when it came to medications.

By the time Hope was six months old, and only nine months since the previous relapse, Wayne went down again. He was such a serious addict, and his body so profoundly chemically altered from his old days of addiction that he could never just use narcotics sporadically. Once he began taking pain pills, it immediately became all-consuming. Within a few weeks, he'd accelerated into his previous out-of-control state. He claimed that he'd been driven to it by the pain of the migraines. I knew that the migraines had contributed, but the problems went deeper. At some level, he wasn't where he needed to be in his recovery. He had stopped talking openly about his addiction, as he had in the first years of our marriage. He again stopped attending AA, and retreated inwardly to typical addict rationalizations and excuses. He wasn't looking for ways to try other treatments for his migraines. Instead, he was looking for reasons why he deserved to take narcotics.

In March I came home one evening to find him out cold on the couch. Though I was very frightened, I was learning healthier behaviors in dealing with him when he relapsed. I decided to leave him alone. I wasn't going to call the college to tell them he wouldn't be in. I was not about to lie and say he was sick. I just wouldn't do anything. He had created this relapse and he would have to deal with the fallout.

I was surprised the next morning that he was still sleeping. I began to suspect something was wrong when I couldn't wake him up. I called my dad to help me make a decision. After Dad saw him, he said we'd have to get him to the hospital. I felt defeated. Wayne would probably wake up after he'd been in the hospital for a while, but meanwhile it would cost a few thousand dollars to be treated there. Then Wayne would blame me for incurring the medical costs, saying it hadn't been necessary to take him to the hospital. We were always concerned about medical costs since Wayne had been laid off from his job the previous year and we didn't have medical insurance.

As we were getting him into the car I noticed there were quite a few empty pill bottles in the trash. When I tallied the possible pills he had taken, it was terrifying. He'd probably consumed 250 over-the-counter pain tablets along with the remaining anti-depressants and other meds he had. I didn't want to accept the truth staring me in the face. He had tried to kill himself.

At the hospital, the doctors told me it didn't look good. Within two hours, Wayne was dependent on a respirator. We'd barely gotten him there in time. Without my dad's intervention, I would have left him on the couch sleeping and he would have died.

Soon Wayne was transferred to the intensive care unit of another hospital in Shreveport. Everyone waited and prayed. When I saw him connected to tubes and the respirator, I hardly recognized his swollen, bloated body. It was agony to look at him. This was the most alarming thing that had ever happened during a relapse.

The doctor came to talk to me as I sat alone in the ICU waiting room.

"Mrs. Thomas, I don't think Wayne will live. If he does live, he may have severe liver damage."

I felt emotionally overloaded. I was numb. That night twelve friends and family came to the hospital and we prayed. *It shouldn't end like this. He doesn't want to do this to himself.*

Wayne did wake up after three days. At first he was very broken. He didn't remember the events of the overdose, or even intending to kill himself. He had done it all under the influence of narcotics.

He initially said he would go to treatment, and that he was leaving the decision to me. Aware that a quick fix was the last thing he needed, I suggested a long-term treatment program that I'd located in Hot Springs, Arkansas. Teen Challenge Ministries had a drug program for adult men that lasted two years. The cost was modest and the length of time in the program didn't bother me. Hope and I would visit as often as permitted.

I knew Wayne's life depended on his getting to the bottom of how he was going to live without relapsing on narcotics, with or without migraines. The suicide attempt had negated any less serious approach. He was relapsing more often, this time after only nine months. The trauma of his near death had broken me emotionally and I was open to any solution that would help him confront himself deeply. Two years in a residential recovery program seemed a small price to pay for a new lease on life.

Wayne was alarmed over the two-year commitment to the program, and unwilling to consider it. He thought I was over-reacting and accused me of wanting to get rid of him for two years. He had no medical insurance, so we could not afford a hospital program. He pushed me to consent to a free local 30-day program, to which I reluctantly agreed. After three days there, he said it wasn't for him. He didn't like being with street people and cocaine addicts; he saw himself as "above" them. I was alarmed at the arrogance this implied.

"You can't just come home and act like nothing happened," I said emphatically. "You nearly killed yourself. You can't keep putting us through this." I felt angry that the addict is often "wiped out" while using drugs and doesn't remember the trauma that the family suffers. I wished he could see a video recording of those three days when I agonized, not knowing if he would live or die.

I wasn't prepared for Wayne's resistance. "I'm going to my mother's house for a few weeks. I'll do some Alcoholics Anonymous meetings there and I promise I'll go to some counseling."

As he left for his mother's house in Houston, our life was filled with uncertainties. Due to his absences and relapse, he had to leave the nursing program. *What now? What would he do for a job?* It was a low point for both of us. Wayne's guilt and fallout from a relapse had hit us again. Now *I* was depressed. I knew what the aftermath of the relapse would look like. I knew the toll it would take on his self-esteem. I feared the future. I felt helpless against his addiction. *Would this demon always come after him?*

I could see that Wayne had lost the momentum of recovery he'd had during the first years when he became a Christian. He'd fallen into fear and lost his hope. Rationalizations had gained a strong foothold in him. The following week was a difficult time as we both ground out the days, one-by-one.

As I rocked Hope and sang to her one evening, I thought of how close Wayne had come to dying. His relapses seemed so incongruent. This addiction didn't fit with the love we had and the good marriage we'd established. Looking in Hope's blue eyes, which mirrored those of her father's, I knew how much he loved her and how much he loved me. But when it comes to fighting addiction, love isn't enough.

> **Chemical dependency is one of the hardest struggles that humans can ever experience.**

Reassessing Responsibility

What I do or don't do does not make another person an alcoholic or addict.
What I do or don't do does not make another person sober.
What I do or don't do does not make another person stay sober.
What I do or don't do makes me *who I am*.

Something I heard at an Al-Anon meeting

CHAPTER 25

A Leap of Faith

In the soul-searching that followed his relapse, we brainstormed our options for income. We both felt Wayne should work in the area he was most gifted. Starting our own business seemed like a way that he could use his jewelry skills to make a living. Given his past criminal record, there was little chance someone else would hire him. Although many small businesses failed, it seemed we'd just have to take the risk. We simply didn't know where else Wayne could work. We both agreed that he would find a lot of satisfaction in goldsmithing and jewelry design.

A retired friend who knew a lot about retailing challenged us with a new idea. What kind of compatible business could we include along with jewelry design and repair that would bring more customers into the store? The answer seemed obvious. Needing a Christian bookstore in our small town had been a recurring topic for years among people I knew. We spent money in Shreveport at one of the larger Christian bookstores there, as did most of the church attendees we knew. It seemed a logical fit. We could launch our store as a dual business…Wayne's jewelry work and a bookstore within the same retail space.

After weeks of planning and research, we discovered that there was actually a workshop we could attend on "How to Launch a Bookstore." We were grateful that we didn't have to reinvent the wheel. We attended the workshop and set out to implement the well-researched business plan. After securing a business loan from the bank, our summer was spent getting ready to open the store. We settled on a name: *The Olive Branch*.

During the bookseller's workshop I attended an evening concert by Rich Mullins, a well-known musician. As he sang, "Hold me Jesus…I'm shaking like a leaf," tears welled up in my eyes. In quiet moments I still felt the trauma of the past few months. I could picture Wayne near death on a respirator. At times I felt that I was still shaking like a leaf. Although Wayne had been attending AA meetings and raising his issues occasionally with me, I knew there were no guarantees. After the suicide attempt, I understood the monster of addiction at a new level. There was no way to dress it up or make it less threatening. It could be life or death. At the concert that night I did the only thing I could…pray for my husband, put his issues in God's hands, and choose to move forward.

Meanwhile, Wayne was struggling with shame regarding his suicide attempt. I remembered how the quicksand of low self-worth could undermine everything. I urged him to talk about it.

"I guess everyone knows I tried to kill myself," his voice often grew quieter when he mentioned anything about that event. I could tell he felt exposed and embarrassed about it.

"Yes, I think a lot of people know, but they also love you, too."

"People probably think I relapsed because I crave drugs," he cut me off quickly, sounding frustrated as he passed over my supportive comment. "They don't know how excruciating the headaches are. I wouldn't have started using pills if I hadn't been in agony." I knew he was afraid others assumed he was acting from the old motivations to just get high.

As usual, Wayne was defensive in discussing his relapses, which he saw as excusable. He felt misunderstood. He remembered the old days, fifteen years prior, when he deliberately set out to abuse drugs. When he told stories about himself from those years, he referred to himself as a "hoodlum." In contrast, he argued now that he didn't intend to abuse narcotics, rather, he *needed* them. Ironically, once he put narcotics back in his body, even for legitimate pain-relief purposes, they still reduced him to an out-of-control state. Chemically, his body would never be anything but the body of an addict. Once he put narcotics in his system, he could no longer make his own choices; the drugs chose for him.

"Wayne, I want you to try that new medication. It helps prevent headaches for some people," I ventured a suggestion. Hope pounded on her highchair, and Wayne fed her another bite of eggs.

"You're always thinking that I should try this or that," he said defensively. "I don't have time or patience to try all those things."

I could see that we'd fallen into predictable ways of discussing this problem, and I didn't want to repeat it every time the topic was raised.

"I'm sure you're doing the best you can. I'll let you handle it." I decided not to make us adversaries that morning. I handed off Hope to him so he could change her diaper. He gave her a wide smile and we easily shifted into the day's activities.

I was learning that giving these supportive comments was the only option I had. He would have to come to the conclusions by himself. To insist on my view was to close off communication between us. I didn't want him to stop talking to me about it.

Wayne found it hard to talk about the suicide attempt and, although he went to some counseling, I sensed that he hadn't dealt with it on a very deep level. I knew counseling would have limited value unless he revealed the depth of his thoughts to the therapist.

I was struggling with the reality of knowing he was capable of suicide. Whether or not he had really intended to kill himself, it was now within the realm of possibilities if he relapsed again. Just as my life had begun to surface from the internal problems that had plagued me in my own recovery, now I had a different set of fears to face. Wayne was now the person in our marriage with the most complex and threatening issues.

Fortunately the positive aspects of our marriage continued. Wayne and I loved each other deeply. We'd invested a lot into one another in the five years of our marriage. There had been gut level honesty. We'd taken some bad hits from Wayne's relapses, but we had a lot going for us. We had dozens of loving friends, a great church fellowship, strong family relationships, a determination to keep seeking God, and a beautiful child. Buoyed by the positive support we had, we opened our store.

Although we hadn't planned it that way, our opening day was on Hope's first birthday. Within a month we had a community-wide grand opening with pictures in the local newspaper. Typical of small town openings, the mayor attended and wished us well. In our town of 15,000 people, we had many customers who came in to see the new store in town.

Business went well. Our artistic skills complimented one another and the store was beautiful. We had refinished several antique showcases and the store had a Victorian flavor. Between the lively contemporary music and the scented candles, the store was a treat for the senses. I quickly adapted to book and music sales. Wayne immediately began getting jewelry business and sales jumped to a positive start. Wayne worked full time and I worked about 20 hours a week. I was also doing part-time counseling work. I had completed my master's degree the previous year. Hope stayed with a babysitter but also spent time at the store with us in her playpen. It was often a family affair.

As we entered the Christmas retail season, we were unprepared for the deluge of sales and the work involved in meeting the holiday shopping schedule. Our Christmas season sales exceeded our wildest expectations. When we got home on Christmas Eve after closing the store, we played with Hope and collapsed into bed. The next morning we phoned my parents and asked to postpone Christmas dinner for a few hours so we could lie in bed longer. Whew! We'd never worked so hard but it was a sweet exhaustion. The community response to the store was very positive. We could tell the business was going to make it. We gave thanks.

Entering 1994 we felt optimism for what we might be able to develop in the store. We enjoyed the four hour trips to Dallas for the gift markets and the bookseller conventions. We were starting to grasp how to do the business and make it succeed. As March rolled around we were enjoying the momentum. We hired an employee. It was quite a contrast from the previous March when Wayne had nearly died. Lately he was working enthusiastically.

"Hey, can you mix up some plaster for me? I'm ready to invest this wax model," he called from the jewelry work room in the rear of the store. Wayne often enlisted me in some of the support work required for casting gold pieces.

"Sure. How did you finish that project so fast? I thought the customer just brought it in yesterday." I was surprised at how diligently Wayne had been working.

"It just seemed to click. I guess I'm feeling creative." His voice was calm and satisfied. I liked seeing him enjoy his talent as a goldsmith. Knowing that he was feeling creative was a sign that he wasn't depressed. This was the real Wayne, I felt, who was creative and optimistic.

While I mixed plaster, Wayne lit his torch and began melting some gold for another project he was ready to cast. We had developed a rhythm of working together. I knew exactly when to take a super-heated mold out of the oven and

Courage for Lambs

place it next to the molten gold in the crucible. Just when the gold had a mirror finish on the surface, Wayne released the trigger mechanism on the casting machine and centrifugal force slung the gold into the mold.

As Wayne extinguished his torch we stood watching the metal cool and lose its glow as it spun slower and slower. We usually turned out the light to highlight the impressive glow of molten gold. It was a tradition with us to just stand and watch it, unhurried.

"I think this is the happiest year of my life," Wayne said.

No other comment could have made me happier. After months of recovering his morale and working hard to establish the store, it seemed he was finding his emotional bearings.

Wayne was minding the customer checkout one afternoon when an eight-year-old girl came in the store alone. She spent quite some time picking out an inexpensive key chain.

"It's a present for my mom," she said proudly as she came to pay for it. She emptied her pocket and laid a collection of coins on the counter. From my desk I could see and hear Wayne interacting with her at the counter.

"How much is the key chain?" she asked innocently. She hadn't seen the $2.99 price sticker on the packaging.

"How much do you have?" Wayne countered her question.

After several seconds she added up her money. "I have $1.27."

"Oh, that's just enough!" Wayne feigned surprise that she had produced just the right amount. The child wasn't aware of his generosity. As she left the store he was still smiling.

That night we picked up Hope from the babysitter's house and headed to our comfortable log home in the country.

"Let's be sure and walk the dogs this evening," I said.

During warmer weather we had started putting Hope in a backpack-style child carrier. Watching her bounce along on Wayne's back made the walks even more fun. The fresh springtime leaves were coming out on the trees and I was feeling energetic. From the back porch of our home I had counted at least 30 blooming dogwood trees. Lately there were so many positive vibes from Wayne that I felt I could really celebrate spring.

> **Although we have influence in the lives of those we love, our influence is often limited.**

"...my life has become unmanageable."

Step One
The Big Book
Alcoholics Anonymous World Service Inc., 2001

CHAPTER 26
Mexico

I had never seen tropical fish so beautiful. As Wayne and I snorkeled, we held hands. This helped us stay together as the current gently moved us around the shallow bay. Occasionally we pointed out a fish by gesturing to one another in the surreal silence of the undersea world.

Our trip to Mexico felt like a second honeymoon. We'd bought a vacation package to Ixtapa, a few hours north of Acapulco on the Pacific coast of Mexico. Mom and Dad kept Hope during our six-night trip.

Driving south down the Pacific coastal highway, we saw a breathtaking sunset. We parked on a bluff from which we could see the fifteen-foot waves crashing on the beach below. I vowed to return one day to see another sunset there.

We had planned a side trip to Taxco, high in the central mountains. This town, renowned for the production of sterling silver jewelry, was a place where we could purchase sterling at wholesale prices for our store, which would nearly pay for our vacation.

It was August, and the air conditioner in our inexpensive room put out only a weak stream of cool air. Wayne became very angry when the hotel manager refused to move us to a cooler room. Impulsively, he grabbed our suitcases and stormed back to the rental car. I followed meekly, but his anger level frightened me.

I had learned that addicts have a saying called "H.A.L.T." When an addict finds himself becoming too Hungry, Angry, Lonely, or Tired, he may be putting himself at risk of relapse. Stressing oneself in any of these ways often leads to impulsiveness and rationalizations about using alcohol or drugs. Although I knew I was powerless to control Wayne's making poor choices about using pills, I couldn't help observing his behavior and noting the danger.

After searching quite a while for an available room, we checked into a high rise hotel on Acapulco Bay. Although there was a beautiful view from our 12th floor balcony, we'd paid a high price for the room. I was irritated that Wayne had forfeited our economy room, even though we would have been uncomfortable for one night.

As soon as we were in our room, Wayne announced he was going for a walk. He was still very angry and restless.

"You're going walking in Acapulco at midnight? You'll get mugged!" I was incredulous and exasperated. After a fantastic morning of snorkeling and later the romantic sunset, this day was ending on a rotten note.

Wayne was sulky and stubborn. "Just go on to bed. I'll be back later," he said as he left the room.

I cried from frustration and anxiety. I had antennae now for the nuances of Wayne's moods. I sensed that he was fighting the desire to go find narcotics. It was hard to pin down, but there was something alarming happening in him. I tried to reassure myself that he was just walking off his anger, but when he hadn't returned in an hour, I decided to go down to the lobby to see if I could find him.

It was 1:30 a.m., and the elevators were shut down for repairs. The desk clerk told me over the phone that I could use the exterior stairs to the ground and walk around to the lobby. When I got down to the street level, however, I discovered that I couldn't exit a locked gate onto the sidewalk. I climbed back to the 12th floor, checking the door on every floor. They were all locked. I was becoming more and more alarmed. It appeared I was locked outside of the building on the stairs. I felt panicky and vulnerable.

This day was taking on the pattern of Wayne's previous relapses: he would do something irrational and then I would try to find him. I vowed that if I got back in the building, I'd stay there. I realized now that *I* was acting irrationally, behaving out of fear, and putting myself at risk. I climbed to a higher floor and finally found an unlocked door. Thankfully, the elevators were operating again, and I got to my room safely.

When Wayne returned around 2 a.m., he didn't have much to say. I could tell he was having an internal battle, but he wouldn't talk about it. I was angry that he'd frightened me by being gone so long. I was honest and told him that he wasn't thinking of my feelings by putting himself at risk like that. He had no reply.

We continued our trip, but there were two other instances when he insisted on walking or shopping by himself. Each time he was gone longer than seemed reasonable. Things weren't adding up. Whether or not he had somehow purchased pills, I didn't know, but he was exhibiting the restless and impulsive characteristics of his previous relapses. His eyes didn't look glazed, but he wasn't himself.

As we flew home I reflected on the past few months. I knew that Wayne wasn't pursuing his recovery with the intentionality needed to remain sober. He was too quick to miss an AA meeting because he was "tired," and he declined meeting with a church recovery group that had started in Shreveport, though he had always said he preferred a more overtly spiritual support group. More than anything, I saw that the damaging emotion of self-pity had taken root in him.

I was also aware that spouses of addicts live without guarantees. Through my own healing I was still learning that I had to detach from his addiction. I had learned to tell myself the truth when I felt overwhelmed: *I can't control him. I can't make him sober. I can provide a supportive environment, but it's his battle. If I stay anxious and fearful, it won't improve his chances of sobriety one bit. It would only waste my energy and put more strain on our relationship. If I spend time arguing with him, he will tell himself that the battle is with me. I am learning that the battle is between Wayne and his chemicals. Lord, he's Yours.* When I prayed to God and talked to myself this way, I could manage the anxiety, at least some of the time.

After our return from Mexico, Wayne's depression returned. This time it didn't seem completely related to the headaches. He seemed to have reached a low point.

A few months earlier, Wayne had experienced several days of heavy depression. He consented to see a psychiatrist to be evaluated for an antidepressant. He'd come home with several surveys to fill out about his depression symptoms and said he'd seen a social worker for a pre-screening. He'd have an appointment with a psychiatrist in a month, and would take the surveys back then. By the time the date came around, the depressive episode had lifted, and he didn't keep the appointment. I'd forgotten about the surveys.

In early October Wayne complained of a toothache which flared over the weekend. By the time he went to the dentist on Monday morning, he had a full-blown abscess. The dentist sent him home with penicillin and pain medication, instructing him to stay in bed and return in three days. The abscess was too serious to open before the penicillin had several days to work. I suggested that Wayne call Tom and give him the pain medication. Tom could administer the prescribed amounts. Wayne rolled over in bed and ignored me. He didn't want anyone interfering with the control of his narcotics.

The phone rang in mid-October with bad news. Ken, a man who had been one of Wayne's close friends and mentors, had killed himself. We had known that Ken was struggling with depression and severe sleep apnea, but we didn't expect this. We were deeply shaken for several days. I worried about the impact this might have on Wayne. Ken's family asked Wayne to be a pallbearer at the funeral.

After attending the service, Wayne seemed to open up to me. "I won't kill myself, I assure you. I know you've been afraid that I would try that again," Wayne was sincere. His straightforward eye contact felt reassuring.

"You don't know how bad I need that reassurance from you," I said.

Wayne took my hands across the table in the restaurant. "I'm going to be all right." He said each word deliberately. "I took some pills last week, but I haven't gotten any more. I'm okay. Really." He didn't seem to be trying to deceive me or himself, and I chose to believe him. I could tell that *he* believed it.

Within two weeks I saw evidence that he was sunk again. He didn't come home from the store on time. He wasn't making eye contact. One evening after we'd closed the store, he told me to sit down; he needed to talk.

"JoAnn, I love you. I mean, I really love you. I want you to understand that. Do you hear me?" His voice was urgent.

I was puzzled at his sudden profession of devotion. Wayne had always told me that he loved me. But what was behind this mood?

"Listen," he seemed to plead, "You've got to know how much I love you."

I nodded. "I know you love me. Your using narcotics isn't about not loving me." I was trying to interpret this speech.

Wayne started sobbing and I held him. His defenses were down. A window was open into his soul. I felt a deep compassion for his struggle. *Fighting addiction is such torture. I see it in him. It causes him agony.* After several minutes of crying, he sat up.

We were in separate cars, and I left to pick up Hope from the babysitter. As I drove I wondered if the display of emotion I'd just seen meant that he was getting honest and letting his real emotions show. He looked broken. I hoped he was going to seek help.

Several days later I realized he had been drinking heavily. Alcohol wasn't Wayne's drug of choice, but he had abused it occasionally in previous relapses when he couldn't get narcotics to satiate himself. When I confronted him, he immediately came clean.

"I'm so tired of fighting this. I want to be with the Lord. I really think of heaven sometimes. I'm so depressed. I feel like I want to kill myself," his voice had an edge of despair. "But I'm not going to do it because I have you and I have Hope."

I was glad to hear the second part of that statement.

"Would you go to treatment before you really hit bottom all the way? You know it's only going to get worse." I was able to say it without any anger.

Surprisingly, he said "Yes."

I called the treatment center in Houston where Wayne had been before. I felt it was the only answer. Somehow we'd pay for it. Our dear friend, Tom, had offered any assistance we needed. I called him within an hour of hearing that Wayne could be admitted.

"Wayne says he'll go to treatment. Can you leave right away and drive us to Houston? I don't think I should try to take him there by myself."

"You bet," Tom was quick to answer. "Pick me up at my house on the curb in 30 minutes." It was already 10 p.m. Again I thanked God for friends who were willing to sacrificially serve us. Tom made the five-hour drive. Wayne was admitted to the treatment unit, and I slept on the back seat while Tom drove home.

When the phone rang the next afternoon, I immediately knew something was wrong. It was Wayne. He had checked himself out of the treatment center after only sixteen hours. He hung up abruptly. I was heartsick.

For three days I didn't know where he was. *Oh, God, this is so scary. If he buys illegal drugs on the street in Houston, he's sunk. He'll be back in prison. God, get him home safely.* I knew he had a lengthy felony record in Texas.

Finally, on the third day, he drove up our driveway at 11 p.m. He'd rented a car and come home. The suitcase and items he'd taken to the hospital were gone. He'd used so many narcotics that he couldn't find the motel where he'd been staying since leaving the hospital. His personal items were in a Houston hotel somewhere.

During the next week, he functioned erratically, but generally stayed either at the store or our house. Several friends called him to encourage him to seek help. He even sought help from a physician who was a recovering addict himself.

I felt helpless against Wayne's addiction. All I could do was to put up boundaries to keep Hope and me safe. I told Wayne that he absolutely could not drive with Hope in the car anymore. He meekly agreed. I had been angry with myself that I'd allowed him to pick up Hope from the babysitter several weeks before, later realizing that he'd been drinking. I promised myself that if he got arrested for driving under the influence, I wouldn't get him out of jail. It was time to get out of the way and let him fail. Maybe this would propel him toward seriously working on himself.

Courage for Lambs

On Tuesday morning, Wayne suddenly announced that he was going to drive to Baton Rouge to see his dad. This seemed impulsive and irrational to me. *Other than chaining him up, what choice do I have?* There was no way to prevent him from going. I'd begun to worry that Wayne would put our store assets at risk when he relapsed. He'd never taken money out before, but I felt it coming. I panicked when he told me he had our gold jewelry inventory in the car and was taking it to Baton Rouge with him. He planned to sell a few pieces to his dad's friends. I knew this was a terrible risk. He might lose the jewelry, inadvertently allow someone to steal it, or pawn it for narcotics money.

While he was taking a shower I removed the jewelry from his truck and hid it in the house. I knew he'd be very angry with me, but I had to protect both of us. I knew losing or abusing the jewelry assets would only be another reason for him to feel guilty when he was sober again. I had grown bold enough to protect our family assets when he wasn't being rational. When I told him he wasn't taking the jewelry, he was livid.

"Give it back to me right now!" Wayne demanded angrily.

"I'm not going to let you do that. Period!" My resolve surprised him.

Within minutes he quieted down. I could see that he was on pills and his moods shifted rapidly. He played gently with Hope on the bed for a while. I stood silently and watched. I knew what a good father he was. *How ironic that drugs can steal so much.*

"Well, I'm leaving now. I need to see my dad. I'll probably be back home by Friday."

I knew it was crazy for him to be leaving for Baton Rouge, but there was nothing I could do. I lay down on the bed beside Hope.

"Well, let me pray for you," I offered. I was resigned to the only option I had.

Wayne surprised me by lying on top of me, and I put my arms around him. For a minute he was humble. For a minute he received my love and the prayer I offered out loud. He kissed me goodbye, then got up and walked out.

It was the last time I would see him alive.

Remaining anxious and fearful about another person's chemical dependency does not improve his chances for sobriety. The hard truth is that you cannot control him or make him sober. You must not allow him to abuse you or the relationship; it will only add to his shame and self-hatred.

For more understanding about the dynamics of confronting other's addictions, see Essay #9: Wise as Serpents.

To let go
is to admit
powerlessness,
which means the
outcome
is not in
my hands.

Author unknown

CHAPTER 27
Human Frailty

When Wayne left a message on the answering machine Thursday evening, his voice sounded positive. "I've been visiting with Betsy and Jim," he said, "and I should be home by 6:30." I was relieved that he'd stopped by to see our friends. I sensed that he'd been avoiding them whenever he relapsed. Going to see them could only be a positive influence. I settled Hope in her high chair and began feeding her supper.

During the past days I'd talked to Wayne several times while he was in Baton Rouge. Once when Wayne was out shopping, his dad reported to me that Wayne had been especially restless, had paced around his apartment at night, and hadn't slept well. I really didn't know what shape he'd be in when he arrived home.

By 10:00 p.m. I hadn't seen or heard anything from him. I was anxious.

"He left here at 5," Betsy said when I called her to check. She said that their visit had been good.

"Well, I'll let you know when he comes in."

As I went to bed alone that night I repeated the exercise in prayer that had brought me peace. *Lord, You love Wayne more than I do. You loved him even before I did. He's Yours, Lord. He's just Yours.* As I repeated this prayer several times a day, I often raised my hands and motioned as if I was handing Wayne to God. It was a simple prayer of commitment and surrender. It was the only prayer I could think of. I talked to myself in affirmations as I tried to fall asleep. *It won't do any good to lie awake worrying. It won't help Wayne. It will only exhaust me. I have a two-year-old to take care of. I've got to get some sleep. I've committed Wayne to God.*

At the store the next morning, Wayne's voice sounded strange on the phone. "I got arrested on the way home last night for driving under the influence. I'm in the jail in Coushatta. My truck is impounded. I need you to bring $280 in cash and post my bond. Come get me OUT!" He had been refused bail by a local bail bondsman because he didn't have enough cash on him.

I was caught off guard by the sudden jolt of his voice on the phone. "I'm not sure what I'm gonna do," I responded tentatively.

"What? What do you mean?"

"I mean that I don't know if I'm coming to get you out. I have to think about it."

Wayne's tone became demanding. I quickly interrupted and told him to call back in two hours. I hung up before he could protest anymore.

I knew immediately that I wouldn't bail him out, but I needed time to strengthen my resolve. I called several friends and asked them to pray for me. This was one of the hardest things I had ever done. I knew I'd have to withstand Wayne's wrath over this one. He wouldn't be expecting me to toe such a hard line. But I knew that rescuing addicts from a crisis was one of the worst things families could do. I was willing to weather the embarrassment of his being in jail. It might wake him up. Everyone I talked to was supportive of my decision.

When he called back later, I delivered the news. He was irate. He said the predictable things: "This proves you don't love me. You must want to divorce me…" and on and on.

I repeated a phrase that I'd actually practiced for such an occasion. "I'm not going to divorce you because this isn't a marriage problem. This is *your* chemical dependency problem." I tried to mask my anxiety with a resolute tone. I told Wayne that I'd drive to the jail the next day and bring the items allowed: toothbrush, Bible, underwear. I ended the conversation as quickly as possible.

I hated the nastiness of his words. Part of me had wanted to wilt and beg him to stop talking like that. Another more mature part of me knew that it was the drugs talking again. I tried not to absorb his anger. I was shaken but had held my ground.

I had been learning during the past six years that I didn't have to live by my feelings. I was still frightened at what was happening and hurt by Wayne's harshness, but I had learned to act for our welfare in spite of being scared.

Without bail, Wayne would have to stay in jail at least a week until he went before the judge and was sentenced or fined. That was good. At least I knew where he was. Maybe he'd detox over several days and would make a decision for long-term treatment. Maybe the judge would order him to a treatment program if I informed him of Wayne's history. I could see several ways that this trip to jail might be leveraged for good. Nevertheless, the circumstances were rotten. We weren't out of the crisis yet. Although I was convinced that I was doing the right thing, I wished that it didn't feel so crummy.

The next day I drove the 40 miles to the jail to deliver his Bible and toothbrush. I took a friend, Brenda, for moral support. I was relieved when I got there to find that he wasn't allowed visitors. I was sure he was in withdrawal from the narcotics and wouldn't be rational. He'd just take out his anger on me again. A deputy told me Wayne had been pacing for hours. Wayne had said that his chest was hurting last night, and the deputy took him to the hospital to be checked out. The deputy reported that Wayne hadn't slept much at all. *He's in withdrawal. I've seen him experience this before.*

That evening I repeated my prayers again. *Lord, he's Yours.* Even though I prayed earnestly, I couldn't shake the anxiety. *I'm so worn down by all of this. How much longer can he keep relapsing?*

At 10:00 p.m. the phone rang. It was Wayne. "I'm at the store," he stated flatly. I was instantly alarmed. *How had he gotten out of jail?* "A bail bondsman from Minden drove down and bailed me out. I paid him when I got to the store," he said with satisfaction.

"Well, I'm coming to get you and bring you home." I figured that nothing positive could happen until he slept. From what I had gleaned from his dad and the deputy, Wayne hadn't slept much in five days. I didn't want him sleeping at the store. Another part of me feared that he might take the money from the store and leave. Although I had no idea what to do next, I wanted him at home tonight.

"I don't want you to get Hope out of bed," he sounded considerate for a moment. "I'll go to bed here on the couch."

For the next twenty minutes our conversation wandered over the topics that I expected him to address. He was insulted that I hadn't gotten him out of jail. Typical of an addict's mentality, he blamed me for everything he'd been through. Didn't I know how traumatic being in jail again was for him? He wondered if we should get divorced. He expressed both sorrow that he was putting me through this and later disappointment that no one understood him.

As he talked, I realized that he wasn't rational and he'd probably been drinking since he got back to the store. I told him several times that I loved him and that we didn't need to divorce because the *real* problem was his chemical dependency, not our marriage. I wanted him to hear my commitment as a wife while stating the problem clearly. He briefly mentioned that he loved God, and I reassured him that I knew this. I could sense the war between his addiction and his heart. After repeating some of the comments several times, I realized that we weren't making any headway. Nothing positive would happen until he'd had some sleep. I said goodnight and hung up.

I'll never get to sleep. Fear came over me in waves. I dreaded this lasting longer.

I did my best to say my prayers and repeat my sleeping affirmations. *If I stay up worrying, it won't prove anything. I've got to stay sharp. I've got to sleep and take care of Hope.* It was hard to shake the fear. Finally I fell asleep.

About 1:30 a.m. I had a terrible nightmare. In the dream I was being led before an execution squad. Someone covered my head with a black hood and in the dream I knew I would be shot soon. I awoke frightened and sweaty. I'd never had such a vicious nightmare. This time I called on God earnestly. I repeated my affirmations, but it took me an hour or so to fall asleep again. I felt helpless and frightened.

I awoke Sunday morning before Hope got up. Within minutes I called the store to check on Wayne. No answer. I thought about it. Maybe he had walked to a nearby grocery store for coffee or breakfast. He didn't have his truck. Another option was even more frightening. Maybe he'd run. I thought of how he'd been in Houston for three days, high on narcotics. He may have taken some store money and left on foot. Finally, I decided that he might be out cold on the couch in our office due to his lack of sleep. The phone wasn't waking him up. I called again an hour later but still no answer.

I had learned from Al-Anon support groups that family members have to carry on with their lives. I needed to see my church family and be encouraged at church. I dressed Hope and myself and headed for town. I'd look in on Wayne briefly. I quieted my fear by concluding he had to be asleep.

I drove up to the front of the store, parked by the curb, and left Hope sitting in her car seat. I was going to jump out, run and check on him, and jump back in the car in 60 seconds. I didn't want Hope to see him because she had been asking for him. She'd cry if she saw him and wouldn't be allowed to wake him up. I quickly unlocked the front door and started around the checkout counter. All the store lights were on.

Immediately, I saw Wayne lying face down on the floor. I froze. I watched for breathing, but there wasn't any. I think I knew, but I didn't want to know. I saw a small amount of blood on the floor. I didn't want to touch him. I ran out and locked the door. I had to get help.

Several stores down I saw a group of people waiting for the discount store to open. I drove up, jumped out and used a pay phone. "I need the police," I stammered to the operator. "I think my husband is dead!"

I called Tom and Dorothy, who only lived minutes away. "Tom, I think Wayne is dead. Please come here now!" I was getting hysterical.

A young man overheard my conversation. "Ma'am, I'm a policeman. What's wrong?"

"My husband is in our store down there. But I think he's dead!" I pointed to our shop. He took my keys and started running toward the store. I could already hear the police sirens coming. I drove back to the front of the store but couldn't bear to go back in. Several police cars and an ambulance arrived. One policeman started taking information and asked me what I thought had happened. I could hardly bear to say it.

"I think that maybe he killed himself."

Tom arrived and I said, "Get us out of here. Take us to your house." After clearing this with the police, we left.

We live in a fallen world. Despite the reality of a God who is good, we must deal with the repercussions of human frailty.

Dear Reader:

I didn't want to break your heart.

You've rooted me on to my healing,
and you want to see my life be good now.

If this were a novel, I would never have written another sad part.

In fiction the character can have a bad time of it,
but if the author makes it too sad, the publisher will say, "It won't sell."

How I wish it were fiction now.

Real life is too painful.

> JoAnn Nishimoto
> (As I'm writing the book, 2003)

CHAPTER 28

Ultimate Pain

Earlier that morning my mother had awakened at her home with a sense of doom. Like everyone in the family, she had reached a feeling of helplessness about Wayne's addiction. Her mind kept returning to the morbid thought: *Where are we going to bury Wayne?* She tried to shake the hideous idea, but it returned several times. She flung open the curtains to let some sunlight in and lift her mood, but she had a sense of foreboding she couldn't shake. Within an hour I phoned with the terrible news.

Word travels fast in a small town. As First Baptist Church was about to begin the Sunday morning worship service, someone phoned my pastor with information about Wayne's death. When Pastor Rick stood up to begin the morning service, he shared the tragic news with our congregation.

"We're going to have a different service this morning," he somberly told the 500 attendees. "We're going to pray for JoAnn and her family." In his sermon he compassionately spoke of Wayne's struggles without being judgmental. The service dismissed early and nearly 30 people headed to the store to support me.

Meanwhile the police were ruling out robbery or homicide. Tom and Dorothy accompanied me back to the store. Wayne's body had been removed. I was informed of the mandatory autopsy in these cases. The police seemed compassionate. They gently confirmed that Wayne had killed himself. The horror of such an act left me bewildered. It was unthinkable.

The coroner reported that Wayne had been dead at least eight hours. I felt jolted. The timing coincided with the evil nightmare I had in the night. In our spiritual unity as husband and wife, had I sensed the anguish of his death?

Walking out of the store, I was moved to see the many friends who had gathered. I walked into their open arms. My parents arrived from their home 20 miles away.

As my mother drove me home the anguish built within me. After several miles I blurted out, "Aren't we HOME YET? I CAN'T STAND THIS!" It was a senseless comment erupting from my overwhelmed mind.

The afternoon passed with compassionate supporters in and out of the house. Wayne's mother and stepfather arrived. Relatives were phoned. My sister, Helen, would fly in tomorrow. Sam, Mary, and the children were coming from Saudi Arabia. I repeated to everyone the history of the last three weeks, trying to remember the chain of events. For most of the day I just sat on my couch with an afghan around me.

Late that evening, Dorothy and Tom drove out to my house.

"Tonight while I was in church," Dorothy said, "I had a vision. It came to me while I was worshipping." She went on to say that, in the vision, she had seen

Wayne running toward a source of bright light, his face transformed with surprise and joy. Dark shards fell off him as he ran, and his clothing became a brilliant white garment. "He was running toward the Lord," Dorothy spoke tenderly.

I already knew that Wayne was with the Lord, but the comforting imagery of Dorothy's vision brought me some peace. *He's at rest now. He lost the battle but he didn't lose the war. He's safe with the Lord.*

In the preceding year Wayne and I had a discussion about people who claim to see visions from God. We had both known hucksters who reported visions to make themselves look more spiritual. I'd had similar experiences with Hansen. Wayne had also witnessed several people who claimed to have visions but had erratic lives which didn't confirm a real commitment to Christ. Wayne stated that he really didn't believe in the validity of visions, but commented, "Now if *Dorothy* had a vision, I'd believe it." Wayne was reflecting on the consistency of Dorothy's spiritual life, humility, and credibility. However, I had never passed the compliment on to her. *How appropriate that Dorothy should come to tell me this. Without the hope that he was at peace now, how could I go on?*

Betsy agreed to stay and spend the night with me. As the person who had led Wayne to Christ, she had loved him for nine years. She felt his death keenly with me. As we laid in bed, we held hands. Neither of us could sleep, and we exchanged words off and on through the night.

Emotionally I felt like Wayne and I had both been in the battle. He had died, but I had an image of myself being carried off the battlefield by my friends and family, having done battle for him. I was exhausted and broken. I had fought valiantly, but lost. Lying in bed, I had pain in my chest. My spirit felt crushed. I groaned in the horror of this unspeakable defeat.

I moved through making the arrangements for the burial and memorial service like a person in a dream. *Am I imagining this? He can't really be dead!* When I walked into a room with 20 caskets, I felt nauseated.

As 48 hours passed, I woke Tuesday morning with a sense of peace. Though it was temporary, it was a welcome reprieve. *I can feel people praying for me.* I knew that I wanted to share at the memorial service. I wanted to tell Wayne's story.

I insisted on being alone when I went to view Wayne's body. There was something that I needed to say to him. I had the overwhelming sense that he had made a bad choice in taking his life. He had been impulsive. Now he had crossed the point of no return. It couldn't be undone. He had ended all the things that God had intended for him to do in his life. His choice had been shortsighted. He hadn't listened or humbled himself. It wasn't an unforgivable sin for him to have killed himself, but it *was* a sin. I felt that God was very grieved that Wayne had made this choice.

"I forgive you," I said aloud while viewing his body. I said it as an act of my will. I didn't know then forgiveness would be an ongoing process that would work itself out through the various parts of my life.

Without even being conscious of it, I was making decisions to face his death in an open and forthright way. I had spent the last six years being honest about life. I would continue. I would be honest about what had happened.

At the funeral service I told Wayne's story: how he became addicted to drugs, was incarcerated, and how he converted to Christ. I wanted people to remember *all* of him, and not to define his life by how he had died. I shared four threads that ran strongly through Wayne's life. First, he was often offended by racial prejudice, especially when churches were still so racially segregated in the South. Loving people of every race had been one of Wayne's strengths. Second, he thought that we should wear blue jeans to church! Wayne had been good at spotting anything superficial about church, and he resisted the idea of emphasizing appearance. Third, he would tell everyone who would listen not to tamper with drugs or alcohol, because from the moment he tried drugs, they controlled him. Last, he would tell others that he knew Jesus Christ to be real.

The day after the funeral was Thanksgiving Day, 1994. Intense pain alternated with periods of numbness.

"Where's Daddy?" Hope asked.

"Honey, he's in heaven now." I steeled myself to answer her question without beginning to cry. "He's gone to live with Jesus," I said slowly, wondering what her reaction would be.

Hope paused, then went on to her next question. "Can I have a cracker?"

I was relieved that at two years and two months old, she didn't seem to understand what had happened. She was preoccupied with her cousins and all the attention she'd been getting. *At least it doesn't seem that she is emotionally suffering.* I was both thankful and tearful that she was so young. I distracted her so she wouldn't see me crying. I felt deeply saddened that she wouldn't remember her own daddy.

Wayne's truck had been impounded because of the DUI arrest, but a friend retrieved it and brought it home to me. Joe mentioned that when he got in the truck and started it, Wayne's cassette tape of the Brooklyn Tabernacle Choir had boomed on. It had been a tape that we played often in the store and I knew Wayne loved it. I thought of the irony of it all. There was the very authentic part of Wayne that was reaching out to God, seeking hope, and hungering for freedom from addiction. Even under the influence of narcotics, he was riding down the road playing that tape. Another part of him had grown weary and hopeless, and he bought into the lie that there was no other way out.

As I picked through the trash in the truck, I found several pill bottles indicating Wayne had been to more doctors during the past week in Baton Rouge. As I had suspected, he had been out of control. He must have thought there was no other way to stop himself.

I thought back to the evening two weeks earlier, when he'd told me so vehemently that he loved me. It felt clear now: he had made up his mind then to kill himself. He wanted me to know that it wasn't because he didn't love me. He had expressed his love so plainly. He was telling me goodbye.

Wayne! Why didn't you reach out and take the help that was offered? Why did you let pride and denial make you refuse the treatment program? You could have worked on yourself! You could have gotten back to that place of victory you once had! But you quit talking and shut down. You turned inward. You listened to shame!

> There are about 30,000 documented suicides in the U.S. each year. In a city of 100,000 persons, approximately 12 of them will die by suicide in a given year. Drug or alcohol abuse is a factor in nearly one half of all suicides. Visit www.cdc.gov for additional statistics on suicide.

When someone you love commits suicide,
he hangs his emotional skeleton in your closet.

> A saying I heard somewhere

CHAPTER 29

An Open Grief

My grief over Wayne was an open grief. Two days after the funeral I had to reopen the store for the Christmas retail season. I knew that if retailers don't make money in December, they go under. I had no choice but to carry on in the store and cry my tears in front of the customers.

Wayne's workbench in the store seemed so empty. Nearly every day a customer expressed deep sorrow over his death and we cried openly together. If I stayed at home in a self-protective cocoon, I could avoid the embarrassment of my red eyes and nose, but I'd be missing out on the love others were offering. I knew I had to stay at the store.

Occasionally someone came in the store who didn't know about Wayne's death, and there was shock and grief when I told them. It was clear that I wouldn't be wearing eye makeup for some time. My face was continually taut, either from crying or from sadness. The grief felt like a mask on my face.

Keeping busy at the store was the best thing I could do. Thankfully, community support was strong. One of my friends said, "I'm telling everyone that I'm buying all my Christmas gifts at the Olive Branch this year." I quickly hired several friends as part-time employees to help with the holiday rush.

The trauma of the "death scene" seemed to haunt me. In that brief moment when I saw Wayne's body on the floor, my mind had taken a snapshot of the scene. This picture was continuously on my mind from the time I woke up in the morning until I went to sleep at night. The movie projector in my head was stuck on that one frame. As troubling as it was, I couldn't shake it. It seemed I couldn't choose *not* to think about it. Even if I was looking at someone, his or her face was just superimposed on the death scene in my head. I tried praying it away and talking about it, but the image remained. It seemed to be part of the shock and trauma of finding him dead. I later learned that this was a trauma symptom pointing to Post Traumatic Stress Disorder (PTSD).

Putting Hope to bed one night, I noticed that it was only 8 p.m. Once she was asleep, the hours passed in slow motion. This was the worst part of the day. It would be at least midnight before I'd be able to fall asleep. I knew that once I went to sleep, I'd wake up after only four or five hours. Sleeping was the only relief from my emotional agony, and I longed for the escape. I understood, for the first time, why drinking oneself numb could seem attractive. Although I didn't consume any alcohol, I longed for an escape from the pain. Facing this enormous grief was exhausting.

I called my white German shepherd, Ellie Mae, in from the porch. I had always found my dogs to be a source of comfort. Lying beside her on the floor, I buried my face in the thick ruff of her neck. I could smell the earthy scent of her fur, and I cried there. Ellie Mae always seemed to offer her compassion.

Restlessly passing the evening, I watched the memorial service on videotape. I was trying to accept it as real. *That's me on the tape and this is Wayne's funeral.* Part of me still couldn't believe it. In the unreality and shock of his sudden death, it was easy to imagine that the phone might ring and it would be Wayne, or a car pulling up in the driveway might be him.

Although I sold Wayne's truck locally about six weeks after his death, the first time I spotted it in town I was shocked. I almost wanted to tail the driver, hoping it would be Wayne. If only for an instant, I could imagine that he wasn't dead. I paused and cried for a few minutes. It was one of the hundreds of "firsts" that happened after he died: the first time I saw his car without him in it, the first time a full moon came and he wasn't there to take me and Hope for a walk, the first time I visited his aunt and uncle without him… The "firsts" went on and on.

Initially, it seemed simple enough to understand Wayne's death in terms of his hopelessness over the narcotics. He'd grown tired of fighting and had given up. In his war against addiction, the balance on the scales had tipped…he had come to believe that there was no going back. However, as the weeks began to pass, the mystery and burden of his death seemed to grow larger. I began to question myself.

The "what ifs" were difficult to wrestle with. They seemed to be rational arguments that confronted my overwhelmed mind and emotions. *What if I had been easier on him and bailed him out of jail? Maybe he felt abandoned by me and this brought him more despair that night. What if I'd been tougher on him and demanded that he go to long-term treatment in Arkansas or I'd file for separation?* Easier? Tougher? I could play the arguments either way.

I thought back to the night he'd called…our last conversation. I couldn't remember if I'd said another "I love you" right before I hung up the phone. *Maybe one more "I love you" would have been the eye-opening one. Maybe it would have held him to life.* It seemed impossible to keep my mind from spinning in this self-condemning argument. I felt guilty for not saving him. I tried to console myself that at least he wasn't struggling and suffering any more with his addiction. *I'm relieved that his struggles are over.* Immediately the toxic guilt bit again: *I feel guilty for being relieved that he's dead.* There seemed to be no answers and no escape from the guilt monster.

In addition to being his spouse and the one who knew him best, I was also a professional counselor. I'd recently been seeing clients who were depressed. *I should have known better than anyone how to help him. Not only have I failed Wayne,* I thought, *but I also don't deserve to be a therapist anymore.* Wayne's death seemed to prove to me that I couldn't help anyone. As a therapist, I now felt disqualified. *I understand if people don't want me as their counselor anymore.* I believed this and told myself that I would not practice again.

By the end of the first month I was plunging into even more questions. They were all dark and scary. I called a female therapist I'd met in town and told her I needed help. Sitting in her office, I exhaled my pain freely. The sessions were helpful. It was humbling to go from being the counselor to being the counselee.

As Christmas approached a month after Wayne's death, I had no heart for giving or receiving gifts. Hope's grandparents had assured me that they had several gifts for her, and nothing else seemed to matter. The only thoughts that brought any comfort were thoughts of Christ being born, coming to earth as our Savior, and making a way for us to have eternal life. *I'm so glad Jesus came. I'm so glad Jesus came.* It was my newest affirmation, and it brought me comfort. I must have repeated it hundreds of times.

About 8:30 p.m. on December 23rd, I had just put Hope to bed. I could hear a truck engine approaching down my gravel driveway, and as I peered out the window I saw the UPS delivery truck driving up. *Gee, those poor delivery guys work late during the holidays.* The driver handed me a "rush" parcel. It was from family friends in Colorado. As I had never received a gift from them before, I decided they must have heard about Wayne's death through my mom and were sending me a love gift to cheer me up.

When I opened the box, I discovered a beautifully wrapped gift embedded in packing noodles. *It looks like it's from an expensive department store.* I studied the elegant bow and attached decoration. *It's really beautiful. The package is so light, I wonder what it could be?* I opened the gift-wrap and peered inside the box, searching through the layers of colored tissue paper. *Where's the gift?* Suddenly I realized that there was only a 16-inch piece of ribbon inside. Lying in the beautiful paper, this was the only item in the box. *Did they forget the gift?* I looked at the ribbon. Lettered in script handwriting were the words, "Tidings of comfort and joy." *I don't get it. They paid to rush this package, spent $10 to beautifully wrap it, and just put this ribbon in?* I paused to try to understand.

In a moment of quiet knowing the meaning began to emerge. *They are telling me that the good news of Jesus coming...the tidings of comfort and joy...is the one thing they can offer me. They know other gifts feel meaningless right now. They wrapped it this way because it is such a precious gift...it deserves to be wrapped like the valuable gift that it is. They rushed it because it is urgent news. Oh, now I get it.*

I rummaged in a drawer to find thumb tacks and immediately tacked the ribbon on the wall of my bedroom. *I'm so glad Jesus came. There is hope to redeem the pain in this life. Heaven feels closer now knowing Wayne is there.* I had always believed in heaven and the promise of redemption, but this Christmas I clung to it like a lifeline.

> **Truths about God and life are often highlighted when pain has awakened us.**

*Suicide doesn't end pain.
It only lays it on the broken shoulders of the survivors.*

Anne-Grace Scheinin

Quoted by Albert Y. Hsu
*Grieving a Suicide:
A Loved One's Search for Comfort, Answers and Hope*
IVP Books, 2002

CHAPTER 30
Solitary Grief

Whenever there was opportunity to talk about Wayne, I did. I didn't want others to forget him too soon. I didn't want people to avoid talking about him, although I could tell that some were uncomfortable with the topic of suicide. I *needed* to talk about him. The negative burden of his suicide had brought such intense pain and guilt. I desperately tried to balance the scales by validating the contributions I had made to his life, and the ones he had made to mine. There was so much to wade through, but as I talked about him, I was able to resolve small pieces of pain at a time.

As 1995 began I realized that everyone else was returning to normal life except me. My agony seemed to be getting more intense as the two month mark rolled around. I had previously thought that I was miserable emotionally, but now it was even worse. The first two months after his death I had been partially shielded from grief and pain by the mechanisms of denial and shock. Now the storm broke in full force.

One morning I awoke and listened to see if Hope was stirring in her room. I checked the clock. Normally she would be awake by now and would have cheerfully called "Maaa-Ma" from her room. I lay in bed with a sense of impending doom. *I'm so afraid that she's dead.* Given the shattering of my life in the previous months, imagining more tragedy seemed rational. I quietly walked to her room where I found her still sleeping. *I feel afraid of everything. When will the next bad thing happen?* I later learned that these obsessive thoughts were part of the emotional aftershocks of trauma.

I had begun reading a book about recovery after the suicide of a loved one. I also wanted to talk to others who had been through it. On a sheet of paper I made a list of people I knew who had experienced a suicide in their family. I searched my memory for the times I had heard suicide mentioned in our community. I could think of one friend's father, someone's brother, and several others. Given the people I knew in my large church alone, I could think of seven people who had experienced suicide in their extended families. I determined to call each of them for help. I wanted to know what they had learned and how they answered certain gnawing questions.

During the next several weeks I made contact with these families. The responses ranged from small consolations to those who didn't respond to my calls. No one offered anything of wisdom or substance. *No one knows how to talk about this. People aren't healed. This is such an emotionally-laden topic. Some of them are avoiding me.* I began to feel the awkwardness of being a survivor of suicide. *People don't know what to do with me.* I longed for someone who wasn't afraid to talk about the troubling questions.

Mom and I went to order the headstone for Wayne's grave. Answering trivial questions seemed intolerable, and salespersons, even though well meaning, felt intrusive. I found myself disliking the salesman.

"And what is your husband's date of birth?" The salesman queried me for the information I wanted on the grave marker.

"January 16, 1953."

"Why, today is his birthday," he said casually.

In my grief over having to even perform this task, I felt that the salesman was insensitive. *What a stupid comment! Doesn't he have any idea how hard it is to face Wayne's birthday without him?* Normally a person who saw and complimented the good in others, I now felt judgmental and cynical. My frayed emotions couldn't cut any slack that the guy was just doing his job.

I explained to the salesman that I wanted the marker to read "Jesus Christ Saved Me" under Wayne's name and the dates. I had thought about this for some time. If Wayne could come back from heaven and say something, this would be the one all-inclusive thing of importance. Regardless of Wayne's addiction, struggles, brokenness, and frailty, the grace and power of Jesus Christ transcended all. It was a statement of comfort that brought me peace. When Hope was old enough to comprehend this, it would comfort her, too. The salesman seemed puzzled, but wrote up the order.

"Did you bring a copy of the death certificate?"

"Here it is." My voice sounded monotone these days. The burden of grief made ordinary tasks like talking feel like hard work.

Whenever I had to show Wayne's death certificate, I felt vulnerable and exposed. I felt that strangers would gawk as they read it. On the line where "manner of death" was checked, there was a large "X" in the "Suicide" box. In another box there was a description of his wound.

Getting the death certificate in the mail had itself been traumatizing. Now I had the official document. Here it was in black and white. After the incident with the salesman, I felt even more self-conscious about the death certificate. I didn't want anyone seeing it or gossiping over the details. When the bank called to say I couldn't close our joint account without a copy of the death certificate, I fretted for weeks about taking a copy to them. I pictured the bank tellers crowding around it to learn the details. Although this was probably exaggerated, it highlighted the pain and stigma that I was feeling about Wayne's suicide.

One day, when I was feeling a little more self-confident, I went to the bank with a photocopy of the death certificate. I had copied the official one and covered the details I didn't want others to know.

"But we need an official copy," the bank officer countered.

"This is enough." I stated with some self-protection.

He took it.

I spent evenings going through Wayne's things. In his dresser drawer I found the survey he'd brought home from the social worker six months before his death.

I was shocked that he'd answered so many questions in a way that indicated he had seriously considered suicide at that time. "Yes," he was having thoughts of ending his life. "Yes," he thought others would be better off without him. *He had been struggling with this for some time. Why didn't he keep the follow-up appointment?* I was beginning to feel angry with him.

As the weeks passed, the number of issues I was wrestling with only seemed to grow. I felt intense longing for Wayne that could snowball during the day to anguish. I couldn't seem to find anything to alleviate it. Sometimes at night I laid in bed and moaned.

I was beginning to have irrational thoughts. I fantasized about going to the cemetery and digging him up, just to see him again. Although I strongly believed that his soul was in heaven with Christ, I would settle for just seeing his body. Part of me knew that I really wouldn't act this out, but there was some satisfaction in dreaming about it. I didn't want to stop this fantasy; it seemed to have its place. In lieu of this, the best thing I could think of to make a connection with him was to put on one of his shirts, spray some of his cologne on his pillow, curl up with it, and cry myself to sleep.

At times I felt the soft love for Wayne that had always endeared him to me. I remembered how he'd supported me in my emotional recovery after the abuse. Someone less honest and broken than he might not have understood me. He'd been such a positive influence in my healing. He'd always cheered me on.

Then, as I hit the third and fourth month following his death, I began to feel mad at Wayne. It seemed my tender feelings were shifting. I had learned from my past recovery that I could give myself permission to feel my hurt and anger. I could be angry with Wayne for choosing this act without vilifying him.

"Wayne left me and he left Hope," I voiced my anger to my friend, Brenda. I appreciated her company several nights a week, especially in the lonely hours after Hope went to bed. "It doesn't fit. How can a man who says he deeply loves you just leave you like that? He could have addressed his addiction and faced it... others do." Brenda patiently let me vent my feelings. "I'm angry that he didn't take advantage of all the opportunities he had."

There was a lot of truth in this. Wayne didn't *have* to die. He didn't *have* to leave Hope without a father. He didn't *have* to leave us with the emotional burden of suicide.

"He was my partner in healing, and he quit on me." I fidgeted around the kitchen, crying while I tried to make popcorn for us. I was too agitated to complete the process.

"Could you stay here with Hope for a couple of hours?" I asked Brenda. "I need to go for a ride and be alone."

"Sure." Brenda could tell I was bursting with a mixture of anger and grief. She knew that although there were some things she could do for me, there were other things I had to wrestle through alone.

When I left the house I wasn't immediately sure where I was going. But as I drove along the idea grew stronger that I wanted to go to the cemetery and give Wayne a piece of my mind. I was furious with him. *How dare he leave me! How dare he quit on his recovery!* I got out of the car near his grave, hot tears of anger streaming down my face. I knew I had to get these feelings out or they would poison me.

I only know three curse words, but that evening I got a lot of mileage out of them.

> **Suicide is so complicated. At least when a loved one is murdered, you can vent your anger toward the killer while mourning the loss of the one you loved. In suicide, this is one and the same person.**

It takes courage to live...
courage and strength and hope and humor.

And courage and strength and hope and humor
have to be bought and paid for with
pain and work and prayer and tears.

Jerome P. Fleishman

CHAPTER 31
Tantrum

After exhausting my anger at Wayne over several months, I felt calmer but more depressed. A certain cynicism pervaded my thoughts. *I won't ever be happy again. No one can be happy after something like this.* Eventually this faded into an obstinate self-defeating attitude.

"I'll show Wayne that he went too far. I don't care if I'm ever happy again. I know that's a sick attitude, but that's how I feel," I told my friend, Ginger, on the phone.

Ginger knew she'd get further with me by acknowledging my pain than by chiding me for being irrational. "Well, honey, I'm sure you sometimes feel like you don't have any hope."

At that same moment Hope started pulling on my leg to get me off of the telephone. She was tired of me being on the phone and wanted my attention. The irony struck me all at once.

"Well, it's funny," I managed a laugh, "But I have 32 pounds of 'hope' pulling my leg right now."

Taking care of Hope did soften the incredible burden of sorrow. At two and a half years old, she was jabbering continuously and learning new words every week. She was outgoing and busy, and it took a great deal of time to chase her around. She was a beautiful child and seemed to attract people wherever we went. I was painfully aware at times that I felt mechanical with her. My grief was often so intense it wouldn't permit room for the normal joy of mothering a toddler. However, as I went through the motions of caring for her, occasionally a little joy broke through. *She deserves an emotionally healthy mother. I've got to get well. I'll do it for her even though I don't always want to do it for myself.*

I continued to read my grief and suicide recovery books. I knew I needed the objectivity of the books to help anchor myself in the truth. Through reading I could see that Wayne's choice wasn't good or rational, but it was *his* choice, not mine. I read that although I had a lot of influence in my loved one's life, that influence was *limited*. I learned that my agony was normal, given the trauma of suicide. Although I was a therapist myself, I had to lay aside my textbook learning and become a real-life student of grief.

Being a suicide survivor was to become a member of a fraternity of people that I never wanted to join. I had read that there are 30,000 documented suicides in the U.S. each year. Now it was *my* husband, *my* life, *my* agony. The impact of

Wayne's death had been like an explosion. It had sucked out of me all my positive feelings about life, God, and myself. Now I had to dedicate myself to working hard to get these back.

As I exhausted my anger at Wayne, I seemed to turn my anger at God. *Why didn't God prevent the suicide? Why were other addicts, with less devotion to Christ than Wayne, still alive and again sober after their relapses? Hadn't I done my suffering in life already?* I knew I was secure enough in the love of God that my anger wouldn't hurt Him, but any phoniness in my faith would hurt me. I'd have to be honest with Him. I wanted genuine healing in the end, not a cosmetic healing that hid a shattered faith or a simmering anger at God.

One evening after I put Hope to bed I decided to have it out with God. I closed all the doors between my room and Hope's and got on the floor. I was ready to throw a tantrum and tell God just how mad I was. I would flail my arms and legs and pound on the floor. I'd seen Hope throw a few tantrums two-year-old style in the last year, so I went at it. After yelling and kicking for some minutes, I exhausted myself. Without conscious effort I opened my mouth and spontaneously said, "I love you, God." I felt a touch of peace, but more of a knowing. God knew. He could hold me through the rage.

As spring turned to early summer, I found myself wanting to revisit places I had been with Wayne, reliving the good years we had. These rituals of mourning gave me something to do. I canoed the bayou again, this time with Brenda, and remembered the early spring day when Wayne and I were just beginning our relationship. I returned to familiar places and reflected on the times Wayne and I were there. I planned weekend trips with Hope to visit friends and keep myself busy. I still found myself fighting depression, but looking forward to these trips seemed to help.

My mind began to clear a little. I discussed my mental battles with friends and family, talking out the issues I was trying to resolve. From my own recovery (after Hansen's abuse) and from my counseling experience, I knew that talking was central to healing. Although rationally I knew that Wayne's suicide wasn't my fault, this truth was taking a long time to work its way through to my emotions. I was learning to give up the illusion that I could have been omnipotent, or could have prevented the choice that he made. *What I did or didn't do did not cause Wayne to take his life.* More and more I was able to think of Wayne's death without irrational guilt. My anger had previously been so strong when I thought: *Why did he leave me?* Now I could ask another question: *Why did he leave himself?*

Our anniversary (it would have been the seventh) passed in July, and it caused more pain to see Sam and Mary celebrate their anniversary soon after. *They're together and I'm alone.* Also, they were having another baby. I felt grief that I might never have more children. I began to look at my friends' husbands and speculate that should a friend die, one of their husbands might marry me. I would have been embarrassed to admit this to anyone, but I bounced in and out of these irrational fantasies. I had a brief crush on a single man in my church. Just a few days into the crush, I collapsed into crying over Wayne again. *I'm so mixed up. I'm lonely. I don't want to be single the rest of my life. I want Wayne back.*

Although I couldn't always see it, healing was happening one day at a time. I kept reading and talking, praying and crying, remembering and thinking. Gradually the agony was decreasing. As the one-year anniversary of his death approached, I decided to hold a gathering. I invited 25 people to my house to share and be with me. Fourteen accepted. It was a healing time as everyone reflected on the past year, their grief, and the interacting influences that had led to Wayne's death. Although I cried through the entire hour and a half, it was a positive experience. I could feel small amounts of hope seeping through. *It will take time, but I can get back to peace again.*

Following Wayne's death I had asked that a memorial fund be established, and during this time I distributed the $2,000 in gifts that had come in. I called the state penitentiary in Louisiana (the infamous one, Angola Prison) and talked to the chaplain. I explained about Wayne's life and asked the chaplain how I could help. It gave me some comfort to mail him a check for $500 to cover Bible study materials needed for the inmates. I sent another check to help cover the expenses for a Christian band to perform at the prison. *Wayne would have liked this. He would want other men to hear the gospel.* I was planting seeds of hope for the future and validating the good things Wayne had done.

I returned to the local prison where Wayne had once been incarcerated and talked to the inmates who attended the chapel. I tried to explain what I had learned about Wayne's life and relapses and what the pitfalls of recovery were. I knew they'd be facing the same things when they got out.

I came to realize that Hope and I couldn't stay at Victory Haven in our log home there. For the first time I contemplated selling the camp and leaving. This felt like a defeat, and one more loss in the long string of things that "might have been." I needed to move to town to be near others. Country life alone with a small child was too isolated. One day I was determined to start the large riding lawn mower and mow the lawn myself, but didn't have the strength to hold in the clutch and operate the shift at the same time. It had always been Wayne's job. I cried in frustration, and then pushed the mower back in the garage. "Why'd you leave me!" I jabbed out loud at Wayne. I couldn't handle the camp maintenance by myself. The board of directors agreed with me that the time had come for us to put the camp up for sale.

One day at church an older lady hugged me and said, "Honey, don't worry. You'll get married to another husband."

I found no comfort in her unsolicited platitude. As I walked away I mumbled to myself: *I liked the one I HAD.*

> **Anger is a predictable part of grieving. Grief usually includes both anger turned inward:** *I'm mad at myself for what I did or didn't do...* **and anger turned outward:** *I'm mad at God and others...*
>
> **We are not in control of the choices that others make. For help in processing this reality, see Essay #11: The Fantasy of My Own Control.**

August, 1997

Dear Sarah:

I admire your willingness to walk toward the pain. In my own grief experience (and as a counselor) I have witnessed that this is the only way.

Grief is a monster, which in its fury overwhelms us initially, but little by little is sapped of its power as we slowly process and face it.

I am convinced that Wayne would change his decision if he could. Unfortunately, it is unalterable. But given what cannot be changed, he would want me *to give myself permission* to heal fully, to live vibrantly, and to walk on with hope. In this way I will influence many for God, enrich both their lives and my own, and one day enter eternity where He has redeemed all our sorrows for eternal purposes.

Sincerely,

JoAnn

> An excerpt from my letter to Sarah, a woman who attended my support group for survivors of suicide. Her son killed himself only eight months earlier.

CHAPTER 32
Blessings Ahead

Slowly I was embracing the idea that I *wanted* to heal, love, laugh, and be positive about life again. I could see that remaining distraught over Wayne's death and being self-blaming wasn't going to prove anything. It wasn't going to prove that I loved him. I had already done that by loving him fully while he was alive. As I approached the eighteen-month mark, hope slowly grew stronger. *I am beginning to believe that there are blessings ahead. Maybe I can be happy again.*

I'd always wanted to go on a short-term mission trip, and as 1996 dawned, I decided to join a small Baptist group on a twelve-day trip to Ukraine. It was ambitious, but it gave me something different to look forward to. I had always felt a burden for those who had lived under the oppression of Communist governments. Since the Iron Curtain had fallen, Ukraine was welcoming outside help and I wanted to see the people I had prayed for over the years. The $1,800 I needed for the trip was supplied three ways: $600 of my own money, $600 from my church, and $600 from friends and family. In April I flew to North Carolina with Hope and left her with my sister, Helen, for the twelve-day trip.

When I stood in a Ukrainian church to give my testimony, I didn't know I was shocking the congregation by speaking so openly about Wayne's death. I later found out that in their closed way of thinking, one never mentioned suicide because it was a shame and stigma on the family. I found myself grateful that I lived in a society that was somewhat more progressive in its treatment of suicide.

An older woman approached me after the service. "No one ever came to see me after my son killed himself," she said through an interpreter. "There was no funeral."

"I'm so sorry. You must have loved him very much."

My heart went out to the round-faced Ukrainian woman. I couldn't imagine having to endure social isolation after a suicide. It seemed so cruel. Although I had sensed some measure of avoidance from others, it was nothing like what she had suffered.

I returned from the Ukraine trip refreshed by new experiences. Besides enjoying the ministry opportunities in schools and churches, I had been able to focus on others who needed help. After eighteen months of focusing inwardly on my grief, I felt it was progress to be able to look outside of myself.

By the two-year mark I had come to a much deeper acceptance of the limitations of my control in Wayne's life. I had permitted myself to hold conflicting feelings in tension, both honor for him and anger at him. I had learned to confront the inner accusing voice that said: *You could have stopped him.* Gradually the truth was taking hold and I was rising above the paralyzing irrational beliefs. *I can tell I'm getting better.*

My optimism had been growing lately. *I guess the future is open to me. Is there something I want to do? Looks like I'm going to be the sole breadwinner. I wonder if I might go back to school and get a doctorate?* I had often admired people who were college professors and I loved teaching. The idea of getting more education was intriguing.

As the months passed, I continued working at the store and went back to part-time work at the YWCA, counseling in their sexual assault center. I began to investigate graduate programs. I dropped a hint to my parents that I might go back to school. They had always valued education and were immediately supportive of the idea.

I knew if I were to go back to school, it could take three or four years. That would be a huge commitment of time and money. After investigating a program at Wheaton College in Wheaton, Illinois, I began to think seriously about more graduate training. I was very interested in their Clinical Psychology program which incorporated theology. I knew how intricately psychology and theology actually played out in real life. This was a program I could be excited about. But I was taken aback by the length of the Wheaton program: five years!

Five years! Good grief! I'll be 43 by the time I graduate! I got out the map to look at the location. Moving to the Chicago area felt intimidating to a person who was used to small towns and rural log homes. I called Wheaton and discovered they had an upcoming visitor's day for prospective students. Despite my fears, I decided it would be good to visit. Slowly the idea grew to feel more feasible. *Well, I plan on living to be 43 anyway. The time will pass one way or the other.* I kept coaching myself mentally. *Do I want to turn 43 years old with or without the doctorate? Yes, I want more training and I want to be able to teach at the college level.*

Meanwhile, I sold the camp including my personal property and log home adjacent to it. It had been hard to come to terms with closing the camp and selling the property. I struggled with feelings of guilt and failure. I felt I was letting others down who had partnered over the years with me to build up the camp. All the dreams Wayne and I had there wouldn't happen. When my friends remarked that it must be a huge loss to sell the log home I had built, I replied that it was small in comparison to losing Wayne. When the property sold, I enjoyed distributing the camp proceeds to 27 other Christian organizations around the world, as directed by twelve people who had supported the camp over the years.

I rented a small house in Minden and moved to town, then was suddenly offered a full-time job as a therapist at our local hospital. I turned over the daily operation of the bookstore to my employees and went to work on a geriatric psych unit. I thanked God for the wonderful arrangement I had for Hope in my church's preschool. It was just a block from the hospital, so convenient when I needed to drop by for one of Hope's school programs. It was an ideal set up for a single working mom.

Two weeks before the visit to Wheaton College, my mother surprised me by saying she'd like to travel with me. I was delighted to think Mom wanted to visit

Wheaton. I had spent a great deal of time with my parents during the three years since Wayne died. They'd been so supportive and helpful about what I wanted to do. I knew they would rather I choose a closer regional school, but saw the value of my doing something that challenged and excited me. What was good for me would be good for Hope. I knew that if we moved to Wheaton, we could fly back and forth for visits. It was hard for my parents, but they knew Hope and I needed a new beginning.

While visiting Wheaton, my mom and I scoped out the preschools and tried to envision what it would be like if I moved there. After the visit, I tackled the lengthy graduate application process, then settled in to see if I'd be accepted. It was a four-month wait. I deeply committed the decision to God. *Lord, show me if this is Your direction for me.*

"The acceptance letter came! I'm in!" I called my folks to tell them that I had been accepted in the Wheaton doctoral program.

I felt a huge surge of optimism about the future. Now I had something to work toward. Now I had some direction for Hope's and my future. Several friends declared that I must have "lost my mind" to be moving to CHICAGO. Chicago evoked feelings of the unknown for me, too. It felt only slightly less foreign than Bangkok or Berlin!

"You'll end up marrying a Yankee," an older friend stated with resignation.

"I'm open to any and all possibilities," I responded with a smile.

It seemed there were a thousand things to do in the six months before I'd move to Wheaton. The most difficult would be selling The Olive Branch. Since Wayne's death I didn't have the benefit of the jewelry repair income in the business. Coupled with the falling economy in the area, it had been losing money and was a serious problem to shoulder. After showing the store to more than 20 potential buyers during the summer, I still hadn't sold it when the time came to move to Wheaton. I had already dropped the selling price several times.

I could tell I'd basically have to sell the store and take the loss. I felt enormous disappointment over taking this big financial hit. This was another repercussion of Wayne's death. I felt angry at him again. Had he lived, I believed the store would have been profitable. The past three years I had reinvested a large amount of the profit and lived frugally in order to try and grow the business. Now I saw that I had actually made less per hour than my employees. I cried. It didn't seem fair. I had shouldered so much risk and responsibility in owning the store. In order to sell, I would barely end up with enough to pay off my debt. I would just have to accept it and move on.

As Dad and I left in the Ryder moving truck for Wheaton, we could see Mom and Hope waving goodbye from my parents' yard. They'd be flying up in a week, after Dad and I had moved in my household stuff and unpacked. I had purchased a condominium for Hope and myself only a mile from the college. In route to Wheaton, we phoned Mom and learned that I had a buyer for the store. The last hurdle had been crossed in starting my new life!

Dr. JoAnn Nishimoto

I was moving 850 miles from all four of my child's grandparents, my support system, my church family, and all I had ever known. I was going to start graduate school as a single mother, make a new life for myself, and work toward something that would challenge and excite me. I was 39 years old, and Hope was about to have her fifth birthday. *What in the world am I getting into?*

Regardless of the intense pain life can bring, if we continue healing we will eventually reach new horizons of hope. There are many blessings ahead.

Your greatest life messages
and your most effective ministry
will come out of your deepest hurts.
The things you're most
embarrassed about,
most ashamed of, and
most reluctant to share are the
very tools God can use most
powerfully to heal others.

Rick Warren
The Purpose Driven Life
Zondervan, 2002

CHAPTER 33
New Beginnings

The school year kicked off at Wheaton and I was delighted to meet my seventeen classmates. I knew we had the potential to be a supportive community to one another. At 39, I was the oldest, and the only one who was a mother. During a sharing time in theology class, several people risked disclosing difficult parts of their lives. I had already decided it was time for me to begin sharing more about my abuse years when the situation was appropriate. When it was my turn, I decided to put my cards on the table. It felt trivial to me to report only the neutral facts of my home state and where I went to college. I wanted to be real about my life.

"I lost the decade of my twenties because I was in an abusive relationship," I began. "Later, marrying my husband, Wayne, was an enormous step forward for me, and he was really a catalyst in helping me to heal from the abuse. Most of you know that I am widowed, but you probably don't know Wayne killed himself." My story was definitely heavy, but I saw supportive looks from my classmates. Although I was trying to keep a professional demeanor, tears ran down my cheeks. "This is my first big step in starting something new in the three years since Wayne died." After sharing a little of how I got to Wheaton, I concluded by adding, "I didn't want to be the only one today who cried."

I felt vulnerable, but safe. I had decided to begin my relationships at Wheaton with openness about all of my life. I didn't want to sidestep a question because it might mean revealing that I'd been in abuse. I was here to become a psychologist, but it felt vulnerable to cry in front of others and look like I still *needed* one.

"Thanks for being real," a classmate said during the class break.

"Is there any other way?" I said.

Hope adapted readily to her preschool class at Wheaton Bible Church. We also began attending there on Sundays. I tried the singles' class, but found it depressing. There were often far more women than men. After a couple of weeks, I was invited to attend a class for married couples. My friend assured me that the group would welcome me, and there were several single adults in the group. I accepted, hearing that many of them had children Hope's age. It would mean families and kids to meet and incorporate into our lives.

My biggest prayer before moving to Wheaton was to find childcare that would be good for Hope. That prayer had definitely been answered. My classmate, Dave, had moved to Wheaton with his wife, Mary, and two small boys. Mary was a stay-at-home mother and she was happy to be Hope's babysitter during the 25 hours a week I needed to be at school. Hope loved being in their home, and when I arrived to pick her up she often said, "Mom, I'm not ready to go home!" I was elated to see Hope happy in her new surroundings.

As I got into the swing of classes, studying, taking Hope to activities, and participating at church, I felt positive. Ironically, when I was alone at night, I was experiencing yet another surge of grief about Wayne. *Why now? I thought I had grieved his death thoroughly, so as not to be haunted about it the rest of my life.* I was tired of crying about him, and it didn't make sense.

The reality was that moving from Louisiana had brought more losses. No one in Chicago knew Wayne and no one remembered him. Here, it was as if he never existed. I remembered times in Louisiana when I noticed someone at church wearing a piece of jewelry Wayne made. No one in Wheaton would be doing that. I thought of the huge amount of change I had been through during the last few years. Now the last chapter had been written on my life with Wayne. I had sold the store we had begun together. Everything here was different. It brought on another wave of grief, and I found I needed to cry and talk about it several times during the first months in Wheaton. It felt strange being both happy with my choice to move and grieved at leaving the last reminders of Wayne.

Meanwhile, my 40th birthday was approaching in June. I remembered planning a 40th birthday party for Wayne five years earlier. We had fifteen friends over, and it was one of the most enjoyable times we'd ever had. Now Wayne wasn't here to celebrate *my* 40th birthday. I didn't have a spouse to plan a party for me. After fretting about it for several weeks, I decided that I needed to *do* something.

"This may sound stupid," I told Dave and Mary, "but if someone doesn't help me have a 40th birthday party, I don't think I can stand it." Dave and Mary were sympathetic. As my closest friends in Wheaton, they knew the waves of grief I'd been struggling with during the last few months. Once they were aware of my feelings about my birthday, they quickly offered to plan a party.

Occasionally, Hope had begun to ask more questions about Wayne's death. She didn't yet know that he had killed himself, and I intended to wait a few more years before I told her. I wanted her to get a little older so she would have more understanding. When she brought up the topic of her daddy, I reassured her that he had loved us very much. I always emphasized his talents and gifts.

We were riding home from the store when Hope mentioned Wayne again.

"Your Daddy made beautiful jewelry," I told her, "and when you are older I will give you some of the items he made."

Riding in the back seat, Hope was quiet. After a few seconds I could tell she was crying. "I miss Daddy. I don't know why he had to die."

"I know, sweetie. We both miss him very much."

Hope was nearing six years old, and it was obvious to her that other children had fathers. "When is God going to give me another daddy?" Hope questioned.

"When it is God's time, honey."

It took faith for me to say this, since I increasingly wondered whether I'd ever marry again. Hope's question tapped into my own emptiness, and I knew she wanted a father as much as I wanted someone to love. I'd been in Wheaton almost a year, and no one had even asked me on a date. Most single men at the

Dr. JoAnn Nishimoto

college were 30 or younger, and they were interested in women who were 25, not women like me who had just turned 40 and who had a child. I hadn't moved to Wheaton to find a husband, but I was certainly open to the possibility if it were to happen. I felt that I had a lot of love to give. I had loved being married, and I wanted Hope to have a father. But things weren't looking too promising.

As I put Hope to bed, she said her familiar prayer. "God, please give me a daddy."

I kissed her and said goodnight. She'd been praying that a lot lately.

I had spent a lot of time the last year doing my self-talk, trying to keep myself positive and my head straight. *I can be happy even if I don't get to be married again. There are many fulfillments in life, and being married is just one of them. Lots of people don't get to have even one happy marriage, and I've had both a happy marriage and a wonderful child.* Just when I talked myself into not worrying about my singleness, Hope would start praying that prayer again and I'd lose my fragile sense of peace. *Oh, God, I really do want to be married.*

Meanwhile, with or without dating, I knew I'd have to be proactive about creating happiness in my life by loving others. I enjoyed entertaining, and my first year in Wheaton I had small groups of people over for dinner and developed a knack for Cajun cooking and showcasing southern hospitality and good food. By the end of the year I had invited more than 80 people to dinner. These included my classmates, their spouses, neighbors, and church friends. Hope shared my excitement about having guests and grew to love setting a beautiful table with my china and my grandmother's crystal. Wheaton was beginning to feel like home.

My first year in Wheaton ended without a date. While visiting in my parents' home during summer break, I told my mother just how bleak I felt.

"There aren't any good men left," I lamented. "I'm afraid I'll be alone the rest of my life."

"It's going to be alright," my mother stated with conviction. Her attitude of certainty seemed unrealistic to me, but I wanted to believe she was right.

"How do you know it's going to be alright?" I pressed.

"I just know." Her face had an expression of firmness that kept me from challenging her further.

I decided to hang on to her faith about my getting remarried because I certainly didn't have any.

We can create happiness for ourselves by reaching out to love others. Why not invite someone to dinner?

It isn't for the moment you are stuck
that you need courage,
but for the long uphill climb back
to sanity and faith and security.

Anne Morrow Lindberg
A trauma survivor

CHAPTER 34
Blind Date

As I hung up the phone, I could scarcely believe it. I actually had a date. My friends from church, Jim and Cindy, had arranged a blind date for me with their friend, Stuart. I didn't know much about Stuart except that he was about my age, a committed Christian, of Asian descent, divorced, and worked for the Navy. Jim reported that he and Stuart had been friends for twelve years. Cindy sounded excited. I could tell she was enjoying her matchmaker role.

In the days before the date I began to get nervous. I chided myself for not working hard to lose at least five pounds. I was developing a bad cold, and my nose was bright red. *Ugh. Not the best presentation of myself.* I mulled over the "ins and outs" of dating. *Dating in my 40's feels different.* I didn't have a lot of dating experience. Ever. Other than a brief high school boyfriend, I'd never dated anyone but Wayne.

I looked down at the ring on my hand. On the first anniversary of Wayne's death, I had moved my wedding ring to my right hand. During the last three years I had worn it there. I enjoyed people's comments on how beautiful it was, and I would tell them that it had been my wedding ring Wayne had made. Tonight, leaving for the blind date, I put the ring in a drawer. It was time for change. Going out on a date marked a new milestone.

Later, as Jim and Cindy hosted us for dinner at their house, the evening progressed smoothly. Stuart seemed relaxed, and the conversation flowed easily. My feeling of "first date jitters" faded quickly as we kept talking. Of course, I was monitoring the conversation for nuances of who Stuart was. I learned that for six years he had been tutoring inner city kids in Chicago one night a week. *Hmm. He's capable of sticking to difficult tasks.* I had done enough "people helping" to know those kinds of ministries lose their glamour after a couple of years. It also told me he wasn't a self-centered person. As we talked and shared about ourselves, I kept listening for content. I noted the ways he seemed to spend his money and his time. I heard traces of his spiritual convictions. After the four of us played a game together, I left to go home.

I picked up Hope from the babysitter and got her ready for bed. I hadn't mentioned to her that I'd had a date. I had only told her I was eating with friends. I didn't want to raise her hopes. I knew she wanted a daddy so much, and that she was likely to throw herself at anyone who came into our life. I acted nonchalant about the evening.

It occurred to me that I had now entered Phase Two of the dating game... better known as the "waiting game." *Will Stuart call me for another date?*

I phoned my friend, Linda, to give the "date report" I'd promised her.

"Well, did he make eyes at you?" Linda was enjoying her chance to be playful.

"I don't know…his glasses were kind of thick."

"Well, did he ask you out again?"

"No. But I feel good about it. It was fine. No fireworks or anything. But it was really nice."

After 48 hours the phone rang, and it was Stuart. He wondered if I'd like to go out again. I accepted readily. This time we'd have a daytime date, and he invited me to the beautiful Morton Arboretum. It was mid-October, so it was a great time to see the leaves and enjoy the outdoors.

Walking in the October sunshine, we began to share more about our lives. I learned that Stuart had been abandoned by his wife after they'd been married two years…two years and forty days to be exact. (I was to learn that Stuart had a memory for numbers and dates.) They'd not had any children, and he'd been single again for six years. He told me about his school, work, and family history. I learned that all four of his grandparents had emigrated from Japan as young adults. His mother was born in Hawaii and his father in Oregon. They met in Chicago in their twenties and married. Stuart was born in the city. He was an only child. He'd been a Christian since childhood. He'd gone to church his whole life.

When it was my turn I reciprocated with my family and school history. I'd already been listening for Stuart's maturity level, and I carefully worded the summary of my twenties.

"I was in an abusive relationship during my twenties," I said, "and I don't have much to show for that decade of my life. I was pretty messed up. It started when the pastor of my church started abusing me. I'll tell you more about it sometime." We were walking, but I turned to look at Stu's face for signs of how he was reacting to this "bombshell." Stu seemed okay with that explanation for now.

I continued, "You know that my husband, Wayne, died four years ago, but I don't think you know that he killed himself."

"No. I didn't know. I'm really sorry."

"Yes, it was awful. He killed himself while he was relapsed on narcotics." I filled in a few details of what had happened.

After about four hours, we said goodbye. We'd covered a lot of territory. All the guideposts for the kind of man I was looking for were matching up well so far. Stu was a teetotaler, and this was certainly important to me. I didn't want to deal with the possibility of drug or alcohol problems again. He had conservative Christian convictions. He sounded thoughtful about the ways he had resolved his divorce. There were no red flags.

This relationship might be promising. A part of me knew it was too soon to be optimistic, but hope is a powerful thing.

Hope is a powerful thing.

Sharing your testimony is an essential
part of your mission on earth because
it is unique. There is no other story just like
yours, so only you can share it...
Personal stories are also easier to relate
to than principles, and people love to hear them.
They capture our attention, and we remember
them longer. Unbelievers would probably
lose interest if you started quoting theologians,
but they have a natural curiosity about
experiences they've never had. Another
value of your testimony is that it bypasses
intellectual defenses. Many people who won't
accept the authority of the Bible will listen
to a humble, personal story.

Rick Warren
The Purpose Driven Life
Zondervan, 2002

CHAPTER 35
Will Love Bloom

The third date Stuart and I had will forever be called the "financial interview" date. After all, as 40-year-olds we were going to have to compare ideas about money. I knew this was one of the largest compatibility factors in marriage. We hadn't planned to disclose our philosophies about money so early on, but the conversation developed naturally at a local restaurant.

"I've never bought a new car," Stu said, "because you often get a better value by buying a good used one." He was eating his lemon pie slowly.

"Having the perfect car isn't on my *Top Ten List*, that's for sure," I said. Stu had no doubt observed that I drove a thirteen year old Buick which my dad had handed down to me. I found out later that he was pleased over my contentment with my older car.

"I believe in tithing," I said, introducing another financial topic. "I've been giving ten percent to the Lord's work since I was fourteen." I wasn't bragging; I was hoping he'd tell me his philosophy of Christian giving in response.

"Well, I started tithing when I was ten," he said, "ever since I got my first job on a paper route."

"You're kidding," I smiled. "I've never met anyone who has tithed from such a young age." *This conversation is going really well.* I decided to keep playing my cards.

"I don't have any credit card debt either," I said. I had been living within my means and I hoped he had, too.

"Neither do I." Stu elaborated on his ideas about frugality. He regularly stopped by thrift stores and only allowed himself a limited vacation budget.

After two hours we'd hashed out everything that had anything to do with money, and we couldn't have been more compatible. I learned that money had been a major cause of friction in Stu's first marriage.

"Over the last ten years I've been giving to a project that I think is one of the most important things that has ever happened in history." I had returned to the topic of Christian giving again. "There's a movie about Jesus' life that has been translated into hundreds of languages. It's called the Jesus Film Project."

Stu smiled and started looking in his wallet. He quickly produced a 2-inch piece of 8mm-movie film. "This is a piece of an actual film reel from The Jesus Film," he said. "When the film gets worn out, they distribute pieces of it to remind people to pray for that ministry." Of all the charitable or Christian giving options available, I was amazed we had both supported this one.

I didn't hide my pleasure. I could see we were on the same page about our money and values. It pleased me that Stuart had a heart for ministry and missions. I called my mother the next day to say, "This relationship looks promising."

I knew that meeting Stuart's friends was going to tell me a lot about him, so I welcomed a chance to be with his longtime friends, Jeff and Laura. Stuart had often babysat their kids and was an honorary uncle to this lively family with five children (all younger than nine). We were visiting in a fast food restaurant while Stu played with the children in the playland area. *Any man willing to babysit this energetic bunch has to have his wits about him.* Laura and I visited and I immediately liked all of them. I was delighted to see that Stuart had such a connection to the children. *He loves these kids. He could be a committed father to Hope.* I couldn't help checking things off my mental list.

Laura proved to be a delightful woman, just as Stuart had said. He referred to Laura as his substitute sister, as he didn't have any siblings. Observing Laura's outgoing personality and loving spirit, I continued to build on my sense that Stu was a solid individual. *If he would pick this kind of wonderful woman for a "sister," then he's got his head on straight.*

Of course, while I was inspecting Stu's friends, they were inspecting me, too. I learned that Stu had two dozen or more friends who wanted to meet me. They must have felt protective of him after his first marriage, and they probably wanted to be sure I wasn't a flighty widow looking to grab a nice man I might not deserve. Not that anyone made this concern explicit, but I could certainly understand why they were loyal and protective. On more than one occasion, after leaving a social occasion with his friends, I sensed I had "passed." Several of his friends, aware of the potential for our relationship, even encouraged me by saying, "Stu's a great guy. He's always been just the way he is now. Solid."

Hmm. Check again. Stuart is a safe person.

After introducing Hope to Stuart, I explained to her that we had a new "friend" and that we'd be spending time with him. I didn't refer to us as "dating," because I didn't want her jumping to conclusions.

Just as I expected, she wanted his complete attention immediately. Before long she was holding his hand and chattering with him during meals. Trying to quiet her six-year-old enthusiasm was useless. *Well, I might as well let him have the full experience of me and Hope together, because if he marries us...I mean, me, it's going to be a package deal.* During a walk along Lake Michigan near the Navy base where Stu worked, Hope wore Stu's jacket and he carried her on his back. Later, looking at a picture I took of the moment, my heart leaped. Seeing them together looked wonderful. *I'm going to have to work hard not to let my hopes get too high. I like him so much. I don't want us to overwhelm him with our exuberance. I don't want to scare him off.*

The topic of marriage had already surfaced during the first two months of dating. I knew Stuart wanted to get married again, "if the right woman came along." He knew that I did, too, so there was an understanding that we were both investigating this relationship for its marriage potential, not just for casual dating. I couldn't afford to let Hope throw herself at someone who didn't want to get married again.

Every week we continued to talk about our life experiences, and I knew it was time to tell him the "big one."

"I'd like to tell you my abuse story," I posed the topic one afternoon. "It's going to take a couple of hours to tell you the whole thing."

"Sure, whenever you want." Stuart seemed relaxed about it. I studied his face, looking for emotions. *Is he dreading hearing this?*

In reality, I was the one who was hesitating. There was a risk here. My story was so weird that he might decide to look elsewhere for a woman with a simpler past. Until Stuart heard it, there were things about me he wouldn't be able to understand. There were pieces of my character and healing that would be a mystery to him without the knowledge of what I'd experienced those twelve years.

Telling my whole history had gotten easier over the years. I had explained my story to two dozen people over ten years, and each time I told it I realized that I had continued to grow in my understanding of myself and the dynamics of the abuse. I'd also found value in reading material that helped people de-program themselves from cults. I'd expanded my reading into topics of manipulation, control and abuse.

A week later we settled in on the living room floor for my "presentation." Stu listened attentively. I told it step-by-step, laying the foundation of Hansen's influence in my life. Stu was quiet. I could tell he was repulsed by the manipulation involved. I opened a notebook in which I had outlined the twelve years. I shared a few of the poems and thoughts from my journal as I concluded. Two hours had passed.

"I know that God wants me to write my story someday. I worked on it about 100 hours last year, but only got as far as making an outline of what happened." As I finished I was feeling emotionally lighter to have gotten through it. Stu had commented only sporadically, but I could tell he was taking in the whole of it.

"I'm so angry, and I don't know what to do with it," Stuart finally spoke his feelings as I finished. I knew he deserved to have room for any and all feelings he had.

I felt validated that he had understood me. I was glad he was angry. I knew good men feel angry when they hear this kind of thing. Overall, I was relieved. He really knew me now. My cards were all on the table. I felt better. Ironically, he didn't. At least not in the short run. Now he had a burden he hadn't had before. I knew the questions spinning in his head: *How does this kind of thing happen? How can someone do that to another person?* Stu asked some initial questions, and then we adjourned to do something lighter for a while. I could see that he was deep in thought.

It was a necessary, but awkward, step in our relationship. Now Stuart had to begin integrating my story into all that he knew of me. Now he could understand what Wayne had meant in my life as my partner in healing. As our relationship continued, we processed his questions together as they naturally came up. I could tell Stuart was an emotionally mature man. Watching him address my abuse in a straightforward way told me volumes about his character. He wasn't afraid of it.

I think I love this man.

> **Healing allows us to be open and vulnerable, which in turn paves the way for intimacy.**

There is nothing in the world so attractive
as someone who will dream with us,
merge their dreams with our own,
clarify the path toward the actualization of the dream,
and lock their arms into ours while walking the path.

Neil Clark Warren
The Triumphant Marriage
Focus on the Family, 1998

CHAPTER 36
A Kindergartner Takes Charge

"How do you spell *really*?" Hope asked me from the dinner table. I was getting supper ready for us, and I saw she had paper and crayons out. She was learning to write all her letters, and lately she had begun making her own greeting cards.

"R-E-A-L-L-Y," I spelled it out for her. She continued her project. I spelled "want," "you," and "my."

"How do you spell 'daddy?'" Now that word got my attention.

"It's D-A-D-D-Y," I said.

It occurred to me that she was writing a proposal note to Stuart. I glanced over her shoulder to see her sentence: "I really want you to be my Daddy." I supposed Stuart might feel this was a bit manipulative, but after all, I hadn't put her up to it. If she happened to be using her six-year-old charm to wheedle her way into Stuart's heart, who was I to get in the way? I pretended I didn't know what she was doing.

When Stu arrived and she gave him the card, I ducked in the kitchen. He read the card with a smile. "We'll see, Hope." He was gracious and hugged her.

The next weekend we went shopping. My toaster had bitten the dust, and I was looking at some $20.00 models. My budget was rather tight, and I was explaining to Hope that we weren't going to buy the $50.00 toaster oven she was pointing to.

"Please, I'd like to buy you a nice toaster," Stu offered. This was one of the first times he'd offered to buy me a gift, but I insisted on the small toaster. Hope was listening intently.

"No, really, let me buy you the nice one," Stu insisted.

"Yeah, Mom, let Stuart buy you the nice one," Hope chimed in.

I cut Hope a look that said, "This isn't *your* decision."

Soon I gave in, thanked Stuart, and we took the more expensive toaster oven to the cashier. Hope was skipping ahead of us. I knew what she was thinking. Our financial status had been rather lean during the last four years, and she was enjoying eating out and the other advantages that dating Stuart had brought into our lives.

When Hope and I visited Louisiana at Christmas, I spent one evening filling my parents in on everything I knew about Stuart.

"Now you've told us all these wonderful things about him," Dad said, "but now you've got to tell us something about him you *don't* like." Dad wanted me to be realistic. Stuart must have at least one fault.

"Well, he's kind of a pack rat," I said. "He saves a lot of stuff."

"Oh, you can live with that." Dad, himself a pack rat, wasn't deterred.

I was well into my second year at Wheaton, and we were busy with kindergarten, church activities, seeing Stuart on the weekends, and a busy graduate school course load. As Stu and I talked on the phone each evening, we told stories of friends, trips, and how our lives had progressed. Occasionally we visited the topic of marriage, sharing our expectations and hopes, but I could see Stu wasn't going to rush things.

As the winter in Illinois passed, I made plans to take Stuart to Louisiana during spring break to visit my parents and meet my Louisiana friends. Now it was his turn to get "inspected." During the trip I showed Stu the log house I'd built, my hometown, and the churches I'd attended. We stopped by the cemetery to see Wayne's grave and Hope arranged the seashells she'd put there before we left for Illinois. It was her way of "decorating" Wayne's grave, and she took pride in it. This was Stu's first trip to Louisiana, and my dad took us down one of the bayou waterways in his boat. It was an introduction for Stu to the "Old South," complete with cypress trees and Spanish moss. During the week Stu met about fifteen of my close friends.

While visiting with my parents, we told them that we were considering getting married. They were delighted.

Mom and Dad were celebrating their 50th wedding anniversary soon, and for the occasion Mom had planned a family reunion in Breckenridge, Colorado, for August. Mom had already invited Stuart to join us. Sam and his family would be coming from Saudi Arabia and Helen and her family from North Carolina. My aunt and several cousins would also be attending.

Within a month, Mom and Dad visited Breckenridge on a planning trip. Mom wanted to see the accommodations for the reunion and plan some activities. When I told her that Stu and I had mentioned getting married while the family was gathered in Breckenridge, she asked for permission to look for a place for us to get married.

"You can get some ideas," I said, "but remember nothing is certain yet."

Stu was a little taken aback by the sudden flurry of wedding interest. He was still praying about whether we should be married. I didn't want to push him, although I was already very sure I wanted to marry him.

Meanwhile, Sam's boss in Saudi wouldn't grant him a vacation in August even though the boss knew it was his parent's 50th anniversary celebration. Mom gave Sam the "heads up" that Stu and I had spoken of possibly getting married at the reunion. Sam decided to use this news to his advantage and went straight to his boss and said, "My sister is getting married, too, and I *have* to go in August." Then Sam e-mailed Stu and said, "Congratulations, Stu! Good decision! Mary and I are excited about the marriage!"

"Is there something you're not telling me?" Stu was perplexed by the congratulatory e-mail from Sam, since he hadn't officially proposed to me yet.

"I'm sorry, Stu, but my family is just so excited about you that they're jumping the gun a bit. I'll tell them to calm down." It was hard to hold back my own enthusiasm, too.

Finally, in May, Stuart made the formal proposal. We were at O'Hare airport putting Sam's family on a flight. At Gate C-23, in front of the cousins, Stuart knelt down and presented the ring. Stuart had planned to present it earlier, but we'd run out of time before leaving for the airport. Now we'd be getting married at the Breckenridge gathering.

"My mom is going to marry Stuart," Hope offered our news to her kindergarten teacher, Mrs. Henry. Mrs. Henry was near retirement. One can only imagine the private information she had been privy to over the years.

"That's very nice, Hope."

"I get to be in the wedding. Mom says I can be a flower girl, or sing a song, or do whatever I want."

"I know you're excited. That's just wonderful."

"My mom was praying that she'd get another husband." Hope's six-year-old exuberance showed no signs of abating. Mrs. Henry must have wondered where this conversation was going.

"Well, he must be a very nice man, Hope."

"My mom knew he would be good for us," Hope concluded, "because he bought us a nice toaster."

When Mrs. Henry related this conversation later, I was truly embarrassed. I hoped she didn't think I was so desperate for a husband that I'd been swayed by a toaster.

If you're worried about your image, don't send your child to kindergarten.

Why had I waited so long,
making excuses to myself
that I needed the perfect moment?

There is no such thing
as the perfect moment.

We *make* all our moments,
and by the love and truth we bring to them,
we make them perfect.

Frances Sharkey, M.D.
A Parting Gift
St. Martin's Press, 1982

CHAPTER 37
Mountain Wedding

It had rained every morning that week, and we could only pray we'd be able to have our wedding on the balcony of the ski lodge. Hopefully we'd have sunshine for our 11 a.m. wedding.

It had been a whirlwind week. Stu met my sister and family for the first time, Stu's parents arrived from their home in Phoenix, and everyone was getting to know each other. Hope had romped all week with her cousins, and we had hiked, canoed, and eaten family meals. Mom and Dad had renewed their own wedding vows in a special celebration the night before, and now we were getting married on the final day of the family reunion.

It was going to be a relaxed wedding. I had purchased a Victorian-style wedding dress. Hope and Anna, my niece, were to be the flower girls. My college friend, Marisa, and her husband, Rod had arrived. He was a pastor and would be performing the ceremony. Counting Stuart and myself, there would be 24 people at our wedding. I had made the silk flower arrangements and we planned a catered lunch after the ceremony. Stu's friend, Paul, would be taking pictures. The night before the wedding I discussed the wedding music with my niece, Elizabeth. She looked over the CD I brought and selected several songs.

The ceremony time arrived and there was no rain! The view up the valley to 14,000-ft. Mt. Quandary was splendid. As we finished our vows and exchanged rings, I felt light-headed. It must have been a mixture of love for Stuart and the 9,000-ft. elevation! We called Hope forward for her part in the ceremony. Stuart knelt in front of her and pledged to love and care for her, too. Then he gave her a small ring, which was a complete surprise to her. I dabbed my eyes. Hope had a daddy. As we were pronounced man and wife, everyone broke out in applause. Then my father came forward and prayed for the three of us as a family. Stuart and I left for our honeymoon and Mom and Dad left with Hope for four days in Denver.

A month later we had a wedding luncheon in Illinois for our local friends, then two months later we flew to Louisiana for a small reception hosted by my parents. Stu's parents also came to visit and to see my hometown. Altogether, we had three separate wedding events and I wore my dress three times. We really felt married!

As we settled into our early months of married life, Stu was wise enough to know he needed a transition period as a stepparent. Although Hope was so eager for a daddy that she had thrown herself at him, she wasn't quite prepared for the fact that he would also be disciplining her. Naturally, she idealized him in the beginning. That was okay. She had wanted a daddy for so long and was making up for lost time.

Stuart, Hope and me at our Breckenridge, Colorado wedding

When Wayne's birthday rolled around the next January, Hope stated that she wanted to have a birthday party for "Daddy Wayne" (as she now called him, since she had begun calling Stuart "Daddy"). I was glad Stuart was an emotionally secure man and didn't feel this was a threat. We made a birthday cake, sang Happy Birthday to Wayne, and ate the cake. Hope was satisfied. I presented Hope with a piece of jewelry that Wayne had made (this became a tradition each January). Afterward, we watched videos of Wayne and Hope when she was a baby.

"Hope, if I had known your Daddy Wayne," Stuart told her, "I know I would have loved him."

Stu's words left me dumbfounded. There was nothing more loving or honoring that he could have told Hope. *Stuart, I'll love you the rest of my life.*

Stuart had always been comfortable when I talked about Wayne. His acceptance of the fact that I had really loved Wayne gave me permission to remember the good years Wayne and I had together. It was nice that I didn't have to censor myself or try not to mention Wayne when things came up naturally. Hope needed to hear the many good things about her dad. I admired Stuart for being secure in himself. He didn't ask me to pretend I hadn't loved Wayne.

I had not yet told Hope that Wayne's death had been a suicide. She was seven now, and I was planning to wait another year. I wanted to give her time to become settled in Stuart's love. I knew this would be a buffer for her against the heavy burden of hearing the truth.

We planned for Stuart to adopt Hope, and we received the blessing from Wayne's parents to change her last name to Nishimoto. They knew Stuart would be a dedicated father and agreed it would be best for her to have his name as she grew up. They knew I had honored Wayne over the years and that we wouldn't let Hope forget him.

In January we had a special celebration for Hope's adoption. We made our courtroom appearance before the adoption judge in Cook County, Chicago. The tall, female judge reviewed the documents while the three of us stood before the bench. Our attorney pointed out Wayne's death certificate, Stuart's and my marriage certificate, and the other legal petitions. It was an open and shut case but the judge made small talk with us so as to not seem that it was moving too fast.

"Hope, I'm glad that you have a new daddy," the judge said. "These are the kind of adoptions I like to see."

Hope accepted her congratulatory lollipop from the bailiff. We shook the judge's hand and asked her to pose for a picture with us. Afterwards we headed across State Street to the famous Marshall Field's Walnut Room for a celebration lunch. It was official. Hope was a Nishimoto. It dawned on us that evening that we hadn't taught her how to spell her new name, so we had a spelling lesson around the dinner table!

Since Stu and I both owned condominiums, we were praying and planning about where we should live. Meanwhile, Stu would be commuting between both homes to be closer to his work during the week. Stu considered a job change, but this never materialized. After nine months we purchased our first home and sold our condos. I still had two years left in my five-year program at Wheaton. Moving to a northwest suburb of Chicago near Stu's work meant that I'd be commuting to Wheaton for another year of classes. We chose a new church and introduced Hope to her new school for second grade. We were feeling like a family.

Meanwhile, as the initial excitement of the marriage settled and we moved into everyday life, I found myself applying the new emotional skills I'd been working so hard on over the past decade. It had taken me years to learn the art of deflecting (not absorbing) another's irritation and being desensitized to the power of anger.

A defining moment happened after Stuart and I had been married two years. I was washing dishes and singing a praise song to myself when Stuart arrived home from work. I pivoted to see him come in the door and saw that his face was tainted with anger. I was tempted, for a moment, to feel fearful. Instead I decided to be purposeful and assume it wasn't about me. I didn't need to fix it. I assumed that it must have been a bad day at work for him. For once I didn't give into the old ways I'd tried to control another's anger. Instead I turned my back on him and went back to singing! I said to myself: *Stuart is mad, and those are his feelings. I am happy, and these are my feelings. I'm going to stay in MY feelings.*

Stuart grumbled for a few minutes, but I continued to focus on my positive feelings. He left the room to change clothes, returned to ask what was for dinner, softened to the smell of good food, and put his bad day behind him. For once I didn't fear anger, over-compensate with apologies, or accommodate him out of fear. I celebrated another blow to my codependent tendencies!

> **Whenever either partner brings a child to the new marriage, it is referred to as a *blended* family. Blended families are even more challenging than when a couple has their own biological children. A stepparent is challenged to accept this "ready-made child" just the way she is. A child is challenged to give up the fantasy that their natural parent who died would have somehow been better.**

You need only claim
the events of your life to
make yourself yours.
When you truly possess
all you have been and done...
you are fierce with reality.

Florida Scott-Maxwell
The Measure of My Days
Penguin Books, 1983

CHAPTER 38

Blue-eyed Courage

It was something I'd been worrying about for five years. I knew I'd eventually have to explain Wayne's death to Hope, but I wasn't looking forward to it. Although I'd never liked it when I heard that families tried to keep suicide a secret, I suddenly felt sympathy for their short-sighted avoidance. Trying to postpone the pain was the easy way out. Although I had developed a deeply held value about walking toward pain and facing it, I couldn't seem to find much courage for this. I'd just have to set a date to tell Hope and then *do* it. It wasn't going to get any easier. She was eight now, secure in Stuart's love, old enough to understand, and asking increasingly more questions.

I didn't like feeling scared. I wished someone could promise me, going into this disclosure, that Hope wasn't going to suffer too much...that she'd not get too broken by the truth. I had a mental picture of myself casting her off a platform, letting her free-fall from innocence. I longed to protect her from the pain of a fallen world.

Although I'd prayed about this event for years, I only felt a small amount of comfort about it. I talked with Stuart about the wisest way to tell Hope, and I'd processed it from every angle I could think of. I decided to tell Hope after Christmas, during the holiday break. We would have a week at home together before she went back to school. Stu and I chose Sunday morning. We'd stay home from church, tell her in the morning, and then have a quiet day together as a family. I decided that the following week would be dedicated to giving Hope emotional support. I had no other demands for a week, and she would have my undivided attention.

I read once, in challenging myself to fully recover from Wayne's death, that I would be able to lead my child to the same measure of recovery I had gained. This thought had been a powerful insight, and it had often motivated me to work on genuine, and not merely cosmetic, healing. I knew parents either teach their children courage or fear about life issues by how they model these things. It seemed a credible theory; now it would be time to test it in reality. I couldn't wait around for the absence of fear. The applicable spiritual truth here was faith. I had done the preparation of *prayer*, planned the "how and when" in *wisdom*, and now I would just have to jump off in *faith* and do it.

The last Sunday in December arrived. I was struggling with anxiety. Hope, Stu, and I piled up in the bed.

"Sweetie," I began, "there are some things I've been wanting to tell you about Daddy Wayne."

It was tempting, even at the last minute, to call this off and tell myself that either Hope or I weren't ready. I monitored my own voice, trying not to convey my anxiety to Hope.

"Remember how I've told you about how Daddy Wayne struggled with drugs in his life?"

I had gradually begun introducing stories about Wayne during the last few years, telling her how he'd struggled with drugs, been in prison, and found Christ there. We'd visited the topic of his drug addiction on occasion during the past year, so this was a starting point for her.

I slowly began explaining Wayne's last relapse to Hope. I glanced at Stu and knew he was praying silently although his eyes were open. Hope sat nervously, aware my tone was somehow more serious than in previous discussions of Wayne's addiction.

"When the drugs are in you, you just can't think right," I continued. "Sometimes you can make bad choices. I know you have always thought that Daddy Wayne just died, but…"

"Mom, STOP!" Hope was frightened, suddenly aware there were things she didn't want to hear.

"I know this is hard for you, but you have to know. Daddy Wayne killed himself, Hope."

Hope was already crying and the pain of the moment hit all three of us. Stuart was crying, too. I stopped talking and we threw ourselves into a family hug for comfort. Hope was in the emotional free-fall to the agony I'd always feared.

During the next hour we continued our closeness in the bed, discussing some of Hope's questions, and comforting her with the answers and peace I'd discovered over the years. We held and patted her, stroking her face and arms, allowing her to cry.

Later in the afternoon, my mother called. She and other family members had been praying for us as I'd told them that we'd be talking to Hope that day.

"Your Daddy Wayne was such a special man," my mother comforted her granddaughter on the phone, "and we have so many loving memories of him. I know this is hard for you."

I wanted Hope to know it was okay to be open with everyone about this. I could tell she instinctively wanted to recoil in silence from the devastating truth she had just heard. It was hard for her to hear that she was the only person who had not known about the suicide. I made the preliminary explanations about why I had chosen it this way, although I didn't expect her to be able to embrace all my logic and decisions at once.

That evening we tried to play a board game and give our minds a rest. As we tucked Hope in for the night, I wasn't surprised that she asked me to sleep with her, and I complied. I'd be sleeping with her for several nights until she felt more steady emotionally.

The next few days Hope initiated more questions about Wayne's death, his funeral, and his addiction. I kept telling myself this was all a process, and that she would recover one day at a time at her own pace. I wanted to give her permission to feel her pain and sadness without rushing her to the resolution I had found.

On Wednesday Hope still hadn't mentioned Wayne and it was already mid-afternoon.

"Well, tell me what you are thinking today, honey," I raised the topic with Hope.

"I think I'm kind of getting used to it," she said matter-of-factly.

Her honest answer touched me. I knew exactly what she meant. The pain of hearing that your loved one killed himself is not a truth that can be easily absorbed. It takes time to get used to it. Everything in you wants to say that it isn't so. Gradually, little by little, you take it in.

By the fifth day I knew she had gotten through the worst of it. The initial terror had been stared in the eye. It had been terrible, but love, prayer, and faith had sustained us. I was relieved that we were getting the initial shock period for Hope behind us. Now would come the ongoing part of processing what this would mean to her. I knew that with each passing month she'd have new questions. Some would awaken spontaneously within her, others would be triggered by events around her. Nearly every month Hope initiated the topic of Wayne's death. If she didn't bring it up, I did. I didn't want to fall into patterns of avoidance. We were tackling the trauma piece by piece.

A year passed. Coming in from school one day with her backpack, I could see in her face that something painful had happened.

"Mom, my friend asked me why my first daddy died," she stated with confusion and sadness. "I didn't know what to say."

I knew this was only one of a hundred discussions we would have in the years to come. With each situation there would be new questions, fresh emotions to process, and fears to face.

"Tell me what you think would happen if you mentioned the suicide." I listened to her view and tried to impart some wisdom about when disclosure might be wise versus premature. Gradually I shared how I faced things when they had come up during the year after Wayne's death. Usually, after these conversations, Hope could deal with things and move back to her cheerful self.

I began to occasionally mention Wayne's death when we were with others, referring to some aspect of the suicide when Hope was present. I intentionally wanted to model being straightforward and mentioning it without shame or fear. I noticed that she was acutely attuned to these conversations, being "all ears" and observing everyone and their reactions. Later, I'd ask her privately what she thought about it. Gradually, we were working our way through Hope's grief and recovery. I felt satisfaction and payoff for all the hard recovery work I'd done myself. When Hope had hard moments I tried to keep the reward in sight. *She'll eventually become as resolved to this as I am. We just have to do it one step at a time.*

Years before I'd read a statistic that initially terrified me. A child who had a parent commit suicide will have a six times greater risk of committing suicide himself. Of course, this information elevated my fears. An initial interpretation of this statistic is that discussing a family member's suicide openly would predispose the child to more risk, so it follows that you'd better keep the subject quiet. But over the years I've come to have a different perspective.

Suicide, like many kinds of painful emotional baggage (abuse, divorce, etc.), often goes unaddressed and hidden by families. The unspoken family rule is: "Don't talk about this because it feels so bad." As a result, family members learn patterns of avoiding pain. Negative emotions are locked in and held under the surface rather than grieved, resolved, and released. When children of these families grow up, they don't have experiences of resolving and processing pain while supported by the love of others. No one modeled it for them. It's no wonder that when they reach adulthood and encounter their own painful experiences, they could feel overwhelmed and become more likely to commit suicide themselves.

In helping Hope process her questions and walk toward the pain, I was actually making it likely she would be *less* vulnerable to suicide. I was modeling openness and emotional healing. I was doing the *prevention*. With this realization my fears dissolved. *My child will be all right.*

Nearly two years later the fruit of healing was evident. One evening the phone rang during supper. A friend from church sounded distraught. Her eighteen-year-old daughter was in agony because her boyfriend had killed himself. She had broken up with him the day before. I said I would come over in a few minutes to speak with her daughter.

As I hung up the phone, I turned to fill in Stuart and Hope.

"I need to go see this teenager. I know this is a terrible time for her." I explained the situation. I turned to Hope. We had just planned a family game after supper. "Sorry to cancel our game, Hope, but I need to go see this girl."

"Mom, I'll go with you. Maybe I could talk to her."

Hope's willingness, at ten years old, to face a crisis situation like this, and the suddenness of a suicide, left me stunned.

It was a golden moment. *Hope is going to be okay. We've conquered the fear. Thank you, God, she's going to be okay.*

Hope's blue eyes were even more stunning when filled with courage.

Emotional healing often has the ripple effect of helping others around you. The most powerful thing you can do for your child is to pursue your own healing.

...every branch that bears fruit, He prunes it
so that it may bear more fruit.

John 15:2 (NASB)

CHAPTER 39

Pruning and Fine Tuning

I graduated with my Doctor of Clinical Psychology degree from Wheaton College in 2002. It felt good to put the stress and demands of graduate school behind me. Nevertheless, it had been a rich experience. My classmates and professors at Wheaton were outstanding.

My marriage had flourished and grown. I had started my relationship to Wayne in a place of insecurity and fragile emotions. My marriage to Stuart began in a place of emotional confidence and peace with myself, obviously a better foundation for marriage. After graduation from Wheaton, Stuart was fully supportive of my taking a year off to write this book and spend some time resting. We agreed that I wouldn't work for a year so that I could focus on writing.

As soon as I finished writing the first portion about the abuse years, I asked my family members to read it and give feedback. It was a relief to have finally articulated on paper what had happened to me. With fifteen years of healing behind me, my education, and deepened insight, I could now convey the understanding I'd gained about my abuse history. Telling pieces of the story to them on occasion over the years had only partially communicated what happened to me. Because some parts of my story were deeply shameful to tell, I had spoken about them only here and there, and no one individual had known them all. Now, hopefully, my family could fully comprehend the enormity of the psychological and spiritual bondage I had been in.

I was naïve in handing the manuscript to my family. While for me it was an emotional triumph to have finally written my story, it made them groan. They had feelings of both apprehension and support for the book. Reading it sent nearly all of them into emotional turmoil. It awoke again the awful questions all families struggle with: *How could this have happened to someone I love? Could I have prevented it? What will others think when they read this?*

Reading my story in black and white, my family experienced a fresh awakening of grief and anger. While they had come to terms with some aspects of my story over the years, reading my book awakened pockets of pain within each person that were still unresolved. Nearly everyone said that while they knew I had been in severe abuse, they hadn't actually known it was that bad. After tears and more processing, everyone came to terms with my story at a deeper level. During 2003 we worked through most of this pain one phone conversation at a time.

My sister related that there were three things going on in her mind while reading my abuse story. First, she viewed it from a rational angle: *Why didn't JoAnn just tell Hansen to get lost?* Then she would shift to the viewpoint as if I'd been in a cult: *This is understandable, it makes sense why JoAnn thought this.* Lastly, she could feel her own emotional response of pain, anger, and grief: *This hurts too much.*

I want to throw the manuscript across the room. Even during the final review of the book, she confessed that she could still hardly read the abuse part.

I had a growing sense of deep recovery from both the abuse and the tragedy of Wayne's death. I began to speak about both freely, using my life as a way to model healing for others. Many times during the past years I've felt "fully healed." There wasn't anything in my conscious awareness bothering me. Talking didn't bring painful emotions to the surface. I couldn't imagine anything that would really stir me up. *How could I have forgotten that God is always interested in growth?*

In the aftermath of the World Trade Center terrorist attack on September 11, 2001, I identified with many of the young widows I saw interviewed on television. I sympathized with their losses, anger, and single-mothering woes, and I focused on the many things we had in common. About eighteen months after the attack, I learned that Lisa Beamer, wife of 9/11 hero, Todd Beamer, who helped overcome the terrorists above Pennsylvania, would be coming to Wheaton College to speak. Lisa and Todd were both alumni of Wheaton, and after 9/11 the Wheaton community had naturally focused on Todd's story.

Although I wanted to honor the heroism of men like Todd Beamer, I didn't want to hear Lisa's presentation. I was invited by friends to hear her speak, but I declined. I had a vague feeling of resentment and jealously toward her, but since everyone was admiring her, I was ashamed to admit this out loud. I told Stuart that I simply didn't want to go, and dropped the topic. Soon afterward my church invited Cheryl McGuinness, wife of the American Airlines pilot whose plane crashed into the World Trade Center, to speak at our Sunday worship service. As the time for her presentation grew nearer, I felt resistant to going. I didn't want to hear her testimony either.

"I thought you felt a kindred spirit with these women because they lost their husbands tragically?" Stuart was puzzled. He was trying to understand my negative attitude toward hearing these women.

"Well, I just don't *like* them."

"*Like* them? I don't get it."

I felt suddenly frustrated with Stuart for pressing the topic and mystified at myself as to why I would want to reject women I didn't know. *Why do I feel threatened by this?* Inwardly, I wasn't ready to admit this to myself. I dismissed the topic and went on with my day. Later that week I began to get more honest with myself.

"I don't know why we're putting these women on the stage and saying they are brave," I couldn't hold back the critical words inside me. "I think they have it easy."

Stuart's eyes met mine and I could tell I had surprised him with my angry spirit. "*Easy?*"

"Yeah. When they tuck their children in at night they get to say, 'Daddy was a hero.'" What's so hard about that?"

As soon as the words left my lips, I felt embarrassed. A part of me didn't want to be angry with these widows, but another part of me felt justified. Suddenly my mixed-up feelings were making more sense. The thing surfacing in me had a name I didn't like: *self-pity*. It was too late to do image-management with Stuart. I might as well talk through this.

"Well, when I tuck Hope in at night, I have to answer questions like, 'Why did Daddy leave us? Why would Daddy kill himself if he loved us?' and stuff like that. I just think they have it easy because they can always remind their children that 'Daddy is a hero.'" It seemed everyone rallied to support the 9/11 widows. In contrast, I knew from experience the hard work widows of suicide have to do in overcoming the stigma.

I could tell Stuart wasn't sympathetic with my self-pity. Since I looked bad already, I decided to spill the rest of my lousy attitude. It couldn't get much worse.

"And one more thing," I rounded out my defense. "Everybody knows that they have MONEY. Good grief, didn't all the families of 9/11 get huge settlements? After Wayne died I was so broke..." I trailed off, half-ashamed I was voicing all of this.

"Aha! *Now* we're getting to the bottom of this!" Stuart isn't usually hard on me, but he wasn't going to gloss over this. He isn't afraid to call a spade a spade. I'm sure he was wondering where all this was coming from.

I'd been honest about feeling sorry for myself, but I knew I couldn't wallow in it. *Lord, You'll have to help me with this one. I didn't know this was even in me.* I'd worked on self-pity years ago and thought it was gone. *Was there more?*

The next week Stuart came home with a book from the thrift store. As always, he felt good about finding a bargain.

"Here, I thought you might like to read this," he held out Lisa Beamer's book, *Let's Roll!* "I got it for three dollars!" Although he didn't say so, I knew Stuart was hinting that reading the book could help me work on my issues.

I forced a pleasant look and "thank you." I was outwardly polite, but Stuart probably knew it was feigned. I didn't voice my sarcastic thought: *Stuart, did I ask you to buy me this book?* As I laid it on my nightstand, I realized I'd need a major attitude adjustment before I'd be willing to read it.

The book sat there for two weeks. Deep down, I knew that to be healed from my self-pity, I'd have to read it. Finally, I started reading, and read it through in only two sittings. I was surprised to learn that Lisa Beamer's father had died suddenly when she was fifteen. *Why had I assumed that she'd always led a charmed life prior to her husband's death?* Like me, she'd also suffered before the tragic loss of her husband. Focusing only on the "advantages" she had, I had never bothered to ask whether I might have blessings she didn't have. *I bet she wishes her father was still alive.* I thought of my own father, aging gracefully at 80. The irony was beginning to hit me. I had been angry that she had something I had been denied: a husband who died a hero and money to ease the stress of widowhood. But I had something *she* probably wanted: a father to serve and love his family and be a grandfather for his grandchildren. My anger was melting as I realized that comparing our lives and suffering was useless.

The deeper roots of my jealousy and self-pity were evident to me now. I still had some remaining anger at God for allowing my life's journey to be what it had been. Ultimately I had to admit that I was still angry with Him that Wayne died by suicide and not in an accident or less troubling way. It was humbling to experience this. *I've got more work to do.*

As I completed Lisa's book, I cried with her. Reading about the lonely nights she cried herself to sleep, I knew we had more in common than not. My anger softened.

When the day came for Cheryl McGuinness to speak at our church, my resistance was gone and I went with an open and humble heart. It was a touching talk where truth was powerful.

This experience took me still deeper in accepting the things God had allowed in my life. Although I wouldn't have chosen or wanted abuse or suicide to be a part of my history, I could trust Him for the ways He would use these things. *God, I can see my history being redeemed for good. I can see Your hand at work in my life. My journey is still being played out as You teach me Your perspective and use me for Your purposes.*

The primary emotion in self-pity is anger. When you realize you're feeling sorry for yourself, try to define what you're angry about.

Are you willing to believe
that God has great possibilities in mind for you,
that the coming years can be the greatest years of your life?

Tim Sledge
Making Peace with Your Past:
Help for Adult Children of Dysfunctional Families
LifeWay Press, 1992

CHAPTER 40
Freedom Dancer

I've done a number of things over the years to expand my emotional healing. In 2011 I decided to attend a women's therapeutic workshop, not as a therapist, but as a participant. I went that day with an open mind, with no preconceived ideas. A unique feature of this experiential workshop was that each participant could experience a role-play or skit about her life. With help from the staff therapists each woman could chose the "actors" from among 20 attendees and a handful of staff, design the scene, then play out the scene to see what feelings and thoughts came up.

The possibilities for life-skits were endless. A participant could select actors to represent herself at different ages, she could play her own self in a drama, or sit back and watch others play her life or family members. At intervals the staff therapist might pause the skit to check in with the participant to see how it was going for her. Some women were in the initial phases of healing from abuse, trauma, or harmful relationships. Sometimes intense feelings of anger emerged, and one could use a plastic bat to pound out the rage (actors protected, of course). I witnessed important moments as women symbolically addressed and confronted alcoholic parents, abusive partners, and life losses.

My turn was approaching. I tried to consider what would be most meaningful for me. *Is there something that I've missed as a component of my healing? Anything I want to symbolically represent?* I'd always wondered what it would be like to have my original church family offer their support to me, confronting my abuser or taking my side in a public confrontation, a sort of moral court. With the passage of time it was impossible to return to my old church family, but I now had the opportunity to create a similar experience within this supportive group.

I explained my idea to the therapy staff. First, I had to choose the actors in my courtroom drama. One attendee volunteered to play *Abuser*. I chose a black cape from the table of accessories for her to wear. The role of *Young JoAnn* would be played by a woman with a baby face, and I draped a pink shawl over her to represent her seventeen-year old innocence. *Jesus* would be played by a woman who had impressed me in an earlier skit because she had a presence of honor. I draped some purple fabric around her shoulders and put a plastic crown on her head.

I would be playing my *Adult Self* in the skit. Although in the early years of my recovery I would have needed an advocate or attorney, I was now a plaintiff who could represent herself. I accessorized myself with a Star Wars light saber, symbolic of TRUTH. The rest of the participants would play *The Church*. I explained to the group that *Abuser* would be reading from a list of statements Hansen had said to me. I'd imagined the satisfaction of having *The Church* believe my story, then mock and shout down the self-justifications and phony "god-talk" *Abuser* used to manipulate me. Feeling their support and power, I'd rebuke his nonsense. They'd represent how an insightful church should respond to the outrageous narcissism of a wolf in sheep's clothing. I decided to have *Jesus* and *Young JoAnn* stand to the side of *The Church* court.

The staff set *Abuser* behind a rope, separating him from me and *The Church*. I signaled that we'd begin by *Abuser* reading his first statement on the list.

"You belong to me," *Abuser* said in a low voice. "God has told me that you are mine."

I held up my hand to halt *Abuser*. He stopped.

"Well, well, let's see." I stepped toward *Abuser* with my sword out. I was confident, slow, in command of the moment. I made small circles with my saber toward *Abuser's* body. I added a tone of sarcasm and mockery. "So you think... you actually think, that God told you I belong to *you*?"

I turned to *The Church* court. "Can you believe this? He thinks God told him I belong to him!" I threw back my head and laughed.

At this *The Church* girls went wild. "You fake-o!" "You wolf!" "You don't deserve to be a pastor!" They talked over each other, yelling and cursing at *Abuser*. I stepped back, motioning for them to take the floor. Their zeal exceeded my expectations.

I felt heady with power. I looked over at *Jesus*. He drew *Young JoAnn* close and nodded with approval. I paused *The Church's* frenzy by raising my hand.

"Go ahead," I jeered at *Abuser*. "Tell us what else God has told you."

"You're supposed to marry me." *Abuser* read another statement from the list.

I coughed repulsively at his comment, grimaced in disgust, and rolled my eyes. "*Really*? Well, I've got a thing or two to say! Did you know Jesus said that it would be better for you if a millstone was hung on your neck?"

Jesus grinned enthusiastically. *The Church* girls were rabid with anger for my defense and started pounding their hands and feet. "You're evil!" they yelled at *Abuser*.

I tapped my saber near *Abuser's* feet. The rope blocking me from getting too close to *Abuser* had gone lax to the floor, so I stepped over it to tauntingly circle behind him. I slapped the saber in my free hand, savoring the position of interrogating *Abuser*. He stood with his hands at his side, his head lowering in defeat with each of his statements destroyed.

The staff therapist intervened to say that I wasn't permitted behind the rope barrier. I could tell that she was afraid I'd literally strike *Abuser* with my Star Wars saber. She didn't need to worry. I wouldn't have wanted to lower myself to literal violence. I was winning the debate on a higher level. I wasn't afraid. The power of TRUTH was the real sword here. I was triumphant.

Young JoAnn had stepped forward from *Jesus'* side. She didn't look fearful now, she was beginning to clap along with *The Church*.

"This isn't lust, its *love* that I have for you," *Abuser* got in another line.

"You should be ASHAMED!" an eager *Church* girl broke the silence before I could reply. More pounding, denouncements, and booing followed. I knew from some of the skits I'd seen that several of the women were also sexual abuse survivors. I paused and took in their faces. They weren't *pretending* to be angry. They *were* angry! I had wanted to experience *The Church's* support that I hadn't felt in Louisiana. That had been the starting point for my skit. I'd imagined that they'd be firm and vocal, but not quite so raucous for righteousness. Although they weren't my original church, they were a *real* church, indignant about the abuse and defending my innocence.

At this point I had what I'd come for. It wasn't that I'd needed to be bold or cathartic toward *Abuser*. I'd achieved that years ago. I'd wanted to feel a church's support without the weakness of small-town fears. I nodded to the staff therapist that I was done. She motioned for *Abuser* to be taken away and everyone to circle around me: *Jesus, Young JoAnn,* and *The Church*. The atmosphere changed to tenderness. Moving prayers were offered for my life and complete healing.

As the prayers were ending, someone put on celebratory music. Everyone started to dance. *Jesus* sort of square-danced around me and *Young JoAnn* was twirling her pink shawl and high-fiving *The Church* girls. Suddenly a young woman leaped up and started dancing wildly only two feet in front of me. I'd never seen such dancing. I tried to mimic her expert moves…part Flamingo, part hip-hop, part belly-dancing…packaged in an energetic, stunning outburst. The intensity of her eye contact told me that she was celebrating me. My freedom. My life. Shame defeated. Thoroughly.

I hadn't planned *Freedom Dancer* as the final character in my life skit. She happened spontaneously. Reflecting on it all weeks later, the exuberance of *Freedom Dancer* was the most meaningful part. She was me…free.

Sometimes you don't anticipate meaningful experiences, they jump up and surprise you. The most healing experiences might not be the ones you plan for.

If there is a book you really want to read
but it hasn't been written yet,
then you must write it.

Toni Morrison
Pulitzer and Nobel Prize recipient

Epilogue

January, 2001, 5 a.m.: I'm doing it again, lying in that state of semi-sleep in the bed, Stuart breathing steadily beside me, and writing the book in my head. If I don't stay in this awareness I'll lose it. I've just spent two hours lying awake and "writing," but it may be lost as soon as my daytime mind starts driving the day.

My eyes shut, in the blackness of the room, I'm explaining a new aspect of my story. I go back 25 years. I'm reliving the narrative of it, giving words to the events. I call it "cooking the book." Like a good pot of navy beans, it's simmering in a cerebral pot, the spices are coming out, and it tastes better than it did an hour ago.

I'm remembering the fear and confusion. The giving up of my sense of self. The disbelief that my abuser could be so cruel, and my plan to change him by being even more loving and giving of myself. Another chapter "written," I fall back asleep, satisfied.

Awakened later by the alarm, I'm absorbed back into the here and now of work, school, or family…sometimes only vaguely aware that I've been writing in the night. As I was doing that semi-awake, sleepy-writing an hour ago, it feels like wisdom emerging, like I'm teaching someone about the dynamics of these relationships. My teaching-mind is always cooking up an analogy, explaining a principle to someone. I'm thinking of you, the reader… how will I explain it to you? I'm the best teacher when I'm not trying to sound smart, when I'm talking off the cuff.

As I write now, I'm closing my eyes as I type, the keyboard my enemy, because I worry that I'll lose access to the thoughts I was having if I open my eyes. Not watching the keyboard helps me get deep in my soul, relate the process, and be real. I must recall what happened. I must set aside any audience. This isn't a performance to be evaluated. It didn't happen on a stage. It's my life. I remember.

I never expected that I'd be reflecting on this some ten years after writing the bulk of the book. The year is now 2014 and I thought I'd have long published it by now. All along, Stuart was approaching the book in an unhurried, non-urgent way. When he mentioned, in 2003, that it might be a couple of years before I published it, I was instantly irritated with the idea, and by extension, him. It was obvious we had totally different timelines. The wait seemed unnecessary. I saw the book as having a mission, something important to get out there to help others. I'd finished it. It was done. When someone read it and even gently suggested that I write more essays or modify some aspect of the writing, I was impatient. My nephew, a thinker and reader, wanted more descriptions…like how the streets looked in the town where I grew up. I had a kind of take-it-or-leave-it mentality. "That's all the book I have in me," I'd say. After so much input and suggestions from my editor-savvy sister, Helen, and others, I had no patience for additions or reconceptualizations.

I once read that you shouldn't publish a book before you're 50. I hit that milestone in 2008. Wisdom says that you might need to retract some of the ideas you've espoused in your less mature, pre-50-year-old ways of thinking. Once published, you can't take them back. By that measure, the book seemed to be holding its own. When I'd reread it once a year, I seemed to like it, and I'd say to myself: *Hmm. It's good.* Meanwhile I read a number of memoirs of various sorts, noting the differences in other's depth of self-disclosure, ability to observe their own emotional processes, and degree of vulnerability. I have my own gold standard for reading in the genre of recovery books. I know what I like.

As with all personal stories, as long as you're alive, they're not done. So I have to ask myself what I've learned in the nine years since I wrote the bulk of the book.

I tried to educate myself about the intimidating world of publishing by attending a writer's conference. I went in humbly as a wanna-be author, then exited the conference discouraged and overwhelmed, realizing that getting my story published in the mainstream American book industry is akin to my neighbor's son making the NBA. Every time I saw that a book was published about abuse I'd feel deflated, as if there was room for only one more book on this topic. *Now that someone else beat me to it, there's no need for my story.* I'd cycle in and out of feeling fearful about the publishing process and then confident again about seeing it through.

If the arena you're trying to enter scares you, and over time you learn to say, "Here's why I do what I do and I'm okay with it," then you've matured and found your peace. In regard to the book, I had to learn to be comfortable in my own skin. After a while I wasn't running scared that I'd be crushed or booed by "real" writers. I saw that there is a meaningful place for what I'm doing and I believe in why I'm doing it. Peace.

I got up my courage and asked four respected, *published* authors if they would read my book and write an endorsement for it. These were people I'd met or had connections to through my education at Wheaton or in the world of Christian psychology. I'd been told it could help me get noticed.

While the endorsements didn't overcome the rejections I got from Christian publishers, they did help me sustain my confidence in the book. The Christian publishing industry is cautious of stories that might be generalized to make all pastors look bad, something I understand, and have worried about myself. I happen to know and like several really solid pastors, and I don't want to make their jobs harder. This problem always seemed unanswerable...my book isn't a novel where I can change the characters or plot. Even I can admit the distaste that just when our society is numb to yet another clergy-gone-bad story, now I've got one to tell.

Are publishers worried about the honor of our faith? The ultimate defense of the faith is the clarity to know the faithfulness of a good God even when you've been fleeced by a wolf in sheep's clothing. This is the real issue at stake here. Jesus said all along that there were impostors among the faithful, tares within the wheat. We're not to confuse the character of God with the religious deception we see.

Bad men don't negate good men. In secular terms, a corrupt Congressman doesn't negate the Constitution. In my case, a corrupt pastor (Hansen) doesn't negate the faith. This book is meant to include an education about pathological men, whether they masquerade in the church or elsewhere.

As I toyed with my options in the first several years after writing, I knew I could self-publish the book. At first it felt like a defeat, a failure for those of us who don't make it into mainstream publishing. Later it felt like vanity: *This is what one does when you're vain and you want to say, "I've written a book" and no one will publish it* (thus the nick-name "vanity publishing" in the industry). Over time I've sorted through my motives and other's imagined responses *(always the crux of fear, isn't it?)* and decided that I'm comfortable, even joyful, over directing what I want. *After all, if I'm paying for it, I can keep the parts of the book I'm passionate about. I can use the quotes I want.* After having counseled 800+ women over the past 22 years, I know the kind of things women struggle with and can picture them reading and relating to my story. *I know what I know.* I know the words that will be an antidote for their shame and fear. *By George, I'll pay for it myself! I'll write what I know works.* Aha! I have scaled another emotional mountain ledge on the fight to the publishing summit. Progress.

Stuart and me vacationing in Wisconsin

Whether it was 2006, 2007, or 2008, Stuart's attitude was: *It will come. We're busy with other things right now.* Stuart knows I can overload myself, in my enthusiasm for everything I want to do in life, with too many projects. He wasn't minimizing the book. Every few months he would make a complimentary statement about the book as if he believed the eventual publication was going to be noted by mainstream America and enrich millions. I'd smile to myself and note how lucky I was to have a husband who believed in me and never reneged on the dream. He just wasn't in any hurry for it. His timetable felt to me like it was moving about as fast as the earth's tectonic plates move…barely detectable. I was becoming desensitized to the urgency I'd felt. I barely sighed when he suggested, in 2009, that I should probably publish it when Hope went to college. "What's another two years?" he said.

Meanwhile, we both agreed that Hope needed to read the book and gain some peace about it. During her high school years she'd developed normal teenage dread at the idea of her mother writing a self-revealing book that could raise eyebrows. I tried ever-so-hard to be patient about this. *After all, what teenager wants others scrutinizing her dad's suicide or her mom's clergy abuse?* Helping her arrive at some peace about the publication was going to take a lot of grace and patience. Over the last five years I adopted the mention-it-once-a-year plan. I'd suggest, "Do you think you might like to read the book during vacation?" Hope's response: "Not really." Hmm. More patience. Wait another year. Although I did some internal groaning: *Doesn't anyone understand how all this waiting is tiring me?* I disciplined myself to keep my mouth shut and not manipulate Hope. At times I did play some self-pitying comments in my head: *I've never been ashamed of you!* Again, Stuart listened to my whining and helped diffuse my impatience with Hope. Support.

Finally, at age nineteen, Hope and her mentor read the manuscript. We debriefed at several intervals as she was reading. I encouraged her to vent all her feelings, even disagreements she had with me. I assumed a posture of relaxation while she cross-examined me, "Mom, *really,* are you sure you didn't know what you were doing?" and "Mom, couldn't you have saved Daddy Wayne by doing such-in-such?" All the healing I'd done on freedom from shame paid big dividends here. I could listen to her confusion without defensiveness. Without fear of being judged, largely because I'd given myself compassion and self-respect, I could give her the grace she needed to accept both my and Wayne's history. I could actually say, with complete compassion for her, "I know this is hard for you. I know you wish it were different." I understood all her questions, because I had asked all of the same ones myself. After respectful sparing and discussion, I saw acceptance settling in. *Alas, when we pray and be patient, God answers the longings of hearts.* Hope even took the manuscript back to college and gave it to a friend. Courage.

Meanwhile, I'd been observing myself grow in a new way. I saw that waiting ten years to publish the book had refined me along the way. First, I had to *get over it,* that is, get over others' responses and non-responses. During the past eight years I've printed 25 copies and had them spiral bound. To my knowledge there have been about 60 readers of my manuscript. It was encouraging that the feedback was overwhelmingly positive. It's been wonderful to see the book open up conversations and growth for others.

There have also been some responses on the negative end. The worst blow came when a Christian leader read the book, then responded with a generic "I just don't understand why women don't get out of abuse." I was stunned, and even defaulted to that "niceness" again. I couldn't think of a comeback. Darn it! Later I was furious. Explaining how women are harmed and even less likely to exit the abuse *is what I explained in the book!* Two years later I was still mad at him.

Eventually, I forgave him and wished him well. I'd be a wreck if I took every rejection personally. I had to work through getting offended.

I needed to get used to the idea that my story wasn't something everyone was waiting to read (something hard to accept ten years ago). My friend, Maureen Lang, a successful fiction author, had adopted the mental position that she never expected anyone to read one of her books. Her surprising comment made me realize that I expected EVERYONE to want to read mine, an assumption which would sentence me to a life of constant disappointment. *Yes, some insanity still remains after age 50!* Gradually, I've accepted the truth that it isn't everyone's cup of tea. Time has tempered my expectations. I've learned to forgive the disinterested. I'm changing from the defensive person to the person who refuses to be offended. More peace.

An energizing development was the addition of my friend, Jen Jao's, illustrations. I first saw Jen's sketches when she began drawing pictures of her own emotional and spiritual recovery. I could see that she was moved to interact with truth through the vehicle of art, unlocking internal emotional doors. *My favorite kind of art!* Although drawing was relatively new for her, I sensed some latent genius emerging in her designs. I asked her if she'd be willing to try drawing illustrations which depicted the principles in this book.

Venturing in unknown territory, she heard me describe, "Let's show my brain in a jar, like it's been pickled by my abuser." I saw nothing unusual about the idea. It seemed an appropriate analogy for my experiences. She looked puzzled, but showed the grit of a brave woman willing to go on an adventure, and went to work translating my ideas into pictures. Working on this wasn't for the fainthearted, and Jen has persevered through our brainstorming sessions and rough sketches to the insightfully creative pictures included in this book. Her partnership gave me renewed focus to bring the book to a higher standard. Her prayers were sustaining. I have deep respect for her.

Now Stuart has taken to pushing me toward completion. To my surprise, I even found the discipline to rewrite some parts of the manuscript and add more essays. When I don't get the finishing touches put on each chapter, he's resorted to talking through the dog, "Sadie says she wants you to hurry up." Tectonic plates eventually shift.

May, 2014, 7 a.m.: It's been twelve years since this all began. I'm finally finishing this book. I fight to keep myself true to the calling. Oh no, I'm doing it again…monitoring the outcome of the book before I'm done…managing my image in some way…worrying that one of my therapist-peers will frown on my self-disclosure…projecting the problems before they've even happened. "Will it sell on Amazon?" is stealing my energy again. I must not reduce the worth of it to such base measures. I must say, "There it is…the story" and not hold my breath. I must not write to promote my career, or defend the faith, or anything. I must write for the defense and honor of my soul.

Well, the simmering is done and the stew is ready. I give it to you now. I do not hold my breath.

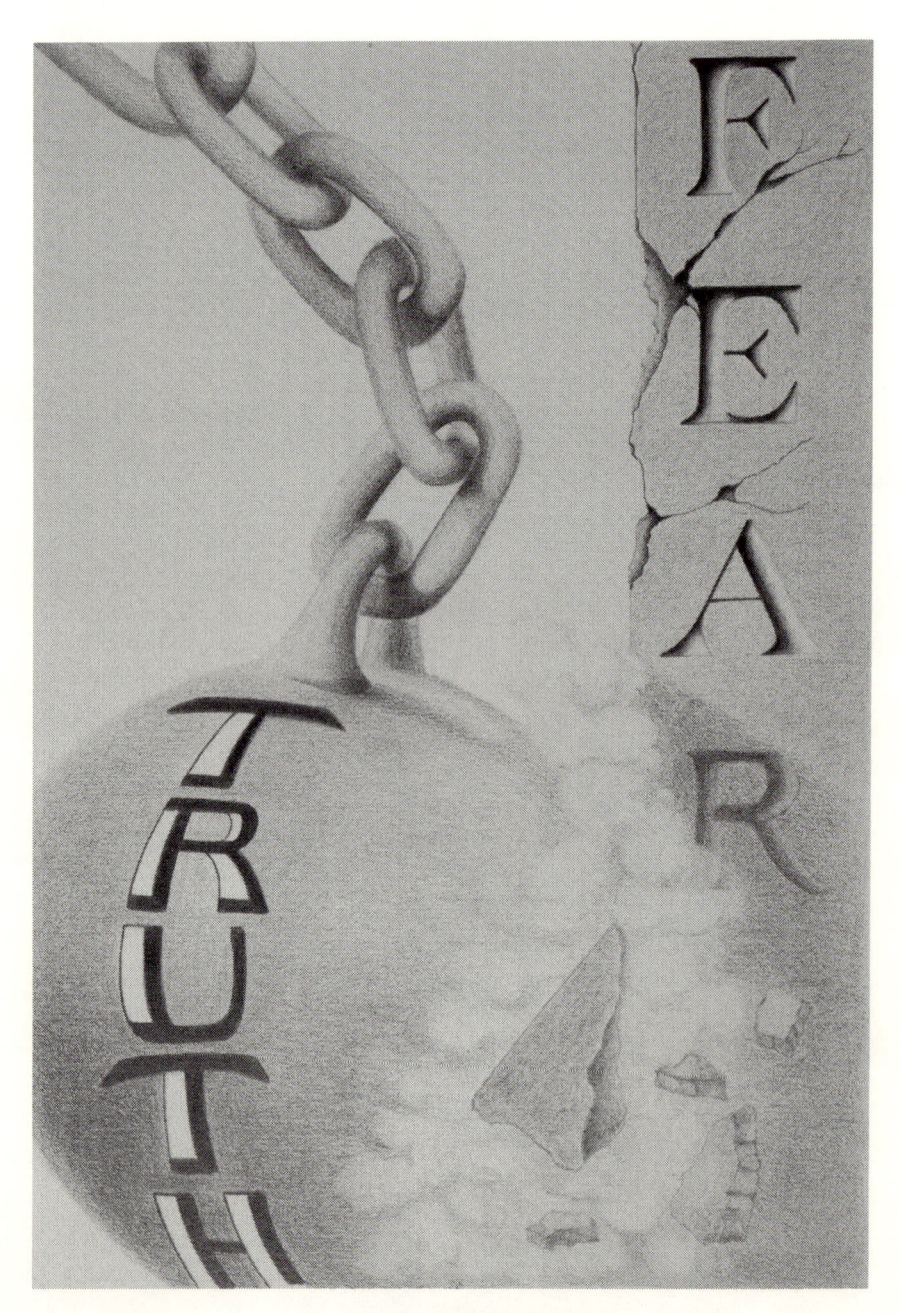

The Wrecking Ball of Truth

Essays

I have written the following fourteen essays because I wanted to address important topics that most people encounter. These are the highlights of the truths that have helped me get well. There is a teacher's side to me, so I'm always working at ways to present these concepts to my clients. Our interactions have shaped these ideas over the past twenty years.

As the picture illustrates, a wrecking ball is an intentional device. It has a mission. You must repeatedly swing the *Wrecking Ball of Truth* against the fears and lies you have believed. Over time, fear will crumble as it is impacted with truth.

Recovery is an active, not passive, endeavor. These essays are a kind of *Wrecking Ball* to help you knock down the fears and lies that may be blocking your growth.

List of Essays

1. The Arch Enemies: Shame and Grace
2. The Compulsion to Hate My Own Life
3. Do I Really Want to Get Well?
4. Put Your Hand to the Plow
5. When I Kept Silent
6. Chase the Robbers!
7. The Shepherd's Gentle Call to Dignity
8. Am I Codependent?
9. Wise as Serpents
10. The Fear of Others
11. The Fantasy of My Own Control
12. Forgiveness is a Messy Thing
13. Who is a Pathological Man?
14. Bathsheba, the Lamb

1 The Arch Enemies: Shame and Grace

> *"...love others as well as you love yourself."* Matthew 22:39 (The Message)

If we want to get to the bottom of the problem, to the real thing that's preventing our emotional freedom, it's the **cancer of shame**. Shame is, in theological terms, the inability to value ourselves in the same way that God values us. Shame is another expression of human brokenness and our tendency to distort truth, especially about ourselves. Shame holds us back from appropriate self-love, and by extension, loving others. **The quality of our love for others is always related to the quality of our own self-acceptance.** Therefore, shame affects both my relationship with myself and my relationship with others.

Shame has many emotional expressions. Some people experience shame primarily as feeling defective, inferior, or self-loathing. Others feel it as being ugly, stupid, or inadequate. For some it is the desire to hide oneself, to fear being known, or to present a false self to others because the real self is insecure.

Shame can be triggered by a thought in our own mind, *I'm inadequate,* or it can be felt as an emotion, flooding one's body. We've all experienced a **shame-attack**. In a second we can feel deflated, defeated, paralyzed. **Shame is nearly any negative moment of low self-value.** Everyone has some degree of struggle with shame, fear about one's value, or low self-worth. All human struggles occur on a continuum, from mild to severe. For some, the shame struggle is mild. For others, it is debilitating.

Shame is surrounded by fear, because it doesn't want to be seen. Fear perpetuates the shame because it makes us keep it hidden. No one likes to talk about their shame, yet revealing the fear in a supportive and loving environment is part of the cure.

I have observed two primary responses when shame is felt:

1) running away to hide (withdrawing, either internally or externally, from others), and **2) lashing out in anger.**

One of my clients is fragile-as-a-mouse when she is flooded with the fear of being judged or seen as defective, and wants to hide when that vulnerable shame feeling hits her. Paradoxically, my most grandiose and defensive client suffers with an equally large self-hatred. He lived by his feelings, which had a very broken "detector." He was inclined to believe that he was being disrespected by others, even when it wasn't their intention. Any trigger (event) which brought on the *perception* of being shamed, insulted, or disregarded by others acted as a catalyst. Like mixing dangerous liquids in a laboratory, the feeling of being disrespected in combination with his chronic sense of low self-worth, resulted in an explosion of rage. Ka-boom! Later he felt self-hatred for the rage, and the chronic cycle continued. He did not gain victory over lashing out when he felt shame, and then emotionally abusing his family, until he accepted God's grace and love for him. This was a process over time requiring humility, hard work, insight, and the intentional application of grace.

A person who is emotionally insecure lives with the liability of always needing others to provide a secure environment. Conversely, a secure person can remain calmly self-confident despite the brokenness of others. We must learn to hold our self-value in the presence of outward attacks (someone embarrasses us) and inward attacks (anger at yourself for a mistake). **Holding our value is the opposite of jumping in the shame hole.**

Shame has many sources:
1) An inborn human brokenness, or sin-tendency, which distorts our ability to love God, ourselves, and others (we all have this)
2) Dysfunctional family issues such as abuse, neglect, rejection, family secrets, or a parent's life-dominating problems (i.e., alcoholism and other addictions)
3) A lack of unconditional love and affirmation from our parents or caregivers
4) Our own broken choices and the ways we've hurt ourselves and others (this legitimate guilt usually is accompanied by shame, too)
5) Life losses (divorce, job loss) where we may feel devalued
6) Vulnerable inborn temperament (some people feel self-hatred more easily than others)
7) False beliefs about oneself which generate shame feelings: *I am terrible because I failed. I do not deserve respect. I cannot be forgiven. I am defective.* This is a chronic habit of making low-self-worth-meanings about everything we do or that happens to us.

Shame defies grace. In fact, grace and shame are arch enemies. Grace is necessary to heal shame. God is offering this grace to us, and we must accept it and apply the grace like a daily salve until shame has lost its toehold on us. It is absolutely necessary to let this self-rejection go so that we can be safe for ourselves.

Let's take a look at some of my clients (the names have been changed for privacy) and how we are combatting their shame issues. Although they come from a wide variety of humanity, their stories illustrate the shame sources I spoke of earlier. Each person's journey is affected by the quality of self-acceptance they have and their freedom from self-rejection. Their identity of self-worth (or lack of it) affects everything else. Any progress they make in their issues is going to be shaky without including the accompanying work on their self-worth. So here's to my clients, my teachers. See if any of these sound familiar to you.

Cindy, the sharp-tongued one: You have shame-roots from your family of origin that you haven't addressed. Your growth out of shame will help you let go of defensiveness and become a powerful, positive influence on your children. They need you to model a secure sense of self.

Rachael, the facing-the-abuse survivor: Regarding the abuse you endured, you must jettison the core belief that you caused it or did something wrong. You absorbed your abuser's shame. Give it back!

Beth, the competent one: You have used performance as a faulty measure of your worth, therefore as you rest from the need for achievement it will stir up any unhealed shame.

Margaret, the afraid-to-pray one: You have denied grace by believing that "the secret" meant you cannot restore the closeness to God you once had. This is a shame-based approach to God. He is waiting to receive your prayers.

Candice, the insecure youth pastor: You mistakenly believed that your mother's rejection somehow equaled God's rejection. This belief was the core of your shame-based identity. Swinging the "wrecking ball of truth" will help you in your quest for authenticity and freedom.

Jim, the adulterer-turned-repentant: You are not disqualified from God's grace and His future work through you. I respect your deep repentance. Now let go of the self-loathing. You can keep humility, but it's time to forgive yourself.

Christie, the perfectionistic mom: You no longer have to function and feel from a core fear of inferiority. Step into the grace-life.

Wendy, the lonely mom: Others struggle, too. Fearing relationships and avoiding community keeps you lonely. Life is a team sport. Return to your support group. Speak authentically. This will help you push against your shame.

Kim, the over-spender: No more "losing yourself" in spending, trying to buy your children's love. This is no antidote for hating yourself. They need an emotionally healthy mom more than the things you buy them.

Jana, the budding therapist: You are not a fraud. It is okay to joyfully pursue helping others while you honestly walk the parallel journey of your own growth.

Jane, the anxiety-struggler: You are a gifted and amazing woman who is temporarily experiencing anxiety. It does not define you. Don't make your anxiety worse by self-loathing.

Lauren, the single parent: Your narcissistic ex-husband injured your self-worth. You must regain it to effectively parent your strong-willed teen. Your child needs you to make your own healing a priority.

Ron, the combat veteran: The black moments of combat cannot overwhelm or negate the beauty of grace. When shame attacks, go to your safe place of grace and sit with God.

Alan, the executive manager: Your fears about your own worthlessness are more likely to generate anxiety than even your stressful job. Your company does not own you. Valuing yourself must always, always trump your career.

Terry, the dominant one: Powering up and intimidating others does not make you worth more. Your grandiosity would not be needed if you could quietly rest in your actual strengths.

Russ, the easy-to-be-defensive one: No need to be heavy-handed with anger to ward off feelings of worthlessness. Self-worth is more satisfying than defensiveness.

Anita, the fearful-of-life one: You may take your place in the world. No more fearing that you're disqualified.

Michael, the compulsive over-performer: Your earthly father demanded the highest performance in order to earn his stingy praise. Your heavenly Father offers a grace-infused sense of security.

Robert, the hopeless-in-his-marriage one: Growth in your marriage will always be held back by your foundation of self-rejection. This maintains a murky, emotional swamp between you and your wife. Keep confronting your shame issues so that you don't project your own self-misery onto your spouse.

Robert's wife, June, the equally-hopeless one: Your self-acceptance must exist independently of your spouse's love (or lack of it). You must understand who you are apart from Robert and claim your identity in Christ.

Jesus Christ is the great **Grace-Purveyor**, the great **Shame-Breaker**. Perhaps you're an outsider examining Jesus (I don't mean examining the Church…the broken, self-professed group who attempt to follow Him). Do not miss the good news: **although you're a broken mortal, you're deeply loved, and Christ has paid for your sins so that you may live in joyful freedom and security in God's love.** This is a free gift and not something you can earn. Life is to be a growth journey of learning to love God, yourself and others. Honesty is required to admit your mistakes and failures, but grace means you're not disqualified from love because you're imperfect. There is always a spiritual facet to shame-healing, and I believe that those who have the most thorough healing have included the power of **His shame-busting gospel**.

May we all grow in a grace-based identity.

2 The Compulsion to Hate My Own Life

"Wash me, and I shall be whiter than snow." Psalm 51:7 (NASB)

During the early years when I began my recovery, I often thought: *I hate my past life.* By this I meant that I hated the events of the abuse that I lived through. I hated that they were a part of my history. I hated that I was deceived. I hated that I wasn't powerful enough to have handled my abuser. I hated that I stayed in the abuse so long. I hated that I lied all those years and lived a double life. I hated that my abuse was so complex and hard to understand. Ultimately, *I hate myself.*

The Apostle Paul was also once a deeply deceived individual. He was zealous for a bad cause, but he thought he was obeying God. When God knocked him flat on the road to Damascus (see Acts, chapter 9), it was an abrupt, well, let's say, brutal confrontation. Paul was busted. Washed up. Lots of bad guilt under his belt.

I'm sure that Paul had an intense period of mourning after he realized that Jesus was the Messiah and that he'd done such damage to His followers. Paul had led a crusade to kill many of them. It must have been difficult to forgive himself. He must have felt unworthy of grace. Although he doesn't specifically say so, I think he must have struggled with intense self-loathing.

During the first two years after Paul was converted, he spent a great deal of time (probably alone) in the desert with God in Arabia (Galatians 1:17). He had to deeply apply God's truth to himself. How he must have struggled with Psalm 51:7: "Wash me, and I shall be whiter than snow." (NASB) I can just imagine Paul thinking: *Who? ME? Whiter than snow? I can't believe that God really could mean this. My sin is too great.* He faced a dilemma: Would he deeply embrace God's truth of forgiveness and redemption? Would he agree with God that the death of Christ was sufficient for his own great sins? Could he dare to believe he was washed whiter than snow?

I used to naively think that Paul was converted and then just skipped off merrily to preach about it, immediately free from guilt, shame, grief, and other diseases of the soul. But that wouldn't be real, and Paul gives us every indication in the New Testament that he was real like the rest of us. I've seen people struggle through the process of forgiving themselves, and I'm sure Paul must have struggled, too. He surely cried hot, bitter tears saying: *I hate my own life.* I'm sure that just when he'd begun to believe in forgiveness, he'd relapse into self-hating, as the vortex of worthlessness sucked him in again. Gasping for a grace-filled breath, he must have battled self-loathing time-and-time again.

Paul (previously named Saul) was in Jerusalem several times following his conversion. Although the Bible doesn't give us the details, we can imagine the inner pain he felt the first time he passed the spot where he'd so gladly condoned Stephen's stoning (Acts 7:54-60). It would have been a sobering moment. Given the many descriptions of shame and pain I've heard in my counseling office, I would imagine that Paul cast his eyes to the ground and bit his trembling lip in sorrow. He may have ducked into an alley to weep. The memory of his brazen, blood-thirsty "triumph" in stoning Stephen now made him nauseous. After laying down that night, the image of Stephen's glowing face intruded on his attempts to sleep. I can imagine Paul in distress, pacing in the wee hours of the night, crying: *I should have been stoned...Stephen should be the one to preach!* The accusing voice of Satan must have whispered that Paul was disqualified from grace. Mixed with his own self-accusations, the taunting inner dialogue kept repeating: *You're NOT worthy!*

Paul eventually resolved his guilt and shame by seeing himself as God saw him... forgiven... clean. It probably came to him the same way it comes to us. Slowly. In fits and starts. Two steps forward and one step backward. The awareness of "whiter than snow" seeping deeply into his self-hatred and changing the core way he saw himself. Paul tells us that he was indeed the greatest of sinners (1 Timothy 1:15), but now in grateful humility he knew that he was a new creature in Christ (2 Corinthians 5:17). I think that a lot of struggle and growth went on between the realizations of those two statements.

The gospel message is that God forgives us thoroughly when we embrace Christ as Savior. We are washed clean immediately. Unfortunately, our shame and self-loathing are not so easily conquered, not because God hasn't forgiven us, but because we cannot forgive ourselves. Grace seems irrational given our sinfulness.

God *does* promise to be with us in the process of facing ourselves. His promise is to see us through this process. While we might have some fear of the way others may see us, the most important thing is to embrace the way God sees us. If we confess our sins...He forgives (1 John 1:9). As we face truth, He supports us, for He Himself *is* Truth. "I am the way, the truth, and the life" (John 14:6, NASB). **In the end we must give God, and not others, the right to define us.**

The truest thing about you is what God says about you. The biggest issue to overcome is not *"How will others see me?"* but *"Will I see myself the way God sees me?"* I had to confront my feelings, which often screamed: *I'm horrible! I've surely forfeited the right to God's plan for my life.* Yes, feelings have to be confronted with the truth of God's Word, which declares: *"I AM LOVED."*

Embracing God's view of you, which is a process over time, is the only thing powerful enough to break the compulsion to hide in shame and hate yourself.

3 Do I Really Want to Get Well?

"Do you want to get well?" John 5:6 (The Message)

When Jesus went up to the sick man, He asked him, "Do you want to get well?" On the surface this might appear to be a rhetorical question, with the obvious answer being, "Yes!" But getting well can be costly, and this isn't a question to be answered too quickly. Let's lay out the costs and advantages of getting emotionally and spiritually healthy.

First, the costs.

If I work on getting well, I'm probably going to experience some pain. Not that my dysfunctional ways haven't already cost me a lot of pain, to be sure, but getting well won't be an easy street. In addition, my house of cards may collapse. I may have to endure a temporary period where I have to face uncertainty about the future. I will likely be reduced to my real truest self, and my "false" self may be stripped away. I may have to endure some embarrassment while I admit to others that such-in-such has been happening in my life, and things aren't as they appear to be. In honesty I come clean and admit my problems. Ouch! Let's not pretend there won't be pain.

Now, the advantages:

*I can have **integrity**. Integrity doesn't mean that I'm blameless, but that I am now being wholly honest. I may have a lot of problems in my life, but I am addressing them honestly, taking responsibility, and facing them. I respect myself for that.*

*I can have a **new resource of emotional energy**. I refuse to be "as sick as my secrets" (as they say in recovery). Now I am not spending my time hiding my problems from myself or others. Being in denial has taken up a lot of my energy. Now I can invest myself in meeting and overcoming the challenges, rather than in trying to suppress the truth.*

*I can **build character and honesty in my life that can never be shattered**. It will feel so good to be honest that I'll wonder why I spent so much time living in that house of cards, anyway! I wouldn't trade my new life of honesty for anything.*

> "Instead of the thorn bush, the cypress will come up,
> and instead of the nettle, the myrtle will come up."

I love this passage from Isaiah 55:13 (NASB). Obviously, thorns are an absolutely useless building material. Wouldn't you rather build with cypress, that beautiful wood from the southern swamps that never rots? Wouldn't you like it if the honesty and growth you're building now would lay a permanent and stable foundation for your life, something that wouldn't rot out from under you?

Have you ever been caught in nettle? That awful, burning plant can cause you misery if it gets on your skin. Nettle represents that terrible trap you've been in by avoiding the truth. Your addiction or secrecy will never bring anything but misery. In contrast, the myrtle tree blooms all summer. The beauty of honesty, humility, authentic sharing, and getting in community is that beauty that blooms and blooms.

Thorns in exchange for cypress. Nettle in exchange for beautiful myrtle. Not a bad trade.

Now cast yourself upon God's **love** for you, His **acceptance** of you despite your failures, and His plans of **hope** for your future. Whenever you are being as honest as you know how, you can bet that God will be in there working to heal you, comfort you, and restore you.

Weighing the costs and advantages above, *do you want to get well?*

4 Put Your Hand to the Plow

"But Jesus said to him, 'No one, after putting his hand to the plow and looking back, is fit for the kingdom of God.'" Luke 9:62 (NASB)

Jesus said, "No procrastination. No backward looks. You can't put God's kingdom off till tomorrow. Seize the day." Luke 9:62 (The Message)

Putting our "hand to the plow" is a way of saying that we have developed some resolve to face the work ahead of us. Plowing is a good metaphor. The purpose of plowing is to follow it up by planting seeds. The purpose of planting seeds is to reap a crop or harvest which makes the labor worthwhile. If we have ploughed and planted, growth is predictable. But we never get the harvest without first committing to plow and plant!

It takes a lot of courage to face a life-dominating problem. When we're getting well from a setback or problem in our life, it takes **perseverance** to stay with the healing process. **Healing happens one day at a time as we work on it by shedding the emotional baggage and draining the tank of pain.** The components of healing are time, talking, reading, feeling, and having authentic relationship with others. These things are the *work*. Doing these things is how we put our "hands to the plow."

It takes courage to say: *I'm going to talk about this. It's not going to go away by itself. It's got to be dealt with. I'm tired of hiding it, trying to save face, and worrying what others will think. I'm going to work on these things which are churning in me.*

A wound on the body must sometimes be drained for healing to continue. This is true on the emotional level as well. **We won't get real healing if we just let it scab over.** There may also be infection eating beneath the surface. The wound must be opened. For years we may have lived in denial: *It's not that bad. There's nothing I can do. I'm not going to tell anyone, etc.* These were ways that we lied to ourselves. Keeping the pain inside has taken a terrible toll on us. We don't want emotional surgery any more than we want to have physical surgery, but the long-term benefits are often excellent. The pain of having a cancerous tumor removed is a small price to pay for the prognosis of a healthy future.

It's true that talking often awakens emotional pain. Remember, plowing can't just be done on the surface. It's got to really turn up the soil! Initially, we can feel worse before we feel better. However, pain must be exhaled. We must give words and voice to it. Think of this again in comparison to physical surgery. Having open-heart surgery is painful. There can be scary moments before and after the surgery when we are afraid of what may happen and of being out of control. But the results can be life-enhancing. We get a new lease on life! Depending on the depth and volume of emotional pain we are carrying, or the extent of the addiction we are facing, emotional recovery can also be grueling. But wow! It feels so good to start experiencing emotional and spiritual freedom.

Ignoring emotional pain is costly. It eats at your body and soul. **It limits your capacity to have intimacy with others.** Although it may be painful to talk about your issues, in the end it is *less costly* than the damage of avoiding it longer and holding the pain inside.

No more procrastinating. I know this may be scary, but the best time to plow ahead and work on your healing is now.

5 When I Kept Silent

"When I kept silent, my bones wasted away through my groaning all day long." Psalm 32:3 (NIV)

"When I'm not open and honest, I make myself sick." (JoAnn's paraphrase)

As a therapist, I often use the phrase: **We can't be healed of what we can't get out of our mouths.** In other words, we usually can't heal from things which we either refuse to talk about or resist talking about. To talk about something requires taking a risk. This can feel very threatening, particularly when we are just opening up. I remember worrying that I'd be rejected, misunderstood, and shamed by others.

Talking is a pathway to healing. The things we hold within the narrowness of our own minds have the potential to become distorted and rancid. Getting it out in the open can be the first step toward healing. A sensitive and caring person (friend, therapist, or spiritual advisor) can extend compassion and mercy to us while we speak about our pain, confusion, or mistakes.

There is something dangerous about holding things in our minds that we are unwilling to tell others. This should be a "red flag" that those thoughts may deteriorate, become exaggerated, or grow into areas of bondage. No matter how crazy, embarrassing, or shameful our thoughts and experiences seem, the pathway to healing is opened when we speak about it to a trusted person in a safe setting.

Holding pain within us, or "keeping silent" has the potential to make us worse off, not better. Mental anxiety eventually plays itself out in the body and can cause physical illnesses. Like King David in the verse above, our "bones will waste away," and we'll make ourselves sick. I credit a large part of my healing and growth to my willingness to keep unloading my thoughts and experiences.

Talking about something once may not be enough. Complex and painful experiences often have to be talked through many times and from many angles. Each time we talk about an experience we resolve small pieces of it. Over time, this adds up, and we start to feel the momentum of getting well.

I meet many people who have extensive pain within them. They think: *I can't let it out. I can't face it.* No, you *can* let it out, and you *must* face it.

6 Chase the Robbers!

> *"And (Jesus) entered the temple and began to drive out those who were buying and selling in the temple, and overturned the tables of the money changers and the seats of those who were selling doves..."* Mark 11:15 (NASB)

Jesus used some rather dramatic behavior when he disrupted the greedy money changers in the temple area. These people were taking advantage of the common worshiper who had come to Jerusalem to offer sacrifices. They used abusive pricing strategies and kept a tight monopoly on the sale of animals and birds for sacrifice. Hardened by years of deception, they didn't mind shortchanging the worshipers either! Jesus disrupted them twice in His ministry: early on when He first began preaching (John 2:13-16) and shortly after He entered Jerusalem for His final week of ministry (Mark 11:15-17).

These "business men," whom Jesus later called thieves and robbers, sat behind their tables, no doubt entrenched there for years. The average person had probably come to see this as normal, however, Jesus couldn't stomach it. He would not accept their presence. He longed to restore honor and dignity to the Temple. The moneychangers would not have responded to a gentle request to leave. They would have to be run out. In an act of intensity, Jesus made a whip of cords and chased them. He also grabbed their tables and dumped them awry. Jesus made no apologies for His intense behavior.

As believers in Christ, we are the present temple of God. There is no longer a temple made of stones where God dwells. Under the new covenant, which Jesus ushered in, **you and I are now the temple**. "...do you not know that your body is a temple of the Holy Spirit who is in you...For you have been bought with a price..." (1 Corinthians 6:19-20, NASB).

I have found that many believers in Christ have allowed the "moneychangers" to remain in their lives. They sit in our souls behind figurative tables labeled **shame, fear, false-guilt, and self-loathing.** They make no apologies for robbing us of joy, self-worth, or dignity, and they are not going to leave without a fight. They are the "robbers" who first gained a foothold in our minds when we believed their lies.

We may have believed that we are to blame for the abuse we endured (perpetrators are so clever at transferring their shame to the victim). We may have accepted living in a general state of fear about life, rather than moving toward life-enhancing and God-honoring goals or relationships. We may have believed that we must continue to feel guilty for bad choices we have made, rather than accepting that we are truly forgiven. We may have been thinking of ourselves in self-loathing ways (*God loves and cherishes others more than me*), rather than standing on the truth that we are uniquely loved. We may have accepted these lies as normal because they have been entrenched within us for many years.

It's time to change your passive approach to the shame you carry. Grab your whip, as Jesus did, and get mad! The temple, which is *YOU,* has been violated by these robbers and it's time to chase them out. They will not respond to gentle requests to leave. Standing your ground in Christ means that you are not going to accept their presence any longer!

Picture yourself running through the temple, as Jesus did, overthrowing the tables of shame, fear, false-guilt, and self-loathing. As you imagine this, make your declaration:

> In honor of the freedom Christ bought for me,
> I will not engage in attacking myself anymore.
> I refuse to carry false-guilt.
> I will not wear shame.
> I will not live in fear.
> Be gone, you robbers!

You reflect holy anger, and the character of Christ Himself, when you honor your freedom in Christ, overthrowing their tables and chasing them out!

7 The Shepherd's Gentle Call to Dignity

> *"Behold, I stand at the door and knock; if anyone hears My voice and opens the door, I will come in to him, and dine with him and he with Me."* Revelation 3:20 (NASB)

Christ never manipulates His followers. He always preserves their sense of personal dignity and choices. This is the hallmark of real love. Notice Christ's humble declaration in Revelation 3:20 above: *I stand at the door and knock.*

Christ is a gentleman. He won't barge in. He knocks. Admitting Him into our lives is *our* decision. We see this over and over throughout the Gospels (which are the first four books of the New Testament and four different writers' accounts of Christ's life). Christ never makes anyone do anything. He honors each person's free will. He respects their choices. He preserves their personal dignity. This truth is particularly important to anyone who has been through abuse, or had someone else's will imposed on him or her. In contrast to Christ, people who manipulate are pushy, and their goal is to achieve their agenda regardless of other's reluctance to participate.

Christ describes Himself as the "Good Shepherd" who "lays down His life for the sheep" (John 10:11, NASB). As a shepherd, He will never drive, force, or push His sheep. In describing authentic love, Christ says that the real Shepherd, in contrast to the imposter, "calls his own sheep by name…leads them out…goes ahead of them…" (John 10:3-4, NASB). This passage is a tip-off that people who push or drive others are demonstrating that their motives are self-centered, and not for our best interest. Instead they have some underlying motive.

In this same chapter the "false" shepherd is called the "hired hand" (John 10:12, NASB). He doesn't own the sheep himself, and he wouldn't sacrifice for them. A hired hand might say that he has our best interest at heart, but he is misrepresenting what the Shepherd's true care for us would look like. By contrast, Christ *leads* us. He goes before us. He walks ahead of us, lovingly calling us.

This thought was very important to me as I tried to resolve the spiritual confusion while healing from the abuse. My abuser had driven me, pushed me, and manipulated me, using the pretense that God was telling him to do these things. These Scriptures helped me to see clearly that God would never have done such a thing. Along the slow healing path, I could open myself to trusting God because He wasn't going to "make me" do anything. I didn't have to be afraid of Him.

As your Good Shepherd, Christ is calling you forward to dignity. He goes ahead of you. In the supreme demonstration of His love, He has already laid down His life for you.

8 Am I Codependent?

> *Don't you remember the rule we had when we lived with you? "If you don't work, you don't eat." And now we're getting reports that a bunch of lazy good-for-nothings are taking advantage of you. This must not be tolerated."* 2 Thessalonians 3:10-12 (The Message)

During the 1970's there was a counseling movement that began to focus on helping families of addicts and alcoholics. Therapists often observed that some people in the family were too tolerant of the addict's behavior, had difficulty enforcing consequences for bad behavior, and even played a role in the addict continuing his addiction. This person was called "codependent" because she played a part in the addict's merry-go-round of chemical dependency. She was a co-participant at some level. That's how we got the term "codependent." Today codependency has a wider application and is understood to be a relational pattern that can take place in any relationship, not just one that includes chemical dependency. The defining question is: *How am I participating in the bad things that are happening in this relationship so that I may even help the pain to continue?*

I've found that it can be hard to distinguish codependent behavior from loving behavior, so let's try to contrast the two. Codependency is an emotional tendency in which a person yields and defers to others at the expense or imbalance of her own welfare, dignity, or identity. Yielding to the other person is sometimes driven by a sense of guilt or fear, and there is usually some emotional manipulation being wielded by the recipient of the help (the emotionally unhealthy person). The helper may be motivated by fear: *If I don't comply, I may lose the relationship or experience their anger.* In addition, the helper may be over-spiritualizing her giving and sacrifice. The codependent is unable to withstand the emotional manipulation based on intimidating factors: fear of the consequences: *My addicted husband might die if I put him out;* level of understanding: *God wants us to be merciful. Helping him isn't really hurting me;* or emotional dependency: *I can't live without him.*

In contrast, an emotionally healthy, loving person has a high value of her own worth balanced by humility and love for others. She makes choices through wisdom and love, not fear. It's true that a loving person may at times deny or inconvenience herself, and even sacrifice for the welfare of another. Galatians 6:2 (NASB) applies in this way, "Bear one another's burdens." This means that we are to help unselfishly during crisis times when others have "heavy loads" (the meaning of the Greek word for "burdens" used here). Christians are familiar with verses that tell us to love others, such as "do to others as you would have them do to you" (Matthew 7:12, NIV) and "love bears all things" (1 Corinthians 13:7, NASB). Clearly self-sacrifice is, *at times*, a mark of being a disciple of Christ.

The trick in all this is ***discernment***. A person must indeed be both loving *and* discerning. **Love should sacrifice only within the bounds of discernment**. The Apostle Paul encourages us to let our love "abound" in "real knowledge and all discernment..." (Philippians 1:9, NASB). We are not supposed to willy-nilly sacrifice ourselves. There has to be discernment about the situation. It's great to let our love for others abound, but what is the real knowledge and discernment about the person whom we are helping? Here is where tender-hearted and generous people need to take note: *We must allow others the personal responsibility of their own lives.* Just a few verses after the "bear one another's burdens" verse I cited earlier, Paul seems to reverse things and say just the opposite, insisting each person should "carry his own load" (Galatians 6:5, NIV). Wow! This means that one's daily life responsibilities (the meaning of the Greek word for "load" used here) should not be put on another. Often an emotionally unhealthy person wants us to carry their load. They do not want to be responsible, grow up, stop using others, or reap their own choices.

It's not uncommon for a woman to over-spiritualize her codependent behavior in the name of "Christian love." Driven by fear, she thinks: *They can't make it without me* or *I'm doing this to win them to the Lord*. However, codependency is often hidden beneath the surface. The helper may lose her identity in the service of trying to change, rescue, or save the other person. Symptoms of codependency may include enabling another person to continue his irresponsible or abusive behavior, thus the helper is sometimes called "the enabler." For example, a parent does not require an adult child to pay rent for living at home ("My son can't afford rent"). Yet on closer examination the son probably spends $600 a month gambling and drinking. In this way the parents allow, or enable, the bad and disrespectful behavior to continue. It's amazing how long family members will shell out money into the black hole of another's entitlement. This is not love. Any behavior that does not give and require respect is not in the realm of real love. Co-dependents can be numb to their own needs and wants and be obsessed with someone else's needs. In a not-so-funny joke I heard, "When a codependent falls from a tall building, someone else's life flashes before her eyes."

In contrast, discernment requires that we set boundaries in our relationships with irresponsible, unsafe, and rebellious people. Setting a boundary means that we should observe limits in helping others. There are times to say "no more." When dealing with an irresponsible or entitled person, consider 2 Thessalonians 3:10-12 (The Message): "If you don't work, you don't eat." When there is an unsafe person, we are to "be on guard against him..." (2 Timothy 4:15, NASB). And we are not to "associate" or even "eat" with a rebellious person (1 Corinthians 5:11, NASB).

There are times we must pull back, stop exposing ourselves to loss and disrespect, and leave the outcome to God. Although there are times to extend mercy unconditionally, a helper should observe when she is met with chronic disregard and repeated poor behavior. It's time to stop excusing the prodigal.

So many times I see a woman trying to use mercy, hoping to move a rebel to repentance. If our mercy is being repeatedly trampled on, it's a sign that this isn't going to move our prodigal spouse, friend, or child to repentance. Pull back and set boundaries.

The codependent woman usually over-values the other person and under-values herself. She may feel a sense of false guilt when trying to set boundaries, and often needs support from a wise friend or counselor to shore up her resolve. I often prepare a client for the inevitable "zing of guilt" that will happen when she finally tells another person "no." The unhealthy person/addict will shoot her with the emotional arrow of guilt: "I thought you loved me!" It's a manipulation designed to move her to give in, feel sorry for the prodigal, and even apologize for attempting to set a boundary. A mercy-prone helper will often feel guilty in setting boundaries, fear making the irresponsible person uncomfortable, and feel that she cannot stand it if she withdraws support from the prodigal. Fear is the undermining force. She may be dependent, need the relationship, and feel unable to set a boundary and put the prodigal in God's hands.

For years I have worked on this tendency in myself… the reluctance to set boundaries when I have been disrespected by someone. Although I still love to extend mercy to others, I have slowly learned to follow wisdom in this sometimes uncomfortable way, rather than serving others out of guilt, fear, or obligation. Some individuals (more often, women than men) have strong inborn temperament traits of almost super-empathy and tolerance. This can lead to emphasizing only the Scriptures about sacrificially loving others without the balance of the Scriptures which tell us about dealing with the foolish or wicked ones. Those who have temperaments like mine don't need sermons on being unselfish! I'm still extremely sensitive to another person accusing me of being selfish or unloving and I've sometimes over-spiritualized this: *I think God wants me to continue helping this person.* It can sound counter-intuitive to the Christian message of love to say "no," but codependent behavior makes one vulnerable to exhaustion, burnout, and abuse when helping others. When I first began setting boundaries I felt mean saying "no," even if a wise person would agree I had already passed the point of generous assistance. I've learned to coach myself for the inevitable guilt-trip the other person may zing me with, spot emotional manipulation sooner, and grow in my discernment.

Like all forms of human behavior, codependency exists on a continuum, from mild to severe. When you combine a woman with very high inborn qualities of compassion, being cooperative, and selflessness with an intimate relationship to a pathological man (see Essay #13), you've just fused the atom! It's extremely hard to split it apart again. The man keeps taking and the woman is convinced she'll change him by being nicer, more tolerant, and more forgiving than ever. She's determined that love will change him, and that she will be able to make him love her through self-sacrificing behavior and example. It doesn't work. If he's capable of change, and not irreparably calloused/narcissistic, he'll be moved to change by her standing for truth, not by her yielding in deference.

Some people cite the fact that Christ was "meek and lowly in heart" (Matthew 11:29, KJV). Before we define our behavior as meek, we should note the Biblical definition. The Greek word translated "meek" here is the same term that refers to the bit in a horse's mouth, such as that used to hold back a strong stallion. The horse has the strength to run away, but the bit in his mouth holds back the strength, bridling it for good. A stallion isn't fearful. The reason he isn't running away with the rider is because his strength is being restrained, not because he's afraid to run. Many times I felt I was being "meek" by putting up with disrespect. However, this was a **false meekness**, especially because I was afraid to address the disrespect. I had spiritualized my fear and given it the name of a virtue (meekness). I wasn't a stallion who was holding back strength. I was acting out of fear and being codependent.

Occasionally we step forward to confront another's behavior but then restrain our strength because the timing isn't right. In addition, the Lord may have us confront only part of someone's behavior, but our meekness (bridled strength) enables us to use appropriate self-restraint and wisdom. We have the strength to confront but there are other issues at stake. This is true meekness. This is something very different than failing to confront another out of fear (my former and incorrect definition of meekness). This is an old sore point with me: *Don't act out of fear and then call it meekness!*

It all goes back to fear. The reason you haven't pulled back after being disrespected repeatedly is because you fear what will happen if you confront the unhealthy person and erect boundaries. To pull back is to give up the influence you believe your love and helping generates. This boils down to giving up control, or your *illusion* of control in another's life. **Control and fear are close cousins who do everything together**. Have you used giving and sacrifice to leverage control over another's behavior? Have you realized, like I have, that it simply doesn't work? It only hurts you.

9 Wise as Serpents

> *"...be ye therefore wise as serpents, and harmless as doves."* Matthew 10:16 (KJV)

As I was growing up, I never had trouble with the second part of that verse that is, being *harmless as a dove*. I seemed to have an inborn tendency to have deference for others. Even as a child, if I had a conflict with someone, I worried that it might be my fault. I fretted over any relationship with a friend that was strained, and I was apt to say that something was my fault even if it wasn't. I used apologizing as a way to avoid the conflict of challenging anyone, and to lower my sense of anxiety whenever I thought someone was mad at me. I can't remember if I ever picked even the smallest fight (well, except maybe with my big brother...but that doesn't count!).

On the continuum of human behavior, I was born with a compliant temperament. While being easy-going is a good trait, I didn't recognize when I'd compromised myself too much. Deference, or yielding to others wishes, was easy for me. Yes, being harmless as a dove was second nature. The danger in this is that one can have poor emotional boundaries, making one too vulnerable to abuses by others. My life is certainly an example of this.

I have often seen this tendency in Christian men and women who have internalized the concepts of being quiet-spirited, submissive, and self-denying in the service of their spouses, families, or others. Some of us have taken this too far. In over-extending ourselves to others who are being selfish or hurtful to us, we often fail to make a stand for our own dignity. In doing so, we can actually block the growth that they should be experiencing. When people in our lives are irresponsible, they are happy when WE take responsibility for bailing them out of their trouble. They savor the exaggerated sense of guilt that we feel when we try to make choices for our own self-interest. They have mastered the accusation "You don't love me" when we try to say "no more." This is a powerful emotional manipulation that tender-hearted people often give in to. However, by allowing others to "mess over us" we actually insure that it will be even longer before they face their problems. In the language of psychology this is called *enabling* others.

Being wise as a serpent has to do with how we should act toward people who DON'T have our best interest at heart, who are failing to be fair, and who keep expecting US to do all the giving. I had to learn that it was okay to take action on my own behalf. I already knew how to be harmless as a dove, but my spiritual and emotional growth needed to emerge in the area of being wise as a serpent. I had to learn that it was prudent to set boundaries, protect myself, and learn to say "no."

It was wise for me to make a stand about being tough with Wayne (my deceased husband) about his addiction. By being tough with him and wise as a serpent, I made the environment more conducive for his growth, even though in the end he didn't choose for his recovery (others' choices are never in our control). Although we can't guarantee that others will make the right choices for recovery or growth in their lives, we can provide the best setting for helping them to "wake up" by letting them face themselves. Acting out of fear and giving in (especially when they threaten us with rejection) will almost certainly allow them to continue longer.

For all you "doves" out there, it's probably time for you to have some tenacity about your own self-interest. If you find yourself always giving in to a person who is demanding, it's time to set limits. It's time to set boundaries. "No, I won't loan you money anymore." "No, I will not continue this phone conversation when you are being rude to me." "No, you cannot live here anymore because…" "No, I will not keep this a secret any longer." This is a spiritual position of wisdom and dignity. It's not selfishness on your part. It's being wise as a serpent.

10 The Fear of Others

"The Lord is my helper; I will not be afraid. What can mere mortals do to me?" Hebrews 13:6 (NIV)

In a sermon recently, my pastor told a funny vignette:

> When you're twenty, you think everybody is watching you, and you really care. When you're forty, you think everybody is watching you, but you don't care. When you're sixty, you realize that nobody was paying any attention to you anyway!

With emotional growth we change the way we view other's opinions of us. We don't need their approval as much. We relax the way we monitor other's reactions to us. We transition (hopefully) from the fear of what others think to the confidence that God is for us. *If God is for me...what does it matter who may be against me?* (Romans 8:31, JoAnn Version). With an increasing sense of security in Christ we are less "rejection conscious."

When I first talked about writing my abuse story almost twelve years ago, I thought: *Only one in ten people will understand it, and the other nine won't believe me or they will just flat out reject me!* Over time, I've changed my formula. Now I'm much less "rejection conscious" and much more realistic. In fact, as I write this, I am assuming that two out of ten readers will directly apply some part of my story to themselves, seven will learn something useful in reading it, and one won't believe me and may even *blame* me. These are good enough odds for me to risk writing this book. I can endure the one out of ten. I have learned that I just can't convince everyone, and I'm learning not to emotionally suffer over those people.

There are elements of my story that are common to many serious problems. Perhaps the most common element is **denial**. Living in denial is a central way we avoid the pain of dealing with something we don't know how to face. Fear can be paralyzing, and it's understandable that we run from facing our problems dead on. We silence truth when it is trying to speak within us, because we cannot see our way out. There is less immediate pain in avoiding the tough questions. We are looking for an easy way out that will save our image and spare us emotional pain. These are the ways our brokenness can undermine our healing.

We'll drive ourselves into more fear if we sit around worrying about who is going to condemn us if we get honest. The flip side of this is that being honest attracts a very nice circle of people around us who are willing to be real. Being with authentic people who are open about their problems is so refreshing. We can learn from each other.

Living for the approval of others, or the fear of their judgmental attitudes, is a bondage that will prevent your healing. Look away from them and toward God. Leaving the critical crowd behind and reaching forward to the authentic friendships before you is a marker of true growth.

11 The Fantasy of My Own Control

"I am the Lord, and there is no other; besides Me there is no God…"
Isaiah 45:5 (NASB)

When Stuart and I had been married a few years I had a vivid dream that Stuart had been kidnapped and that he was being held in a corn silo across a dark field. Under cover of night I set out to rescue Stuart. As I walked toward the distant silo I noted that I felt powerful. I had all kinds of gear attached to me. I wore a combat-style suit. I had ropes and a gun strapped on. I felt bold.

In the dream I entered the silo. Looking up I saw Stuart hanging by his ankles, upside down. He was tied up and gagged. The silo had an old, abandoned feel to it. The wet moss growing between the stones gave it a creepy, deserted feel. I went right to work. I fired my hook/gun with attached rope (I don't know what they call these things) to a ledge above Stu. With a kind of grandiose strength I pulled myself up 30 feet to Stu's level. Swinging out with perfect balance, I scooped Stu on my back in a sort of fireman's carry, using only one arm. My power continued. Bearing our weight, I lowered us to the ground and cut Stuart loose. We hugged and then went home. It was all very tidy. A Green Beret-style rescue executed without a hitch.

At breakfast the next morning I laughed while I told the dream to Stuart. "It's like nothing could stop me!" Sighing and grimacing, Stu conveyed that the dream was preposterous, noting also that it didn't make him look manly. After musing at my vivid imagination (Stu's dreams aren't nearly so creative), he left for work.

Several days later Stuart matter-of-factly said, "I know the interpretation of your dream." I'd never experienced Stuart as an interpreter of dreams, but there was something confident and convincing in his voice. "Okay. Let's hear it," I said. "Well, it's clear," Stu began. "You want to believe that although you weren't able to save Wayne, you'd be able to save me."

I instantly teared up. The truth of it was piercing. Yes, that's exactly what the dream depicted. That's exactly what my inner psyche was playing out. Although I had suffered an irreparable defeat and couldn't save Wayne, I wanted to believe that if anything ever tried to take Stuart away, I'd somehow succeed in saving my husband this time. Somewhere below consciousness the dream was playing out my fantasy of control. Its subtitle could read, "I *refuse* to lose another husband! Next time I'll be powerful. Next time I'll be in control. Next time…*I'll be God!*"

I suppose one of the enduring topics of life is: *Why can't I control or stop bad things that happen?* Even though I've made a great deal of peace with Wayne's death, my dream showed me that the desire for control runs deep. I don't like feeling vulnerable to the unknown in this world. In the end I'm a mere mortal, not an all-knowing and all-powerful deity. As the verse above says, there is no God but Him.

It was hard for me to accept that I had done everything I should have done for Wayne. I focused, for some time after his death, on the possibility that I had failed to do all I should. The "what ifs" were daily on my mind: *What if I should have confronted him more? What If I confronted him too much?* The only path to peace was the acceptance that I had done all I knew. No one does more than that.

As this acceptance grew stronger and put down its roots in me, I began thinking of the positive ways I had loved Wayne more than the possible ways I had failed. I imagined a field of beautiful yellow flowers. Looking at the thousands of flowers, I had the thought: *Each one of those flowers is a beautiful act of love that I did for Wayne. Each flower represents a smile I gave him, a kind deed or word, or a prayer on his behalf.* Then a question followed: *Would that field be any more beautiful if it had one more flower?* Rather than meditating on what I didn't do, I would sit with the truth of the thousands of acts of love I *had* done.

In the affluent Western world, where predictability and control are assumptions of life, we add another burden to our grief process. We're always thinking: *Someone should have done something.* We're either blaming ourselves or someone else. We seem to feel, when anyone dies for any reason, that the right medicine, science, and professional intervention could have prevented it. We live in a societal mentality of blame: *Someone has to be at fault. Someone should have controlled for this loss!* We've taken this too far.

We're as prone to blame ourselves as we are others. Ironically, if I decide something is my fault, there is a kind of morbid relief in believing that. The reasoning goes like this: *If I caused the bad event, then next time I'll learn what I did wrong and I won't do it again. Thus I can prevent anything bad happening again.* This is yet another way we play into the illusion of control…a way we seek to make life feel safer.

The field of flowers pictured in my mind helped me see that there is great beauty in what I did do, and focusing on what I didn't do isn't even necessary… and it doesn't change the picture. That's just my over-responsible and control-seeking humanness looking for a way to feel less vulnerable in a world where loss and grief intrude. **No one loves perfectly, and even if there were mistakes I made, peace wouldn't be found in rehearsing my mistakes or omissions.**

How would your loss feel different if you weighed the things you DID do, and remembered the beauty of the love you showed? Perhaps there are many flowers in your field.

12 Forgiveness is a Messy Thing

"And forgive us our debts, as we also have forgiven our debtors."
Matthew 6:12 (NIV)

I cannot think of another topic which arouses as much fear, confusion, anger, and resistance as the topic of forgiveness. I know, because I have personally wrestled with each of these feelings. It isn't a topic to be treated casually. It isn't tidy. **Forgiveness is messy.** There are no neat formulas. When we have been through numerous hurts in relationships, and there are literally hundreds of hurtful experiences, it may take some time to process forgiveness.

Forgiveness was a five-year journey for me. Conceptualizing forgiveness in the early stages of my healing was nearly impossible. The only initial commitment I made to God was that I was willing to end up at forgiveness eventually.

Many people who have been through abuses have a fractured sense of self. There is little dignity within them, and they live feeling fearful of those who have hurt them. The abuse has left them internally wounded and humiliated. If their abuser(s) walked in the room, they would want to run. Fear is still a very present monster to them. This essay on forgiveness is written to those of you in this category. I am not writing here to those who are stubbornly holding onto bitterness or who somehow savor holding hate.

I have seen Christian women rush to forgive too soon. Now I know that this sounds nearly blasphemous to some of you. Forgive *too soon*? You're thinking: *Aren't we supposed to make forgiveness the first thing?* Some women, while still internally broken and wounded from their abuse, are encouraged to forgive their abusers. You cannot, and should not, try to forgive out of this state of being. You aren't ready. **This is the wrong order of healing and freedom.** First comes the slow process of restoring dignity, increasing self-esteem, and reducing fear.

I have counseled many Christian women who felt obligated to deal with forgiveness in the early stages of healing. Later they reasoned that they had already forgiven their abusers, therefore they would not allow themselves to voice the pain, hurt, and anger that were still pent up inside of them. They had achieved only a pseudo-forgiveness. This may have also been a way to run from feeling the pain and avoiding the hard work of recovery. They wanted to escape the pain of abuse quickly, so they rushed to say, "I have forgiven my abuser," as if trying to take a shortcut to healing. But they were still very broken in their souls and fear was still a powerful presence in their lives.

One of the premier signs of recovery for a victim of abuse is the recovery of **dignity.** As dignity comes in, usually anger comes in with it. This is a healthy anger signaling a restored sense of God-intended self-honor. Yet this can be troubling to women who have never allowed themselves to feel mad, or who have not been allowed by others to exhibit anger. The anger can feel sinful to them, but it is not. It is really the beginning of freedom.

Some victims who are healing are confused by the anger they feel. They start to reclaim their dignity, but they also start to feel angry at their abuse or abuser. Then a false-guilt whispers: *Oh, this can't be a good thing, because I have been saying that I forgive my abuser, and talking about my abuse is making me angry, so this can't be good.* They go back to focusing on forgiveness, backing off the anger, and shutting down the recovery of dignity. This short-circuits the most authentic kind of healing.

Real forgiveness will arise eventually from a restored sense of self, not a broken numbness that merely disregards the offense. **Real forgiveness is done from an internal emotional position of dignity, not fear.** Once my dignity was restored, I felt protected emotionally from my abuser. Anger at the abuse and the unjustness of it came in like a flood. Over time I could let it go, but not prematurely before anger had lifted me to a place of dignity. Holding onto anger at my abuser indefinitely would have actually kept me tied to him. Any forgiveness I thought I did early in my recovery turned out to be rather shallow. The reality of forgiveness didn't come until years four and five of my recovery, after my dignity had grown solid.

Some would justify rushing to forgiveness by citing Jesus' example. As Jesus died on the cross He actually extended forgiveness to His attackers immediately: "Father, forgive them..." (Luke 23:34, NIV). However, please note that Jesus died without fear, **HE KNEW WHO HE WAS,** He knew who was at fault, and His dignity was not broken. In contrast, it often takes years for victims of abuse to reach this same position of inner security. This is a process over time.

When I counsel abuse victims, I allow each person to articulate what forgiveness means regarding her own history. For me, forgiveness meant that I committed my abuser to God's judgment, whatever that would mean. I came to trust that, when I arrive in heaven and hear God's decisions about how He dealt with my abuser, I will be satisfied with the rightness of His choices. If I had ultimately refused to release the anger, it would have poisoned me with bitterness. I surrendered the anger over time, but without feeling rushed to do so. I have not lost anything in this surrender, because I kept my dignity.

13 Who is a Pathological Man?

> *"Your tongue devises destruction, like a sharp razor, o worker of deceit. You love evil more than good, falsehood more than speaking what is right. You love all words that devour..."* Psalm 52:2-4 (NASB)

A pathological man is a man who repeatedly harms people in relationships. An estimated 4% of all men are pathological, known by various names: sociopathic, anti-social, strongly narcissistic, or psychopathic. If a woman walks into a room of 25 men, whether a bar or a church, one of them probably fits this category, usually undetected until she is in a relationship (either professional or personal) with him.

Pathological men exist in every setting, but because they are often highly intelligent, they may rise to leadership roles. The settings vary: abusive husbands, narcissistic bosses in work settings, arrogantly-entitled family members, manipulative professors preying on female students, church leaders masquerading as trusted believers, or anger-driven intimate partners who lack remorse and guilt. Those of us affected by these men have more in common than not. A pathological man extracts a similar toll, no matter what the setting. In fact, a darkly pathological man will harm many women in his lifetime.

A pathological man is, in biblical terms, an evil man. In spiritual language he has a hardened heart, a wicked tongue, devises evil, and has seared his conscience. He enjoys gloating about those he has exploited. He lies. He cheats. He twists the truth. Goodness will not win him to repentance. He loves evil. Do not try to change him. You won't succeed. You will end up being dominated. Even if he temporarily appears to change and grow, by definition he cannot sustain positive change. He lacks emotional depth and insight, and is simply incapable of empathy and understanding how he hurts you.

Most people have difficulty in understanding why a woman does not leave an abusive relationship with this kind of man. The understanding comes when we see into the inner world of her mind and emotions. In research by The Institute for Relational Harm and Public Pathology Education, an organization committed to raising awareness about pathological men (see resource page), the women most vulnerable to these relationships scored extremely high on the personality traits of cooperativeness and empathy. Did you know that these inner personality traits, so lovely in normal relationships, will predispose her to stay in abuse? *The basic formula goes like this: Combine one pathological man with one very cooperative and empathetic woman and you get a prolonged, unhealthy, destructive, miserable relationship.*

When you manage to leave the relationship, you will face a long road of recovery. You have probably been harmed financially, emotionally, sexually, and spiritually. Your experiences most likely fit the psychological criteria for trauma. You, like many women, may even experience Post Traumatic Stress Disorder

(PTSD), both during and after the harmful relationship. There may be an aftermath of anxiety, hypervigilance, and lowered ability to cope with life issues.

As you heal from a pathological relationship, it is essential that you sever contact with the pathological man. Don't do this alone. You deserve the assistance of a professional counselor. You need to create a safe, gentle life for yourself, one as free from stress as possible. Fill your life with things that matter most and give you enjoyment, such as supportive friends, wise counselors, the unconditional love of pets, the beauty of nature, authentic spiritual community, etc.

14 Bathsheba, the Lamb

...Why your college professor or therapist shouldn't be sleeping with you and other things you can learn from a 3,000 year-old story...

> *"But the poor man had nothing except one little ewe lamb which he bought and nourished; and it grew up together with him and his children. It would eat of his bread and drink of his cup and lie in his bosom, and was like a daughter to him."* 2 Samuel 12:3-4 (NASB)

Perhaps you're startled by the title of this essay. For years I assumed that Bathsheba was more suited to a "bad girls of the Bible" list than deserving of an association with lambs. *Isn't this the same Bathsheba,* you're thinking, *that we've always paired with King David?* Yes, it's the same Bathsheba. In 50 years of Sunday sermons I've heard many references to David's "adultery" with Bathsheba, an explanation too general to explain the story at hand. Perhaps we've been overlooking some important aspects of the narrative that could explain why, when God delivered His commentary on their relationship, He saw Bathsheba as an innocent lamb, not a guilty adulteress. Would you stick with me while I review the story?

First, some quick comments about King David. Facts about David's life are laid wide open to us in the Bible, practically unmatched in detail by other Bible characters. We have a record of his entire life (the historian Josephus says he died at age 70). When he was anointed as the future king of Israel he was only a humble, youthful shepherd. He was chosen, the Scripture says, because the Lord "looks at the heart," letting us know that David began his calling, as at least some great leaders do, in wholesomeness of soul. Sermons often emphasize the idea that David was a "man after (God's) own heart" (1 Samuel 13:14, NASB), a reference to David which occurred even before his being chosen as king. We have record of King Saul's murderous pursuit of him, his genius as a minstrel and poet, and his military conquests which eventually established his kingdom on a scale of the great rulers of Egypt and Persia. This is the same man who fought Goliath as a youth and authored the familiar 23rd Psalm, which includes the beloved phrase "The Lord is my Shepherd, I shall not want..." (Psalm 23:1, NASB). This essay isn't a comprehensive review of David's life, but a look into his darkest moments.

In contrast, let us look at an ordinary young woman named Bathsheba. She was married to Uriah, who was a soldier in King David's army. No children are mentioned, so they might not have been married very long. Bathsheba could have easily been fifteen or sixteen, an age when many girls married in that time and culture. Uriah and Bathsheba seemed to have been poor folks with no connections to power or influence (implied, as we'll see later, in Nathan's parable).

David had the idea to sleep with Bathsheba when he saw her bathing on her roof. I've heard implications from writers and speakers that Bathsheba was somehow luring David. It then follows, given this assumption, that her encounter with David was adultery, implying two consenting adults (at least one is married) who willingly have sexual relations. However, the Bible doesn't say anywhere that Bathsheba was acting as a temptress or that this was adultery. Let's consider for a moment that David's sexual contact with Bathsheba wasn't brought on by her.

Bathsheba had begun a bath, apparently during the night, because the text says David saw her when he got up from his bed during the evening and went out on his roof (2 Samuel 11:2). This hardly could have meant that Bathsheba was plotting anything, but it was a chance coincidence that David saw her. Rather than her bathing nearby in an exhibitionist way (the "intentional temptress" viewpoint), it could be that David saw the form of a woman in the moonlight, 100 yards away, apparently stepping into a bathing trough. In this narrative it seems natural to view Bathsheba as minding her own business, cooling herself in a middle-of-the-night bath.

Nevertheless, the appearance of a woman bathing set David's mind on a path to satisfy his agenda. He sexualized this opportune moment. He inquired who she was and, although hearing that she was married to Uriah, sent for her to be brought to his chamber. It's obvious that he was told or else he recognized Uriah's name as a soldier in his own army, away from home under Joab's command, because David knew exactly where to send for Uriah later. He logically would not have sent for a woman whose husband would have been home to answer the door!

Was David without a wife of his own? No. David had taken at least seven wives after he came to power as king. Their names are listed in 2 Samuel 3:2-5 and 3:14. At some point he had also legally acquired his predecessor Saul's wives (2 Samuel 12:8). After several years David took even more wives and concubines after he set up rule in Jerusalem (2 Samuel 5:13). He was accustomed to sending for one of his wives at his pleasure. Were they not enough? Earlier in his life David was humble and grateful to God, considering himself as a poor man not worthy to be King Saul's son-in-law (1 Samuel 18:18). But now David had slowly grown into a sense of entitlement. The emotional stage was set for David to abuse his power. Never mind that Bathsheba was someone else's wife. He wanted her. David dispatched an escort to bring Bathsheba to his chamber.

I can imagine the surprise when the palace escort knocked at her door in the night, saying "You are summoned to the palace at once." Following the envoy, what must have been passing through Bathsheba's mind? *Has something happened to Uriah? Is something wrong? Is this the way I would be informed if he were wounded or killed?* The shock of being summoned would have thrown her into unknown emotional territory. As she walked behind the escort, she tried to remember just what she'd been told. *Had the envoy really said that the King wanted to speak with me?*

She must have felt a sudden grip of anxiety. Her breathing quickened and she could feel her heart pounding.

Imagine being abruptly told that you've been summoned to the Oval Office of the White House just fifteen minutes from now. *WHAT?* You're not sure you've heard this correctly. *The President wants to see me? WHY?* Before you've had a chance to process this turn of events, you're suddenly in the presence of the President of the United States. Your deep respect for the office of the President would likely put you in a state of deference and meekness. You don't have a plan. You haven't had time to think about what this means, why you're here, or what choices you'd want to make in the moment. You probably didn't even consider refusing the request to come. Whether you're a man or a woman, you simply obey the summons and yield to the authority of the President. The supremacy of his role, internalized deeply since you first learned as a child who the President was, has carried the moment.

When young Bathsheba arrived in the chamber of the king, the most powerful man in the country, I can imagine she felt quite mute. She found herself face to face with an authoritative man, one for whom she had great respect and was most likely 20 years her senior. This was her king, deeply revered by her countrymen for his courage and leadership. She felt, as all her countrymen did, gratitude for his leadership, endearing him on an emotional level to her. Perhaps she had been present in a Jerusalem crowd when the country recently celebrated David's defeat of their national enemy, the Arameans, who had just come against Israel with 40,000 horsemen. Had she caught a glimpse of King David from a distance, or ever felt the excitement of being in close proximity to him? This sudden invitation to his presence must have put her in shock. In respect for the nobility of his office, I can picture Bathsheba being quiet and submissive, lowering her eyes in deference to David. She'd never dared to think that she would have personal contact with him.

David held all the cards and all the power. His authority and leadership status as the king would make it more likely for someone to go along with his wishes and harder to refuse his advances. With his advantages of age, power, sexual experience, and Bathsheba's emotional gratitude and indebtedness to him, he would have easily been able to coerce sexual contact. **This wasn't adultery, it was sexual abuse**. It was the exploitation of Bathsheba for David's sexual appetite. We don't know if David was drunk with alcohol, but he was no doubt intoxicated by his own power.

The fact that David may have been persuasive rather than violent is irrelevant. He wouldn't have needed to physically manhandle her. **The intimidation of his status was sufficient.** You can see how ridiculous the question is (often asked of women in sexual assault situations): "Did she *resist?*" What an inappropriate question that misses the truth of what is happening here. How predictable for a young woman of her humble position to be timid in the presence of a powerful man. Once it occurred to Bathsheba why she had been summoned, I imagine that

Bathsheba was exploited, precisely why God portrayed her as a lamb.

she found little or no voice to object. Remembering sexual abuse scenarios I have heard from my counselees, where men in power have made up their minds to coerce sex, I can imagine that Bathsheba came and went meekly.

I've heard women in these situations say, "I felt frozen," "This can't be happening!" or "I didn't know what to say or do." Blindsided and ambushed, Bathsheba may have doubted her own reality after she was dismissed that night. I have known women to be stunned and confused for days afterwards in similar situations. My guess is that Bathsheba told no one what really happened to her in the King's chambers. If anyone was aware she'd left her house that night, she likely lied about the events. How would she have known how to explain this to someone else? She couldn't even explain it to herself. It would have been easier to blame herself than to blame the King. Alone with her thoughts in the weeks to come, how terrifying to admit that her menstrual periods had stopped. How hard to face the undeniable truth…she was with child.

When Bathsheba told David some weeks later that she was pregnant, David conspired for a masterful cover-up. It seemed simple enough to bring Uriah home from the battlefront. David was sure that Uriah, happy to see Bathsheba, would have relations with her, providing a cover-up for her pregnancy.

When Uriah arrived home from the war front, David inquired how the war was going, pretending this was his foremost concern. *Can you stomach David's pretense of honorable motives?* As if esteeming Uriah for his service, David granted him a temporary leave from military duties and told Uriah to go home to his house. To cinch his deception, a servant followed Uriah out with a gift from the king, another effort at making Uriah emotionally pliable to the King's wishes. It seemed simple enough…a done deal.

David didn't bank on the fact that Uriah was such a principled fellow that he refused to go home to his wife, knowing that his fellow soldiers on the field didn't have such pleasures. Instead he slept nearby with the palace servants in a show of selflessness for his country and solidarity with his comrades back at the front. Obviously, Uriah had honor on his mind. David had deceit on his.

David tried again. The next day David ate with Uriah, no doubt filling his cup often and urging him to drink indulgently. Assured that Uriah was drunk, David ordered him home once again. Even an overdose of alcohol didn't change Uriah's self-denying values, and again he slept with the servants nearby. David's ploy to make Bathsheba look pregnant by her own husband wasn't working. David's anxiety was growing. Saving his own neck was the priority. He wanted to spare himself the accountability to the righteous prophets, priests, and leaders who might learn of this.

The next day David resorted to the ultimate treachery. He wrote a letter instructing Joab, the military commander, to put Uriah on the front line, then to deliberately pull back from him so Uriah would be killed. David's villainy was full-blown. Trying to make the appearance that Uriah would be killed in battle, David's order to Joab was really a plot to murder. In a gesture that chills the Biblical reader, David sent the sealed letter to Joab *by Uriah himself.*

When Bathsheba heard of Uriah's death, she mourned. She thought that he had died in the line of duty. But she had more problems than just being widowed. Eventually everyone would know that she wasn't having a baby by her husband. She was going to look like an adulteress to everyone. Bathsheba's life circumstances had been manipulated at the hands of a powerful man.

It may have actually been a relief, knowing she was widowed and pregnant, to have been summoned by David to be his wife. "David sent and brought her to his house" (2 Samuel 11:27, NASB). Now perhaps he even wanted to appear noble in taking Uriah's poor widow into his harem. Perhaps the baby could be born and few people would question the timing of the birth. The chapter closes with the summary, "The thing that David had done was evil in the sight of the Lord" (2 Samuel 11:27, NASB). David had abused his power to quench his sexual appetite, and then murdered to cover it. God was watching.

Just when David thought that the cover-up was done, and things had quieted down, he got a surprise visit from the prophet Nathan. "The Lord sent Nathan to David" (2 Samuel 12:1, NASB). Nathan had come to see David before (2 Samuel 7), telling David that God was going to give him unlimited blessing as David served the Lord. When Nathan appeared again at the palace, David probably wasn't on the defensive. The "situation" with Bathsheba was tidied up and taken care of. After greeting Nathan, David probably sat down, expecting to hear another blessing from the prophet.

Instead, Nathan presented a legal case for David to judge. Nathan began a story about a rich man and a poor man. The rich man had flocks of sheep. The poor man had one…only "one little ewe lamb which he bought and nourished" (2 Samuel 12:3, NASB). The story showed the poor man's devoted care for the lamb and the tender relationship they shared. The little lamb even slept in his own bed and drank from his cup. Sometimes a loved pet can touch a part of one's soul that is deeply meaningful; it may have been a rare love for this man.

The story continued…when a traveler came to the rich man's house, he was unwilling to take from his own flocks to feed the guest. Instead, he took the lamb away from the poor man, killed it, and fed it to the guest. **The glaring message of Nathan's story was the rich man's sense of entitlement, his blatant abuse of power, and his heartless narcissism.** This wasn't a message about adultery. It was a message about the abuse of power.

In the characteristic way which humans can deny their own guilt while self-righteously lashing out at others, David was furious. "David's anger burned against the man, and he said to Nathan, 'As the Lord lives, surely the man who has done this deserves to die!'" (2 Samuel 12:5, NASB).

David had unwittingly passed sentence on himself. It was a clever way for God to intervene. After David walked into the divine trap, Nathan delivered the ultimate commentary, "Thou art the man!" (2 Samuel 12:7, KJV). In modern language we'd say, "You're busted!" I don't think there could have been a more terrifying moment for a man on this earth. In an instant David's soul was completely stripped. The truth hit so deep that David did not attempt to wheedle out of it. He inwardly (perhaps even physically) collapsed in the divine spotlight agreeing, "I have sinned." He groaned with intolerable pain; the impact of truth felt as if it broke every bone in him.

To David's credit, he repented deeply. Psalm 51 is a glimpse into David's genuine brokenness. I believe this kind of repentance is rare. I have seldom seen it. "Let the bones which you (God) have broken rejoice" (Psalm 51:8, NASB). However, his repentance didn't erase the damage the sin had caused. Among the vast effects of David's sin was that he had also "given occasion to the enemies of the Lord to blaspheme" (2 Samuel 12:14, NASB). Other people would mock God's name because of David's evil act. God also took David's scheme as a personal affront, *"Because you have despised Me* and have taken the wife of Uriah the Hittite to be your wife" (2 Samuel 12:10, NASB).

My main point in telling the story is this: When Nathan delivered the parable, which was God's commentary on this situation, **Bathsheba was portrayed as the lamb in the story.** God chose to characterize Bathsheba by a symbol of universal and theological innocence: **a little ewe lamb**. She hadn't plotted anything. She wasn't a temptress. She had been manipulated. She had been a pawn in the hands of a powerful person with his own agenda. In God's eyes she wasn't responsible. **This wasn't a tryst between lovers; it was the abuse of power. It was the exploitation of Bathsheba for David's sexual gratification which is sexual abuse.** I think that God acknowledges the losses to her when, in the story, the lamb was portrayed as being killed. All her rights had been taken. There couldn't be a clearer burden of proof. God held David solely responsible for the sexual encounter and the events that followed. David was the party who had to seek forgiveness, not Bathsheba. She wasn't guilty.

The Scripture does not disclose to us if or when David confessed the truth about Uriah's death to Bathsheba. If he did not, he kept a terrible secret his whole life. Although the baby she carried died after birth, they later had another child, Solomon, known as the wise king. If David eventually told her of his murder of Uriah, I can't imagine her confusion and pain.

Adult victims of abuse by professionals or clergy are sometimes blamed as being the temptresses because it is so hard for others to see a leader or pastor as capable of sexual manipulation. However, sexual encounters are frequently started by a clergyman pushing against the sexual boundaries of the parishioner or counselee. Most of the time, the pressure to sexualize the relationship comes from the professional person in power: the clergyman, the doctor, the professor, the attorney, the therapist, the employer, etc. The women who seek their services are in dependent roles. Those who are in the positions of power *always* hold the responsibility to maintain the sexual boundaries.

Sexual abuse happens when a person uses any advantage in the relationship (age, power, dependency by one party, or the lack of understanding of what is happening) to exploit the weaker person for sexual purposes. In the same way that being affirmed by an important person encourages us more, being disapproved of by an important person (authority figure) hurts us more. It's harder to tell an important person "no" because there might be negative consequences for you. This is precisely the dynamic which gives the person in power an advantage.

Let me be blunt here: Young women, this is why you shouldn't be sleeping with your college professor. It isn't the love relationship he's led you to believe it is. You're being exploited. Counselees, you aren't having a sexual relationship of equality with your pastor or therapist. He's abusing you and has done this with other women. You aren't the first. Women, your employer or supervisor has no right to threaten your job by inferring that you must have sex with him. This is sexual harassment, no matter what he tells you. None of these relationships started in freedom of choice and equality. In each case the man leveraged his power for selfish reasons. Run! Report! These relationships are predisposed to failure anyway. Most men who start relationships by leveraging their power quickly feel sapped of the euphoria of sexually exploiting the woman and then feel disgust and contempt towards her. Sadly, she may have believed his advances were genuine offers of love, and she may debase herself trying to keep a sick relationship going. In the end she's stripped of dignity. Many smart women (including myself) have found themselves here.

There are several reasons why Bathsheba's story is misconstrued as adultery. First, most people (including pastors writing their sermons) are undiscerning when it comes to the recognition and naming of sexual abuse, especially when it happens to adult women. They seem to spot abuse only in the most obvious cases such as forced rape by strangers or the abuse of children. I've also seen that pastors of good character can't imagine the frequency of manipulation of women. They don't realize the breadth of the problem. They think it is rare, so they never discuss it. Conversely, narcissistic church leaders may be silent to protect their own guilt. Finally, I've seen that men have often been negligent to challenge other men about their sexual improprieties and sins. It may be easier to preach against adultery than to confront a man about using his power to abuse a woman. I've never heard a strong sermon on it. Clearly I'm on my soapbox here, but **Bible teachers should have tried to make sense of God's view of Bathsheba as a "little ewe lamb," the unavoidable message of Nathan's challenge to David.** In the story Nathan delivers God's viewpoint, always the central issue in Bible interpretation.

I've found that abusive men often emit attitudes of contempt for women that infect other men. David may have infected his sons with an attitude of entitlement too, because his son, Amnon, raped David's daughter, Tamar (they were half-siblings). Our heads are still spinning from the egregious manipulation of Bathsheba in 2 Samuel chapter 11. Now we're nauseated to see Amnon's narcissism and obsessive plotting to sexually take his half-sister by chapter 13. Sadly, Tamar internalized the fear, worthlessness, and shame of being raped. It affected her permanently, as such a tragedy can (without support and healing help), and she lived in another brother's house, a "desolate" woman (2 Samuel 13:20, NASB). Suffice it to say that other abuses happened in David's family.

It's true that we have often mentioned David's sin but we have neglected to preach about Bathsheba's innocence. **In my opinion, the story about David and Bathsheba should have been presented over the years as God's condemnation for those who abuse power and God's view of the innocence of those who were sexually exploited.** There are other passages to use in preaching against adultery. This passage should be used to denounce sexual abuse.

Those of us who have been manipulated by powerful men can find a great deal of comfort and spiritual freedom here. In seeing this, I gave myself even more permission to be free from the last pieces of false guilt I had carried. I wasn't an adulteress. I was a lamb. I knew *that God knew* that I was innocent. I cut loose the last threads of shame. I refused to carry it any longer.

May this book bring courage and freedom to all of you who are lambs.

Helpful Resources

Recovery and Healing Books/Workbooks

Search for Significance by Robert McGee. (Thomas Nelson Publishers, 2003)
This book is a classic for addressing the false beliefs that lower self-esteem, the application of Christian spirituality to low self-worth, and the psychological healing that authentic faith can produce.

So Long, Insecurity by Beth Moore. (Tyndale House, 2010)
This is an easy to read book in Beth Moore's refreshing, honest style. She is a warrior of sorts who knows how to fight the battle against insecurity! A companion workbook for group experiences is also available, as well as a teen edition.

Making Peace with Your Past by Tim Sledge (Lifeway Press, 1992)
This insightful workbook is one of my favorite resources ever. The workbook leads adults to identify, understand, and come to terms with the feelings and problems of growing up in a dysfunctional family. There is a leader's manual for those who wish to lead a short-term support group using this member workbook.

Shelter from the Storm by Cindy Kubetin Littlefield (McGee Publishing, 1995)
This is the best sexual abuse recovery workbook I have seen. A recovery group for sexual abuse is often the single most healing experience for survivors. If you can't find a support group, you could gather at least two other abuse survivors and ask a trained therapist to facilitate a group using this workbook.

Breaking Free by Beth Moore (Lifeway Press, 2010)
Beth Moore is known for authenticity in her video messages and the engaging way she teaches the Bible. I love her self-disclosure and straightforward honesty about life. This is a video-driven Bible Study in which group members complete workbook assignments and can view videos, easily downloaded, which enhance the study.

Recovery Organizations

Celebrate Recovery (www.celebraterecovery.com) is a Christian 12-step program useful in addressing any life-dominating problem, such as chemical dependency, anger, codependency, sexual abuse, eating, etc. Over 19,000 churches worldwide offer free small and large group meetings, led by trained volunteers. Per CR, this is where attendees bring their "hurts, habits, and hang-ups" and experience the love and healing of God.

Alcoholics Anonymous (www.aa.org) continues to impress me with the potential for personal growth and spiritual healing it offers. Any individual who faithfully attends the free meetings for several months would come to understand how freedom from alcohol and chemical dependency is possible. "Open" meetings are for those touched by someone with an addiction. "Closed" meetings are for those who have alcohol and drug addictions.

Suicide Recovery Books

Healing After the Suicide of a Loved One by Ann Smolin and John Guinan (Fireside Books, 1993) is excellent.

After Suicide by John Hewett (Westminster Press, 1980) was helpful to me in resolving spiritual issues.

Recovery from Harmful Relationships

The Institute for Relational Harm Reduction and Public Pathology Education (www.saferelationships.com) offers many helpful resources such as a free e-magazine, books, counseling, retreats, etc. The founder, Sandra Brown, M.A, and her colleagues offer the best resources I have found for the education and healing of those harmed by pathological relationships.

About the Author

JoAnn Nishimoto, Psy.D., is a Licensed Clinical Psychologist.

She began her counseling career after graduating from Liberty University with a Master of Arts in Counseling in 1993. Dr. Nishimoto then worked for the YWCA Sexual Assault Center in Shreveport, LA, and the Minden Medical Center in Minden, LA.

After completing her internship at the Veterans Administration Medical Center in North Chicago, IL, she earned her Doctor of Clinical Psychology degree at Wheaton College in 2002 and joined the team at Meier Clinic in Wheaton, IL.

Dr. Nishimoto has served as an Adjunct Professor and Intern Supervisor at both Wheaton College, Wheaton IL, and Trinity International University, Deerfield, IL.

She is an active member of the American Association of Christion Counselors.

She opened her private practice in Mundelein, IL in 2006. She specializes in individual, family, and group therapy, for the treatment of depression and anxiety disorders, trauma, Post Traumatic Stress Disorder, and self-esteem transformation. She is particularly passionate about the dove-tailing of emotional and spiritual healing.

JoAnn enjoys serving at her church as a small group and seminar leader. She loves to hike, cook, entertain, visit antique stores, take road trips, appreciate original stained glass pieces, view the sky, and walk Sadie in the woods.

To contact Dr. Nishimoto, visit her at www.courageforlambs.com.

Made in the USA
Las Vegas, NV
29 October 2020